More praise for *The Myth of America's Decline*

"Among the pleasures of Mr. Joffe's book is the sheer accumulation of silly comments by smart people about America's many impending dooms . . . [and his] explanation for why declinism seems to have such a grip on the American mind. . . . But the heart of the book lies in Mr. Joffe's vivisection of the China myth. . . . [A] lively, convincing, salutary argument."   —Bret Stephens, *Wall Street Journal*

"Brave and bracing. . . . Joffe makes a strong case that a mix of Chinese vulnerabilities and American strengths means it is unlikely that China will replace the United States anytime soon as the center of the global system. Yet, as Joffe notes, constant anxiety about the United States' prospects might be one of the cultural forces responsible for the country's persistent strength; rather than resting on their laurels, Americans continually and even neurotically poke at their social fabric, looking for tears that need mending."   —Walter Russell Mead, *Foreign Affairs*

"Joffe compellingly traces the history and strategy of declinism. . . . [His] detailed analysis of China's economic challenges, including corruption and the wealth accrued by its leaders, is a fascinating read. . . . The strength of [his] argument and the joy it brings are equally compelling."   —Jay Lehr, Heartland Institute

"One book you must read if you are feeling unhappy with the nation's present and future is Josef Joffe's *The Myth of America's Decline*. . . . [Joffe] is not only comfortable with real facts, but also has the talent to present them in an entertaining fashion that makes

for easy and compelling reading. . . . I recommend you read this excellent book."
—Alan Caruba, Bookviews

"In his excellent new book, *The Myth of America's Decline*, [Joffe] . . . has gathered together the facts of America's economic ups and downs to present a realistic and optimistic view of the future."
—*Canada Free Press*

"German intellectual Josef Joffe makes a stirring case . . . that America is strong and getting stronger. . . . While acknowledging that anything is possible and America's best days may yet be behind us, Joffe is adept at explaining the intangible factors that will likely ensure America's preeminence for ages to come."
—James Kirchick, *Daily Beast*

"Josef Joffe is fascinated by these bouts of self-doubt that 'torment the American imagination.' In *The Myth of America's Decline*, he examines five decades of this malady, leading us to China, the latest bogeyman lurking under the bed."
—Carlos Lozada, *Washington Post*

"Solid. . . . [Refutes] the declinism so feared by the right and perhaps welcomed by some even farther to the right and left. Along the way, Joffe cites some little-discussed statistics, such as the fact that China's aging population and the need for a replenished labor pool to support it fall into 'ratios [that] are far worse than any in the West.' So much for China as the rising dominant world power. There is no triumphalism here, for Joffe notes that there are plenty of problems for the United States to overcome, such as 'the breakdown of bipartisanship . . . intractable deficits and rising debt . . . [and] social polarization.'"
—*Kirkus Reviews*

"Joffe's counter-argument that indeed America is not in relative decline is persuasive. . . . Joffe's detailed catalogue of economic and civil weaknesses in the Chinese police state is the book's high point, however, with the author observing that repression has been the Chinese way since the Ming Dynasty. . . . For readers tired of blame-America-first critics or who want to find out what a smart, influential European thinks of the country's prospects, Joffe's book is a useful place to begin." —*Publishers Weekly*

THE Myth
of America's
Decline

ALSO BY Josef Joffe

Überpower: The Imperial Temptation of America

The Future of the Great Powers

*The Limited Partnership: Europe, the United States,
and the Burden of Alliance*

Ending Empire (coauthor)

*The Political Role of Nuclear Weapons: No-First-Use
and the Stability of the European Order*

THE Myth of America's Decline

POLITICS, ECONOMICS, AND
A HALF CENTURY OF FALSE PROPHECIES

Josef Joffe

LIVERIGHT PUBLISHING CORPORATION
A DIVISION OF W. W. NORTON & COMPANY
NEW YORK | LONDON

For information about permission to reproduce selections from this book,
write to Permissions, Liveright Publishing Corporation,
a division of W. W. Norton & Company, Inc.,
500 Fifth Avenue, New York, NY 10110

For information about special discounts for bulk purchases, please contact
W. W. Norton Special Sales at specialsales@wwnorton.com or 800-233-4830

Manufacturing by Courier Westford
Book design by Fearn Cutler de Vicq
Production manager: Louise Mattarelliano

Library of Congress Cataloging-in-Publication Data

Joffe, Josef.
The myth of America's decline : politics, economics, and a half century of false prophecies / Josef Joffe. — First Edition.
pages cm
Includes biographical references and index.
ISBN 978-0-87140-449-7 (hardcover)
1. United States—Civilization—1945– 2. United States—Politics and government—1945–1989. 3. United States—Politics and government—1989– 4.
United States—Economic conditions—1945– 5. United States—Foreign relations—1945–1989. 6. United States—Foreign relations—1989– I. Title.
E169.12.J63 2014
973.91—dc23

2013019764

ISBN 978-0-87140-846-4 pbk.

Liveright Publishing Corporation
500 Fifth Avenue, New York, N.Y. 10110
www.wwnorton.com

W. W. Norton & Company Ltd.
Castle House, 75/76 Wells Street, London W1T 3QT

1 2 3 4 5 6 7 8 9 0

To Samuel P. Huntington

teacher, friend, and giant among his peers

Contents

CONTENTS

CONTENTS

List of Tables and Figures

America as Has-Been

"Decline" is as American as apple pie, the theme antedating the birth of the American Republic. Already before the founding, America was doomed, as some towering figures of the French Enlightenment claimed. Even the animals were smaller on this huge continent. The title of a book by Georges-Louis Leclerc de Buffon, *De la dégénération des animaux* (1766), tells it all. Another early critic targeted the "pernicious" climate of the New World, reporting on a people who were "astonishingly idiotic, enervated, and vitiated in all the parts of their organism." Americans were both feeble and feebleminded. European settlers were "degenerating" with "every successive generation." Youthful vigor would run out of steam before these Anglo-Americans had reached maturity; hence they faced but "decrepitude and old age."[1]

Mainly homemade, the modern version originated in the America of the 1950s, when Decline 1.0 came to grip the land. The drama has been reenacted about once every decade, the most recent wave—Decline 5.0—rising in the first decade of the present century. The trigger was always real—a brutal recession or a geopolitical setback. Yet each time, crisis spelled foreordained doom, a fate insistently painted on the country's wall by Americans rather than by foreign observers. Either there was something fundamentally wrong with this New World, or other nations were better—more ambitious, capable, and dynamic. The starring candidates changed, or returned to center stage, from decade to decade. The first was the Soviet Union; it was followed by Europe, Japan, and most recently China—with other unstoppable risers like India trailing right behind.

This author remembers the first wave of Declinism, also known as Sputnik Shock, only dimly. Yet in retrospect, the late 1950s came to stand out as premiere—as Decline 1.0, the first instance of a recurring phenomenon. As a student in the United States, the author took part in Decline 2.0. He lived through the turmoil of the late 1960s and early 1970s, participating, as his generation did, in the civil rights and antiwar upheavals that scarred and transformed the nation. He observed Declines 3.0 and 4.0 from abroad. First, it was the Carter "malaise," then the rise of Japan and the resurgence of the Soviet Union.

These acts in the never-ending drama offered particularly rich evidence in support of the Declinist thesis. As Japan threatened to overtake the United States economically, while Soviet Russia was again forging ahead strategically, the United States was sinking fast on both accounts. Declinism took a break in the 1990s, but only to return with a vengeance in the 2000s. Now, with the author teaching U.S. foreign policy at Stanford, China was going to dethrone the reigning superpower, propelled by unbreakable growth rates and the world's largest population.

In retrospect, a vantage point granted only by hindsight, this observer was struck by the cyclicality of the phenomenon; decline unfolded not over centuries, as in the case of Rome, but as repertoire theater season by season. Recurrence formulates its own questions. What triggers the surge, and why does it wane? The next issue is the difference between the cyclical and the secular. Cycles, like the tides, betray regularity, but in the history of nations, the next downturn might well presage the deluge. So prophecy is a tricky business; both doomsters and Pollyannas may in the end prove only their reckless ignorance.

Yet students of contemporary politics and economics cannot milk the benefits of hindsight. They can only make a calculated bet on the future by picking the right variables. Which are fleeting, which are enduring? We can reason by analogy, culling from the past half century what was exaggeration and short-lived despair, on the one hand, and what proved to be long-term strengths, on the other. This book tries to separate the short run from the long run by looking at the postwar careers of the United States and a slew of contenders slated to outcompete it.

Above all, the focus is on power—the central, but cloudiest, concept of political analysis. We can count the sources of power, but can at best only draw inferences about the causal relationship between what a nation has and what it can get with it in terms of making other nations do what they would otherwise not do. Exhibit A of the Declinist debate is economics or, more accurately, rates of growth. Destiny would catch up with the United States because other nations, from Soviet Russia to China, were forging ahead faster. If history has one certain message, though, it is the transience of spectacular growth—a fate that may have already moved in on China, as it had earlier on Russia, Europe, and Japan. Nor is this the only problem of instant Declinism, for the power of nations—"hard" and "soft"—flows from many sources.

After surveying the history of Declinism, this book looks not only at the many-shaped assets of power such as GDP, population, armed strength, projection forces, and technological prowess. It also factors in what cannot be easily quantified: political system, culture, ideology, and tradition. Add more tangible advantages: the sinews of diplomacy and alliances as well as networks of commercial and financial influence. Then look not merely at "cash in the bank" but also at the sources of future power such as education, research and development, immigration, and demography.

Such a "catholic" tally reveals a more complex portrait of global power than growth rates, size, and population, the favorites of Declinism. By way of metaphor, this canvas displays the United States, beset as it is by its many flaws, as "Decathlon Power." It is not first in all disciplines, but in most—in more, at any rate, than any of its rivals. Another term that highlights the unique position of the United States is "Default Power," meaning the one and only to which other nations turn when they cannot take care of the international business on their own. It strains the imagination to cast Moscow, Beijing, Brussels, Tokyo, or New Delhi in this role.

Growth, transitory to begin with, is not enough; that is the long and short of our tale. This book tries to explain why this is so, drawing on history, economics, politics, and strategy. On its side, the argument has a slew of false prophecies from Decline 1.0 to 4.0 that announced America's demise in short order, 5.0 being threatened by the same fate. Against this counterprophecy stands the worst enemy of all soothsayers: the future, which the human mind can never penetrate. In between stands an analysis aspiring to be both pertinent and persuasive.

Josef Joffe,
Stanford, Spring 2013

THE Myth
of America's
Decline

CHAPTER ONE

"It's Decline Time in America": A Short History

Halfway into the last century, America was finished. Or so it seemed. On 4 October 1957, the Soviet Union became the first space power in history, launching its Sputnik ("satellite") into orbit and striking terror into the American soul. This was "a shock which hit many people as hard as Pearl Harbor," recalled a commentator for the Mutual Broadcasting System, then one of the Big Four networks. It was "a frightful blow." America had grown "soft and complacent," believing that it was "Number One in everything." Yet now the country had been upstaged by its mortal rival.[1]

Sputnik stopped transmitting after three weeks, tumbling out of the sky two months later. Short-lived as it was, the wobbly contraption—a mere twenty-three inches across—had a devastating impact on the American psyche. Soul-searching and self-deprecation turned into a national obsession—and into a chronic reflex as the century progressed. In the midst of a crashing stock market and a deepening recession, the October surprise gave birth to a school of thought that would outlive Sputnik and regularly return to torment the American imagination all the way into the twenty-first century. Let's call it "Declinism."[2]

The basic theme—America as has-been—is recycled about every ten years. "It's decline time in America," the stock drama trumpets, and it is staged anew at the end of each decade— typically, as the sun is about to set on an administration while presidential candidates begin jockeying for position. As in the hand-wringing over Sputnik, the alarm does in fact spring from real trouble, be it economic hardship or military misfortune. Economically, this first wave of Declinism bears an uncanny resemblance to the last, which rose after the Crash of 2008. In the fall of 1957, the economy shrank by 4 percent; in the spring of 1958, by an appalling 10 percent. The numbers for 2008 and 2009 were minus 5 percent and minus 6 percent. So there is always a rational basis for this kind of angst attack. Just as regularly, though, anxiety expands into Spenglerian visions of foreordained decay. A crisis is not just a crisis but a portent of doom akin to the writing on the wall in the Book of Daniel. Just change names and places, and the prophecy is up to date.

Doom is one of the oldest stories of mankind. The Book of Daniel is the biblical original that has set the pattern for a rich tradition of decline and destruction in Western thought. When the *"Mene, Mene, Tekel U-Pharsin"*[3] appears out of nowhere, Babylon's astrologers and soothsayers—the policy experts and pollsters of that time—are flummoxed. Daniel, the captive Jewish sage has to be summoned. He quickly deciphers the eerie script on the wall. King Belshazzar and his courtiers had committed blasphemy by praying to idols. The "God in whose hand thy breath is," Daniel informs the king, "hast thou not glorified." Divine retribution was at hand. Belshazzar had been "weighed and found wanting."

Therefore, "God has numbered the days of your kingdom." In that night "was Belshazzar, the king of the Chaldeans, slain."

The modern version of this legend, retold decennially, follows the biblical model: Having gone astray, America will be called to account for the sin of pride or sloth. Like Babylon's, its best days are over. As this is a secular saga, punishment will be handed down not by the deity but by other nations. Meaner and leaner, they will dethrone the "last best hope of earth," to recall Lincoln's famous words in the worst days of the Civil War. The Soviet Union was first in this tale of woe. It would be followed by Europe, Japan, India, and China. The characters changed, the drama became part of the American repertoire. Sputnik marked Decline 1.0. Versions 2.0 through 5.0 would follow.

THE 1950S: THE RUSSIANS ARE COMING!

The first in a long line of usurpers was the Soviet Union. A few months after the "Sputnik Shock," *Life* magazine, then selling for a mere twenty-five cents, launched an "urgent series" titled not *Mene, Mene*, but "Crisis in Education." The editorial intoned, "What has long been an ignored national problem, Sputnik has made a recognized crisis." To drive the calamity home, the author Sloan Wilson put onstage two generic American high school graduates. One was "Johnny," who "can't read above fifth-grade level." The other was "Mary," who "has barely mastered the fourth-grade arithmetic fundamentals." On the cusp of adulthood, this duo couldn't even handle the three R's. How, then, could the country face down the Soviet Union? Even gifted American children "are nowhere near as advanced in the sciences as their opposite numbers . . . in Russia."

In a nine-page spread, the magazine laid out the "frightening scale of the problems the U.S. now faces" by contrasting the lives of two real-life students—Stephen in Chicago and Alexei in Moscow. Distracted by sports and dating, Stephen has "little time for hard study," but for Alexei "good marks in school are literally more important than anything else in life." The achievement gap was staggering. Though one year younger, Alexei is two years ahead of Stephen academically. While Stephen fritters away his young life with trivial pursuits, "more than half of Alexei's classroom time is given over to scientific subjects."[4] It is hard physics over soft pleasure, with the moral all too clear: The Russians are bound to prevail.

Half a century later, a best seller by the Yale professor Amy Chua made the same point, but this time Chinese education was the model held up to America. The message of *Battle Hymn of the Tiger Mother* (2011) was academic performance *über alles*, no play dates, no sleepovers, no TV. What *Life* did in 1958, the *Wall Street Journal* replicated fifty years later, running a short version of the book under the tell-it-all title "Why Chinese Mothers Are Superior." It was young Alexei all over again. Compared with their Western counterparts, "Chinese parents spend approximately 10 times as long every day drilling academic activities with their children. By contrast, Western kids are more likely to participate in sports teams."[5]

"This is our generation's Sputnik moment," intoned President Obama in his 2011 State of the Union address. Except this time it was not Soviet Russia but China and India. Otherwise, it was déjà vu all over again, to recall Yogi Berra's malapropism. Like the Soviets, people in these two countries were "educating their children earlier and longer, with greater emphasis on math and science. They're investing in research and new technologies." The United States would thus have to "reach a level of research and development we haven't seen since the height of the Space Race."[6]

Back then, *Time* had piled on the metaphors in a cover story on the Soviet leader Nikita Khrushchev as its Man of the Year: "In 1957, under the orbits of a horned sphere . . . , the world's balance of power lurched and swung toward the free world's enemies. On any score, 1957 was a year of retreat and disarray for the West."[7] So the Soviet Union, barely industrialized and bled dry by twenty million lives lost in World War II, was poised to outgun and out-produce the United States before Stephen and Alexei would reach middle age. But that was just for starters. In fact, the crisis was much graver than Johnny's and Mary's shabby performance suggested. America's very survival hung in the balance.

In the Year of the Sputnik, a presidential panel produced a top-secret report, "Deterrence and Survival in the Nuclear Age,"[8] which went down in history as the Gaither Report. Though focusing on the Soviet Union, the language of doom could easily be applied to China today, the most recent challenger touted as more dynamic and disciplined than the United States. The economy of the USSR, warned the panel, is just a bit "more than one-third of that of the United States," but "it is increasing half again as fast." So how long would it take for the Soviet Union to demote the United States? Careening along on its straight-line projection, the report predicted that by 1980 Moscow's annual military spending "may be double ours," unless, of course, the United States finally woke up to the deadly threat. Today's doomsters similarly point to the double-digit annual expansion of Chinese defense spending, and the more strident Cassandras target 2025 as the year when China will leave the United States in the dust economically. Others give the United States until 2050 to drop to second or even third place in the GDP race.

Worse, the Gaither Report claimed, the Soviets had "probably surpassed us in ICBM development"—missiles of intercontinental reach. "Probable" is another word for "don't know," but in the annus horribilis of 1957 the report found a grateful reader in the freshman senator from Massachusetts, John F. Kennedy. Up for reelection in 1958 and eying a presidential run two years later, he began to stoke the national angst. For him, the day of America's disgrace was practically at hand. By 1960, "the United States will have lost . . . its superiority in nuclear striking power." The slothful policies of President Eisenhower and his Republicans would produce "great danger within the next few years," ran his mantra.[9]

This was the fabled "Missile Gap" that never existed; it would take years before Soviet missiles based at home could effectively hit the continental United States. Estimates vary widely, crediting the USSR with anything between four and thirty liquid-fueled missiles at the turn of the decade. Tanking them up would take ten hours, longer than it would take U.S. forward-based bombers to reach and destroy them. Meanwhile, the United States had amassed over three thousand strategic warheads and almost two thousand launchers by 1960. In the same year, the first missile submarine, the USS *George Washington*, took to the deep, where its sixteen nuclear-tipped Polaris were immune to a Soviet first strike. Whether by number or technology, the United States was far ahead of the USSR.

Facts, unfortunately, don't deliver prophetic punch. So Kennedy painted Armageddon in the most gruesome colors. The Russians were forging ahead, and the Missile Gap would deliver to them a "new shortcut to world domination."[10] In the presidential campaign, Kennedy orated like a fully blown Declinist: "That is what we have to overcome . . . [the sense] that the United States has reached maturity, that maybe our high noon has passed, maybe our brightest days were earlier, and that now we are going into the long, slow afternoon."[11] *Finis Americae* was practically at hand in 1960. Henry Kissinger, then a young professor at Harvard, concurred: "Only self-delusion can keep us from admitting our decline to ourselves."[12] He would return to this theme again and again.

This was in the midst of another economic downturn, with a worst-quarter drop of 5 percent in the fall. But the United States did not ride off into the sunset, and the Soviets never managed to take that "shortcut to world domination." A mere thirty years later, the USSR was no more, having met a fate worse than what history had supposedly reserved for the United States. It did not just decline; it literally disappeared on Christmas Day 1991, leaving behind the Russian Federation and fourteen orphan republics. Yet Kennedy's agitation made the fictitious missile gap real enough to serve its domestic purpose. He kept his Senate seat in 1958 and beat Richard Nixon to the White House two years later.

Ten years later, at the end of the Kennedy-Johnson era, the drama of decline was reenacted once again, this time by Kennedy's Republican disciple Richard M. Nixon, when he was mounting his second run for the White House. Except that this time the story was not about a fictitious missile gap but about a real war in Vietnam, a campaign that originated in hubris and ended in tragedy. Somebody had to lead America out of desolation, just as Kennedy had promised a decade earlier. This time, the story came with a new twist.

The 1960s: The "Unraveling of America"

As always, pride goeth before the fall. Pummeled by Sputnik and oppressed by the nightmare of Soviet superiority, America's spirits would soon soar again. Only a handful of years after Sputnik,

America was No. 1 again, having reduced its mortal rival to a distant second in the stylized passage of arms that was the Cuban Missile Crisis in the fall of 1962.

All narratives of national decline turn on the nature of power: who is losing, who is gaining it? In the traditional great-power world of the eighteenth and nineteenth centuries, war was the truest measure, delivering swift and conclusive verdicts. It took upstart Prussia just ten months to demote mighty France to a has-been in the War of 1870–71. In 1967, Israel routed all three of its neighbors—Egypt, Syria, and Jordan—in less than a week, establishing itself as a regional superpower. In the nuclear age, however, war can no longer serve as a test of strength. Overkill has eliminated great-power war from the repertoire, and so crises have become the yardstick of power. The most dangerous and decisive one was the Cuban Missile Crisis, when Kennedy had been in office for less than two years.

The outcome proved how empty Kennedy's doomsday rhetoric had been, and how frenzied the alarm over Moscow's unstoppable rise. America was back on top—and triumphant, to boot. By taking on the United States on its home turf, the Soviets actually proved that the Missile Gap was in fact *their* problem. Why else move up so close to the American mainland, engineering a threat that risked devastating preemption against the Soviet homeland? The naval confrontation in the Caribbean waters did not last long—thirteen days, to be exact. Kennedy prevailed, and Nikita Khrushchev, Russia's ruler, had to pledge withdrawal. He would later pay with his political life for his "adventurism," as his Politburo colleagues called the Cuban gambit. America's strategic and conventional superiority had carried the day, in a flash that revealed the true distribution of power, and without a shot being fired.

Freshly vindicated, America was again safe and sound. The temptation wasn't long in coming. Hubris followed triumph as night follows day, notably in Vietnam, where Kennedy, flush with victory, sent some sixteen thousand American servicemen as advisers. By mid-decade, his successor Lyndon B. Johnson had dispatched half a million combat troops. At the end of the 1960s, the war was not going well, though much worse at home than in the Asian theater. Many years later, Harvey Mansfield, a political philosopher at Harvard, would describe the Vietnam years as "comprehensive disaster."[13] This time, the calamity was for real, not a deliberate dramatization, as in the Sputnik years.

It was war in Vietnam and war at home, a crumbling dollar and rising inflation, burning cities and generational revolt. It was the longest and darkest chapter in the history of American self-doubt. Lyndon B. Johnson thought he could do it all—the War on Poverty and the war against Ho Chi Minh, but without raising taxes, let alone reining in civilian spending, which actually climbed to new heights. He told his biographer, "I was determined to be a leader of war and a leader of peace. I wanted both, I believed in both, and I believed America had the resources to provide for both."[14] Although the mightiest nation on earth, America did not.

Jerry Rubin, the counterculture hero and leading Yippie, who in a very American career would morph into a wealthy entrepreneur in the 1980s, wrote on the country's wall (note the German spelling to evoke the Nazi parallel),

> The war against Amerika
> In the schools
> And the streets

By white middle-class kids
Thus commenced.[15]

In 1966, the demonstrators marched by the thousands. By April 1967, some 400,000 thronged through New York; in October, 100,000 massed at the Lincoln Memorial in Washington. One year later, Martin Luther King Jr. was murdered, and so was John F. Kennedy's brother Robert. It was "the unraveling of America," as the title of a book on the period had it, or more ominously, "America's suicide attempt."[16] Vietnam was to Sputnik what viral pneumonia is to a hiccup. Running for the Democratic nomination in 1968, Robert Kennedy naturally invoked the classic prophetic motifs of transgression and perdition: Guilty were those "who have removed themselves from the American tradition, from . . . the soul of our nation." It was a "failure of national purpose," which stemmed not just from bad policies but from the "darker impulses of the American spirit."[17] Thus spoke Daniel to King Lyndon.

Robert Kennedy was not alone in uttering such sentiments. Richard Nixon, the Republican, was also running for the presidency. Like JFK exactly a decade earlier, he sounded the alarm over America's fall from grace. "Let us look at the balance of power in the world," he orated in 1967:

Twenty years ago the United States had a monopoly on the atomic bomb and our military superiority was unquestioned. Even five years ago our advantage was still decisive. Today the Soviet Union may be ahead of us in megaton capacity and will have missile parity with the United States by 1970. Communist China within five years will have a significant deliverable nuclear capability.

Finally, let us look at American prestige:

Twenty years ago . . . we were respected throughout the
world. Today, hardly a day goes by when our flag is not spit
upon, a library burned, an embassy stoned some place in the
world. In fact, you don't have to leave the United States to
find examples.[18]

This was Declinism Lite—not the end, but the shrinking of
America in terms of global power and prestige. The theme would
resurface through the decades. America was sinking slowly, while
others were rising; its influence was on the wane. This would
become the leitmotif of the Nixon administration, and it foreshadowed the "rise of the rest" that suffuses the present-day celebration
of China, India, et al. Its fullest expression was a rambling speech
by the president in Kansas City in 1971.

America is no longer the economic "number one," Nixon
decreed. There are in fact "five great power centers in the world
today." These are the United States, followed by Western Europe, a
"resurgent Japan," the Soviet Union, and "Mainland China," which
"inevitably" is growing into "an enormous economic power" and
eventually a global strategic player. "So, in sum, what do we see . . .
as we look ahead 5 years, 10 years, perhaps it is 15? We see five
great economic super powers."

The diagnosis didn't quite pan out. Fifteen years later, in 1986,
Japan was about to peak. At the end of the decade, it was slid-
ing into long-term stagnation whose end we have yet to see. The
Soviet Union was sinking even more rapidly, its empire collapsing
shortly thereafter. But at the end of his speech, Nixon sounded
like Oswald Spengler and Arnold Toynbee, the twentieth century's most famous Declinists, rolled into one.[19] "I think of what

happened to Greece and to Rome . . . , great civilizations of the past," which first became wealthy, then "lost their will to live, to improve." So they succumbed to the "decadence which eventually destroys a civilization." And "the United States is now reaching that period."

This was the buildup. Like any good prophet, Nixon concluded by switching from doom to deliverance. America's fall from grace was not yet, he told his audience; the country was still "preeminent" as "world leader." It had the "vitality," the "courage," the "destiny to play a great role," but the "people need to be reassured." [20] Like all prophets, the president was the man to do so; "trust me," so to speak. Henry Kissinger, who had been tutoring Nixon in foreign policy, did not sound quite as sanguine.

For Nixon's national security adviser, the end of the two-superpower world was already here, and America had to adjust to the new reality. "Political multipolarity" was at hand, he wrote in 1968, which "makes it impossible to impose an American design." [21] The nation, in other words, had to scale back. In yesterday's two-power world, the United States had held at least one-half of the voting stock; in this new five-power world, that share was bound to dwindle to one-fifth.

This prospect apparently gave rise to melancholy reflections. According to the retired navy chief Elmo Zumwalt, Kissinger had confided to him in 1970 that the United States had "passed its historical high point like so many earlier civilizations." Thus, it was Kissinger's job to "persuade the Russians to give us the best deal we can get, recognizing that the historical forces favor them." Americans "lack the stamina to stay the course against the Russians," Zumwalt quoted Kissinger as saying; they are " 'Sparta' to our 'Athens.' " Kissinger would later denounce the report as total "fabrication," adding that Zumwalt had "misunderstood the points I was making."[22]

Given his political agenda, the admiral surely did misrepresent the conversation. A Democrat running for the Senate in Virginia in 1976, Zumwalt may have used Kissinger as a whipping boy in order to discredit Nixon's foreign policy. On the other hand, Nixon's and Kissinger's perorations weren't pulled from thin air. The United States was hemorrhaging blood, treasure, and reputation. The Vietnam War could not be sustained at home; a wounded nation, the United States had to move out of harm's way. Declinism—heartfelt or instrumental—was the way to prepare the nation for the coming U-turn in grand strategy. This could have been the larger purpose of the "we are down, and they are up" oratory.

The new strategy was détente with the Soviet Union and the "opening" toward China, the two powers that were arming and abetting North Vietnam. Rapprochement with the two Red giants would give the United States leverage over Hanoi. But how to persuade a nation that had been weaned since the late 1940s on a steady diet of "godless communism"? To legitimate the new diplomacy, a new domestic consensus had to be forged. And the issue was "whether the new balance which the Administration sought abroad would balance at home."[23]

So the quintessential Cold Warrior, Richard Nixon, had to change stripes. He had to persuade the nation to scale back, especially since Congress would no longer support this or any other imperial venture. The United States could not play the world's policeman; it had to bring high-flying ends in line with dwindling means. Hence it was high time to avoid direct involvement in favor of regional power balances. Let the locals carry the burden. This was the gist of the new Nixon Doctrine.[24] In order to justify down-sizing and dealing with yesterday's mortal foes, it might help to paint the nation smaller than it was. Declinism, as always, was an educational exercise.

Did Nixon and Kissinger intend to vacate America's exalted place at the top? The "China opening" and détente with Moscow actually added up to a classic of realpolitik, in which deft diplomacy compensated for an apparent or genuine loss of power in these try-ing days. With America in the middle, Washington would play the Soviets against the Chinese, and both against North Vietnam. In either case, the United States would act as the concertmaster.

Alas, neither China nor Soviet Russia would play second fiddle to the United States in East Asia. They kept on arming and shield-ing North Vietnam, and Ho Chi Minh went on to conquer the South after the United States had ended its direct military involve-ment in 1972. Five years later, just before leaving office, Henry Kissinger harked back to his 1968 article about adapting to "polit-ical multipolarity," ending on a melancholy note: "In the nature of things, this task could not have been completed—even without Watergate."[25] But if by "this task" Kissinger meant transforming the world into a pentagon of power, with the United States volun-tarily sinking to *primus inter pares*, the project was neither neces-sary nor part of the plan.

The United States, though it did not prevail in Vietnam, was hardly facing decline in the late 1960s. It did suffer from the revolt of the young, from a crisis of the spirit, and the plight of an econ-omy charged with producing too many guns and too much butter (aka social spending) all at once. But by any measure of power—economic mass, military clout, and diplomatic weight—the United States remained preeminent. Those fabled "dominoes" didn't fall across the length and breadth of Asia; North Vietnam's conquest of the South was socialism in just one more half country.[26] Losing a war without having to suffer strategic demotion—this is the mark of a truly great power. Lesser powers have not been so lucky. After its mauling by Prussia-Germany in 1871, France could no longer claim strategic primacy on the Continent. After 1945, it was Germany's turn to fall from power. After the Soviet Union lost the Cold War, it disintegrated. Defeat spelled disaster for all of them.

THE 1970S: AMERICA'S "MALAISE"

At the end of the 1970s, real calamity struck once again. After the second oil shock, in 1979, gasoline prices in the United States almost doubled in twelve months, a rise that took ten years to work itself out in the first decade of the twenty-first century. By the summer of 1979, Americans again faced long gas lines at the pump, as they had during the first oil shock, in 1973, when price controls, as they always do, led to infuriating shortages. Inflation kept accelerating: from 6 percent in 1977, when Jimmy Carter took office, to 11 percent in 1979. It peaked at almost 14 percent in the election year of 1980. Two years later, U.S. unemployment shot up to almost 11 percent—the highest level since the Great Depression, and more than one percentage point higher than at the worst moment of the 2007–09 recession. At the end of the 1980s, a dollar was worth less than half of what it was worth at the beginning. Abroad, the dollar had dropped likewise against major European currencies, like the deutsche mark. In contrast to those of the Carter years, the economic woes of the Obama years looked more like a nasty migraine—painful and protracted, but not deadly.

The contrast sharpens when the political humiliations of the

time are added to economic catastrophe. Nicaragua fell to the San-
dinistas in 1979, becoming Cuba's first Latin American satellite.
The Shah, America's longtime pillar in the Middle East, escaped
for his life from the Khomeini Revolution in January 1979. And
this time, the CIA and Britain's MI-6 could no longer engineer a
coup to bring him back, as they had done in 1953. Iranian students
occupied the U.S. embassy in Tehran, terrorizing their American hostages for 444 days. A halfhearted attempt by the Carter
administration to rescue them ended in the bloody disaster of Des-
ert One, forcing the abortion of the mission. Soviet and Cuban
forces were marching across resource-rich Central Africa. Finally,
during Christmas 1979, the Soviets invaded Afghanistan.

Nothing could underscore America's fragility more than Jimmy
Carter's famous "Malaise Speech" of 1979, as the media would dub
it. He diagnosed "a crisis of confidence . . . that strikes at the very
heart and soul and spirit of our national will. We can see this crisis
in the growing doubt about the meaning of our own lives and in
the loss of a unity of purpose for our Nation." That "erosion of our
confidence" threatens to "destroy the social and the political fabric of America." It all added up to an assault on our "heart, soul,
spirit, and will."[27] No other American president has ever painted
the country's fall from grace in such gruesome colors.

At the end of the year, Declinism was rampant throughout
the land. *Newsweek* ran a cover story titled "Has the U.S. Lost Its
Clout?" The magazine had unearthed proof positive of the "erosion
of American prestige and power." There was the Soviet bogey again.
Once America had held a nuclear monopoly; now it was struggling
"to maintain something called 'parity.'" The country was "slipping."
To prove the point, *Newsweek* trundled out a Japanese professor
who had always been "eager" to travel to the United States, but

now he didn't "even want to go again this year." The spokesman of the German government wouldn't exactly gloat; "rather we feel pity" for the United States—schadenfreude masking as solicitous concern. A French analyst did not see the "American way of life" as "so absolutely superior" any more.[28] Adjust the names and the dates, and you have a one-size-fits-all-decades diagnosis of inescapable decline.

In an acrid review of the Nixon-Carter era, Robert W. Tucker of Johns Hopkins wrote, "Though disputed until recently," America's "decline" was "no longer a matter of serious contention." Following the ancient prophetic tradition, which sees perdition as the wages of sin, the noted scholar brandished the "unpalatable truth that we have betrayed ourselves."[29] America wasn't quite finished, opined Helmut Sonnenfeldt, previously Kissinger's counselor in the State Department. But the "American dream . . . needs a good deal of revision. We can do less than we have tended to think." Winston Lord, another former aide, put it *tout court* in his new role as the head of the Council on Foreign Relations, which in those days served as unofficial central committee of the U.S. foreign policy establishment: "Our era of predominance is over."[30]

The great riser was again the Soviet Union. Could Missile Gap II be far behind? Henry Kissinger, now out of office, warned that America's strategic "superiority has eroded." If the country did not get back into the race, "then in the '80s we're going to pay a very serious price. The first installments are already visible."[31] The sequel of the first Missile Gap was called "Window of Vulnerability," and the script was written not by an aspiring presidential candidate, as in Kennedy's case, but by the Committee on the Present Danger. This was an assembly of influential private personages, which had already played Cassandra in 1950 and was rising to renewed prominence in the Carter years.[32] Ronald Reagan, the Republican candidate in 1980, had joined the executive board of the committee a year earlier.

Again, Declinism came with real decline. The 1980–82 recession saw the worst single-quarter plunge—almost 8 percent of GDP—since the Great Depression. The Window of Vulnerability built on previous doomsday scenarios that had painted the United States as prey-to-be of the Soviet bear. These were the Gaither Report of 1957 and the National Security Council's NSC-68 memorandum of 1950. The latter, an in-house document, had spelled out to President Truman: Rearm or retreat! Now, thirty years later, the Soviet Union was again reaching for nuclear superiority, and this time for keeps. Or so the Declinist agitation had it. The Soviets were arming to fight and *win* a nuclear war, the Committee on the Present Danger trumpeted. While hardening their own silos, the Soviets were building heavier and more accurate missiles capable of taking out America's retaliatory force in a first strike.

This scenario was hyperbole verging on irreality, given that the Soviet Union could not take out America's undersea strike force or those bombers that were on constant airborne readiness. For *Newsweek*, however, this was "the most alarming forecast in years."[33] *Time* brought onstage defense experts who warned that the "Soviets are ahead or gaining in almost every category."[34] An "even more menacing prospect is a shift in the world balance of power toward the Soviet Union," *Time* wrote on America's wall two years later.[35] The columnist Joseph Alsop, reaching deeply into his grab bag of gloom, placed America right next to ancient Carthage, which was destroyed by "Rome's warlike manpower." Russia was Rome, and "we have reached the stage when we must expect disaster in the long run, unless we make painful efforts to redress the balance without undue delay."[36]

That alarm, which had been sounded twice in the 1950s, turned out to be false once more. At the time, the United States had almost three times as many strategic warheads as the Soviet Union. But as myth, the Window of Vulnerability was as effective as its predecessors—NSC-68 and the Gaither Report. It triggered a wave of rearmament in the latter days of the Carter administration, and the tide rose mightily under Reagan.

Reagan was the greatest profiteer of the Declinist agitation. He appropriated the panicky language as deftly as had John F. Kennedy, the Democrat, twenty years before. "Mr. Carter," Reagan recited in the presidential debate of 1980, "had canceled the *B-1* bomber, delayed the *MX* [missile], delayed the *Trident* submarine, delayed the cruise missile, shut down . . . the *Minuteman* missile production line. . . ." In other words, his rival was guilty of sloth and neglect. It was high time "to restore our margin of safety" and to stop "unilateral concessions" to the Soviets.[37]

"America's defense strength," remonstrated Reagan, "is at its lowest ebb in a generation, while the Soviet Union is vastly outspending us in both strategic and conventional arms."[38] The Harvard political scientist Samuel Huntington summed it all up: "Feelings of decline and malaise, reinforced by another oil price hike and inflation, generated the political currents that brought Ronald Reagan to power in 1981."[39] With the American hostages still held in Iran, Carter lost in a landslide. And true to the prophetic tradition—first Jeremiah, then redeemer—Reagan's most famous campaign commercial three years later intoned, "It's morning again in America. And under the leadership of President Reagan, our country is prouder and stronger and better."[40] But not for long.

THE 1980s: JAPAN'S "RISING SUN"

In previous decades—from Sputnik to "Malaise"—candidates and committees had crowded the stage where the stock drama "Decline Time in America" was played out. The 1980s belonged to the academics, analysts, and thriller authors. The starring role also changed. After three decades of "The Russians Are Coming," the Soviet Union was faltering, and it would go on to lose the Cold War in 1989, when the "Velvet Revolutions" swept away Moscow's decayed empire in Eastern Europe. So who would push aside the United States now? Enter Japan in the lead and Europe in a supporting role.

Japan had been fingered as a power to watch since the early 1970s, in a language almost identical to the hoopla about China three decades later:

> Of all the various postwar economic miracles, the Japanese is the most spectacular. Japan . . . has become, in less than a quarter century, the free world's second-ranking industrial power. Since 1950, Japan's GNP has grown an average of 10 percent per year. From 1960 to 1969, it rose at an . . . average of 11.4 percent per year . . . The Japanese GNP [might catch] up with the American by 1985 or 1990. The year 2000 . . . will begin the "Japanese century."[41]

Percentages are destiny, this classic of Declinism suggested, and with growth numbers that dwarfed even China's performance (around 10 percent) a generation later. Japan was soaring, now and forever more. So first a reality check on the trends as they actually unfolded. In 1985, when Japan was supposed to overtake the United States, its GDP was $1.3 trillion (in then dollars); the United States' was $4.2 trillion, three times larger. Five years later—this was the next predicted draw-even point—the tally was 3 trillion vs. 6 trillion; so Japan was coming closer. In 2000, it was 4.6 trillion vs. 10 trillion; so Japan was evidently slowing. Now shift forward to the present, and it is back to the future and to the original three-to-one gap.[42] In real dollars, the gap was even larger (see figure 1). Such is the fate of linear, tomorrow-will-be-like-yesterday projections.

1. Real GDP, 1969–2011 (2005 U.S. dollars)

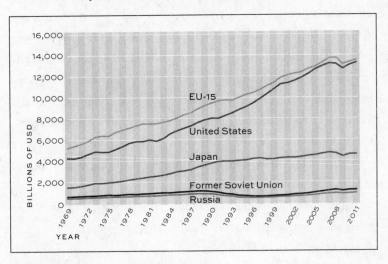

SOURCE: U.S. Department of Agriculture, Economic Research Service, http://www.ers.usda.gov/Data/macroeconomics/Data/HistoricalRealGDPValues.xls.

Yet linearity—the idea of Japan's unbroken rise—would feed Declinism for the next twenty years. Among the first to turn the "Japan über alles" theme song into a long dirge for America was the Harvard sociologist Ezra Vogel with his *Japan as Number One: Lessons for America*. This was in 1979, at the height of Jimmy Carter's "malaise," and it set the tone for unending hero worship. For its admirers, Japan was Hercules and Einstein rolled into one. This giant's strengths and brains were superhuman, as China's are said to be today.

The choice narrative unfolded like this: Japan's bureaucracy planned with meticulous foresight. These wise samurai knew everything, and what they did not know, they studied obsessively to unearth. Government and business worked hand in glove for the greater glory of the nation. Japanese firms could draw on limitless capital, and because the funds were provided by bank loans, not by equity, corporations did not have to please shortsighted stockholders. The educational system was celebrated as the Soviet one had been in the Sputnik days, and as China's is today: no nonsense, hard work, ruthless competition to promote the best and the brightest. Even better, Japan shared none of America's pathologies. Its crime rate was minuscule; its cities were clean and safe. Vogel's *Japan as Number One*, noted an admiring reviewer, was a monument to "Japan's steamroller eminence."[43]

Another typical paean was sung by *Time*: Japan's "power elite practices a democratic ideal" that Americans ignore: "the spirit of compromise and consensus." Business and government are not adversaries; they "work together." State-owned banks make "low-interest loans to manufacturers," and private banks "know that the government expects them, too, to give easy credits." The government does not yield "to the pleas of special interest groups." Bureaucrats and executives jointly manage policy. The two sides "understand one another . . . because these leaders usually have the same roots of culture and class."[44] Hence a culture as messy and self-absorbed as the American one could never live up to such perfection. Today's China admirers use similar language when praising the advantages of "authoritarian modernization."

American admiration for this No. 1 soon degenerated into sheer paranoia that would oppress the American imagination for years on end. In 1992, Michael Crichton published the best seller *Rising Sun*, which was made into a movie with Sean Connery and Wesley Snipes one year later, grossing $15 million ($24 million today) on the first weekend. It was a perfect testimony to America's dread of Japan, the China of the 1980s.

During World War II, the Japanese had never made it beyond Pearl Harbor; over the next three years, its Asian empire was shattered by America's military machine. But in the 1980s Japan looked truly indomitable. It was amassing not just a regional but also a global empire—peacefully and with beachheads right in the heart of the American economy. In 1989, Mitsubishi bought one national treasure, New York's Rockefeller Center; one year later, a Japanese businessman grabbed another, Pebble Beach in California. Fear and loathing exploded in a famous scene in Congress in 1987, where a Japanese VCR was smashed in front of the cameras to make the point.

Rising Sun, the movie, would gross $60 million ($100 million current). On the surface, the book and the movie were spinning a gripping whodunit. But the real message was a remake of Daniel's deadly prophecy. Like Babylon's, America's days were numbered. The plot: A young woman is raped and murdered during the grand opening of a Japanese company headquarters in Los Angeles. In short order, though, the chief of police orders the two detectives to drop the investigation. So the Japanese, the plot whispers, had already corrupted a mighty American city. Undeterred, the intrepid duo goes on to uncover a wider conspiracy: The Japanese want control over the U.S. electronics industry, but only for starters; the ultimate stake is political power. So the invaders try to pin the murder on an anti-Japanese senator who is mulling a presidential run. In the end, the righteous sleuths confront the real culprit, a Japanese executive, with the damning evidence. He meets his just deserts by jumping to his death, and America is saved.

The off-camera realities should have been more heartening still. At the peak of the paranoia, the Japanese economy was in free fall as well, plunging into the "Lost Decade" of the 1990s—into contraction and deflation. Yet nobody noticed how Japan's economic miracle was evaporating. In an afterword to *Rising Sun*, the author Michael Crichton insisted that the United States still had to "come to grips with the fact that Japan has become the leading industrial nation." It had "invented a new kind of trade—adversarial trade, trade like war." In *Debt of Honor* of 1994, the thriller author Tom Clancy went to the summit of all fears, laying out a U.S.-Japanese trade war escalating into the real thing with a nuclear-armed Japan. This movie was a blockbuster as well.

Lovers of irony might have a field day by comparing the fiction with the figures. While Crichton and Clancy were profiting handsomely from their nightmare tales, Japan was sinking fast. The country had boasted double-digit growth rates in the 1950s and 1960s, which at several points had exceeded the 10 percent of China's a generation later. Double-digit expansion ended in 1970. At the close of the 1970s, growth was down to less than 3 percent. In the 1980s, the Japanese economy oscillated between a low of 2 percent and a high of 7 percent. Growth peaked in 1988, the year that marked the beginning of a relentless slide. Yet in the same year, Clyde Prestowitz, formerly assistant secretary of commerce in the Reagan administration, predicted, "The American century is over. The big development in the latter part of the century is the emergence of Japan as a major superpower."[45] The United States was a Japanese "colony in the making."[46]

In fact, it was downhill for the colonizer. In 1992, the year of the *Rising Sun,* growth nosedived below 1 percent, and in 1994, when *Debt of Honor* came out, the rate was lower still. The "Lost Decade," with two dips below zero, was in full swing. Ever since, Japan has been growing at about half the American rate.[47] As Japan's economy worsened, so did its press; this is how the nimble-footed media work. Shiny pillars of excellence suddenly crumbled into piles of rot. The politicians? Poodles of entrenched interests, incompetent and self-serving. The administration? "Japan's bureaucratically guided capitalism . . . demonstrates an increasing propensity to corruption." The banking system that once gushed forth limitless capital? "It is mired in bad debt and cover-up."[48] The school system? An inhuman pressure cooker that is good for rote learning, but flunks on fresh thinking.

Thou shalt not mistake a rapid rise from a low base for an everlasting boom was the lesson of the 1980s, which also applied to East Asia's other shooting stars. Japan's economic miracle resembled South Korea's, Taiwan's, and today's China's (for the parallels, see chapters 4 and 5). Throw in the catch-up economy of Germany, as well, laid low just as Japan's was in World War II—different cultures, similar paths of redevelopment. The steep rise of Japan et al. was fed from the outside by exports and at home by underconsumption and its flip side, high saving.

The surpluses in the trade and savings accounts made money extraordinarily cheap. Funds became even more plentiful as a rising yen swept in foreign monies in search of easy profits from further revaluation. This will happen in China, too, if the country unfetters its currency and keeps it free-floating. The predictable result in Japan was explosive asset inflation (which is already biting in China today). The Nikkei index hit an all-time high of almost 39,000 on 29 December 1989. Choice properties in Tokyo sold at $1.5 million per square meter (or $180,000 per square foot in current dollars). When the bubble burst, trillions were wiped out in the collapse of the stock and real estate markets. Twenty years later, the Nikkei was creeping along below the 10,000 mark.

The year of the *Rising Sun* was good for yet another object lesson. In the United States, 1992 marked the birth of the longest expansion since the mid-nineteenth century, when reliable statistics became available.[49] Essentially, it lasted until 2007, the year before the crash. The boom was interrupted only briefly by an eight-month stumble below 1 percent growth in 2001. That was in the aftermath of the "dot-com bubble" pricked in March 2000.

The Declinists were not impressed.

Just five years before America's fifteen-year boom, the Johns Hopkins academic David Calleo had called the United States a "hegemon in decay." It was "set on a course that points to an ignominious end," he predicted.[50] Now, at the threshold of America's fabulous long run, the scholar devoted an entire chapter of *The Bankrupting of America* to "Decline Revisited." Why another round of gloom? His answer was "de-industrialization." It occupies a place of honor in the Hall of Declinism, next to the theories of many other authors who argued that "making stuff" beats inventing and designing, moving and marketing, trading and banking. "Most of the new service jobs" were not in high-tech or high value-added, Calleo claimed, but "in fast-food chains, discount retail stores . . . and similar low-wage sectors."[51]

In short, America's best days were over—again. It was evolving into a land of hamburger flippers, pizza boys, and big-box retail clerks. In fact the opposite was true; the majority of new jobs were adding value above average. The simplest and best measure of value creation is "real GDP per worker." In the past fifty years, the United States has consistently outranked its nearest competitors, including Japan and Germany, by impressive margins, as is shown in figure 2.[52]

2. Real GDP per Employed Person (2010 U.S. dollars)

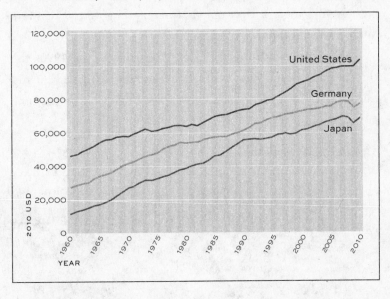

SOURCE: U.S. Bureau of Labor Statistics, Division of International Labor Comparisons, 15 August 2011.[53]

Another favorite of 1980s-style Declinism was Western Europe. In 1987, Calleo and other admirers of the Old Continent thought that the European Community was poised to outstrip the "hegemon in decay." The United States was "no longer supreme."

Its edge gone, the United States was floundering amid great dangers. "If there is a way out, it lies through Europe. History has come full circle: the Old World is needed to restore balance to the New."[54] The problem with America was too much military spending, an "undisciplined budget," "financial disorder," a glaring lack of "creative investment." How much better positioned were the Europeans with their "stable policies favorable to business investment"! Hence America should draw "inspiration" from Western Europe. With its healthier economy, the half continent was moving toward a more perfect union. To boot, its governments were "more efficient than the American."[55]

The problem with this assessment was that in the 1990s the United States would grow at an annual average of 3.5 percent and Europe (EU-15) by less than 2 percent (see figure 3). By the time

3. Real GDP Growth Rates, 1991–2011

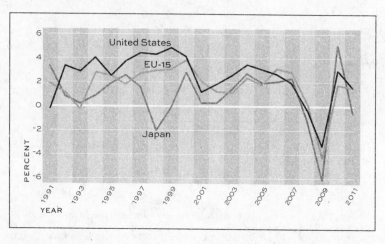

SOURCE: U.S. Department of Agriculture, Economic Research Service, "Historical GDP and Growth Rates," http://www.ers.usda.gov/Data/Macroeconomics/Data/HistoricalRealGDPValues.xls.

the decade was over, unemployment in the United States had fallen to below 4 percent, which is defined as full-employment. In the EU-15, it stood at 9 percent. So much for the *End of Work*, a stew of Malthus and Marx, cooked up at the time by Jeremy Rifkin. As his book had it, the entire globe would soon run out of jobs because of automation and information technology.[56] The United States stubbornly refused to obey what was offered as an iron law of history. So did the Asian economies.

The preeminent Declinist of the 1980s was Paul Kennedy, the Yale historian, who published *The Rise and Fall of the Great Powers* in 1987. The central argument of the 700-page tome was this: "The United States now runs the risk, so familiar to historians, of the rise and fall of previous Great Powers, of . . . 'imperial overstretch.'" Overstretch meant "that the sum total of the United States' global interests and obligations is . . . far larger than the country's power to defend them all simultaneously."[57] In an op-ed version, Kennedy provided this checklist of decay: "overall growth lagging behind that of its chief rivals," the "social problems of its inner cities," the "eroding infrastructure," and the "shortcomings of its educational system." It all added up to "relative decline," just as in the case of Britain, which once was also No. 1. Now the "new number one power is faltering."[58]

History had spoken, and there was only one decent choice left for the about-to-be-defrocked superpower: to "manage" its affairs so that the "erosion" progressed "slowly and smoothly."[59] Get your house in order, cut back on profligacy and imperial ambitions, counseled this former Briton. The most trenchant critique of Kennedy's Declinism was Samuel Huntington's seminal *Foreign Affairs* article in 1988.[60] He reserved his sharpest attack for a classic of Declinism: the steady shrinkage of America's share of the global economy. To lose GDP was to lose greatness, was the gist of Kennedy's indictment.

But it all depends on how the numbers are parsed. If 1945 is the base line, the United States was indeed on the skids. At the end of history's most murderous war, the American share of the global economy is commonly estimated at one-half. Naturally, as Europe, Japan, and the Soviet Union recuperated, that abnormal take was bound to shrink.[61] By 1950, the weight of the American economy was down to 27 percent, which is still enormous when compared with another baseline: the eve of World War I. At that point, the United States was good for only one-fifth of the world's total. In the 1970s, the average share was nearly 27 percent and at the end of the naughts of the twenty-first century a bit more than 26 percent.[62] The data demonstrate obstinate continuity once the anomaly of post-1945 is ignored.

The more general problem lurked elsewhere. When Kennedy looked at the two nations at the top, the United States and the USSR, he discovered a kind of "competitive decadence," a term coined by the Sovietologist Leopold Labedz some forty years ago. Both were declining, but the United States was sinking faster, Kennedy concluded. Actually, it was the other way around. The Soviet/former Soviet share halved between the 1970s and the 1990s, which is an enormous plunge by any historical standard. Kennedy certainly did not think the Soviet Union would "collapse at the first serious testing"[63]—very few people thought so[64]—but collapse the USSR did, a mere four years after *The Rise and Fall* came out. And why? Because whatever symptoms of decadence the United States displayed, the Soviet Union had them in multiples. Kennedy had so much right, except for the name of the loser.

Muscovy *was* overstretched. It had to police and subsidize its impoverished East European empire. It had to keep afloat its Latin American satrapy in Cuba, and pay for Castro's advance guard in the heart of Africa. It was fighting an unwinnable war in Afghanistan. It spent anywhere from two to three times more on its military (as a share of a much smaller economy) than did the United States, straining under the added burden of keeping up with Reaganite arms racing. Totalitarian industrialization under Stalin had brought victory over Nazi Germany. Now the model was grinding to a halt, colliding at every step with the demands of a modern economy. The Soviet Union lacked capital markets and capitalists; it stifled competition and globalization—conditions abounding in the United States. Worse, the Soviet Union suffered from cultural pathologies that made the United States look like an exemplar of strapping health. The list was endless, ranging from alcoholism as a national disease via plummeting fertility rates to the lowest life expectancy in the developed world.

The Soviet Union was the proverbial time bomb waiting to explode. The trigger was the price of oil. In 1980, crude fetched $100 per barrel (all figures in 2012 dollars). When Mikhail Gorbachev was anointed as general secretary five years later, oil stood at $57. When the Soviet Union committed suicide by abolishing itself on Christmas Day 1991, oil sold for $37, dropping to its lowest low, $17, seven years later. At that point, oil was cheaper in real terms than it had been just before the first oil shock, in 1973.[65] This "Upper-Volta with nuclear weapons," as the German chancellor Helmut Schmidt liked to quip, was in effect a Third World extraction economy chained to the prices of raw materials, especially of oil and gas. The source of its power had been minerals and nukes, as the long slide after Gorbachev's rise demonstrated.

Russia was more like Habsburg without Latin American gold and silver, which had paid for an empire "on which the sun never sets" until it ran out. Or like the Ottoman Empire, once a formidable war machine that drove all the way to Bosnia in the west and Basra in the east, but proved immune to modernization. And so the Soviet Empire was not at all like the United States. It did not possess the countless "renewable energies" of an economy that was the world's largest and most sophisticated, hence blessed with myriad sources of rejuvenation. In July 1990, Mikhail Gorbachev conceded to the West what Stalin and successors had ferociously refused for forty years: Germany's reunification within the West. The titanic struggle began and was played out in Germany, and so Gorbachev's "yes" was nothing less than Moscow's capitulation in the Cold War. To give away East Germany, the strategic brace, was to give away the entire empire.

The summer of 1990 thus opened a new chapter in the annals of "imperial overstretch." As the Soviet Union, for forty years the bear at the door, began to limp away, the United States merely stumbled into a short recession. Yet to dwell on this snapshot is to miss the larger point, which was a revolution in international affairs.

Suddenly, the rarest moment of international history was at hand: when one international system gives way to another. The two-power world, known as "bipolarity," vanished, and the last man standing was the United States. The strategic consequences came just as swiftly. As the Soviet Union was collapsing, the America of George H. W. Bush began to prepare for war against Saddam Hussein, and this in a region where American forces would never have dared venture while Moscow's power was still intact. Eventually, 700,000 troops were fielded in Iraq, a quasi-ally of Moscow, and they won handily. The draft was not reinstated, nor was the economy put on a war footing. Instead, it moved into the longest expansion ever, in spite of two more wars: in Afghanistan after 9/11 and again in Iraq in 2003. Such was the "relative erosion of the United States' position" predicted just a few years earlier.

The Twenty-First Century: The Chinese Are Coming!

Declinism mercifully took a break in the 1990s, perhaps because the United States was enjoying such a nice run after the suicide of the Soviet Union. Japan, the geoeconomic "killer app" of the 1980s, was still alive, but out of the race, where it has been ever since. Stuck in the "Lost Decade," the superstar of the 1980s no longer stoked American angst. Though Japanese automakers continued to decimate Detroit's Big Three, the ballyhoo about Japan had dwindled into embarrassing footnotes to history. "Gloom is the dominant mood in Japan these days," reported an Asian commentator, while "American capitalism is resurgent, confident, and brash."[66]

It doesn't take much to vault from Declinism to triumphalism when the geopolitics is right. Hadn't America just won the forty years' war, aka Cold War, the longest in modern history? What other country could win a hot war, as the United States had done in Iraq in 1991, from six thousand miles away? With a high-tech, spaced-based panoply worthy of World War IV? There was no new No. 1 creeping up on the United States—nowhere on the horizon. Why even think about a military threat, as in the Soviet days? U.S. Secretary of State Madeleine Albright crowed that America's clout was so daunting as to render its use unnecessary. "But if we have to use force, it is because we are America; we are the indispensable nation. We stand tall, and we see further than other countries into the future. . . ."[67] Depression had turned into self-aggrandizement.

After the First Iraq War, which cost only 294 American lives out of a total of 700,000 deployed, the *Washington Post* columnist Charles Krauthammer poured sarcasm on yesterday's Declinists: "If the Roman empire had declined at [our] rate, you'd be reading this column in Latin."[68] The U.S. economy, boosted by Reaganite deregulation and Clinton's welfare reforms, was soaring. As the budget went into surplus, unemployment virtually vanished. In Europe, by contrast, it rose above 10 percent in the late 1990s.

Decline was yesterday; now the United States had all the bragging rights. "The defining feature of world affairs" was "globalization," exulted the *New York Times'* Thomas Friedman at the 1997 World Economic Forum, "and [if] you had to design a country best suited to compete in such a world, [it would be] today's America." Forgotten was MITI, the all-knowing and all-powerful Japanese Ministry of International Trade and Industry. Japan was no longer the rage, though top-down modernization would soon be eulogized again as China became the new model. Now the heroes of the dot-com age bestrode the earth. They were the new masters of the universe, and they were all Americans. Those who used to go on a pilgrimage to Japan now invaded Silicon Valley. Friedman concluded on a triumphant note: "Globalization is us."[69]

The occasional Declinist harrumph in those days sounded either quirky or generic like a finger exercise at the piano. Edward Luttwak, a prominent strategist in Washington, thought that the United States would turn into a "third-world country" by 2020. The path seemed straight enough—"straight downhill." At any rate, the country was already adapting to its fate "by acquiring the necessary third-world traits of fatalistic detachment."[70] This was in

1992, on the cusp of America's longest boom, which extended all the way to 2007.

At the end of the naughts, decline was back with a vengeance. Back was Paul Kennedy with a remake of *The Rise and Fall*, this time because of the global financial crisis triggered by the fall of the house of Lehman on 15 September 2008. While Russia, China, et al. might be suffering "setbacks," the "biggest loser is understood to be Uncle Sam." Chronic fiscal deficits and military overstretch—the twin scourges of his 1987 book—were finally doing in the United States, and the "global tectonic power shift, toward Asia and away from the West, seems hard to reverse."[71] This shift was one reason for America's slide; the other was "American political incompetence." There was but one consolation: great powers "take an awful long time to collapse."[72] The nice thing about prophecy is that doom never comes with a date.

"The crash of 2008 has inflicted profound damage on [America's] standing in the world," warned Roger Altman, formerly the deputy treasury secretary; "the crisis is an important geopolitical setback."[73] German finance minister Peer Steinbrück predicted, "The U.S. will lose its status as the superpower of the global financial system [which] will become more multipolar."[74] The Harvard historian Niall Ferguson went halfway. On the one hand, "the balance of global power is bound to shift." On the other, "commentators should always hesitate before they prophesy the decline and fall of the United States."[75] He remained as sibylline two years later. "Empires," he wrote, "function in apparent equilibrium for some unknowable period. And then, quite abruptly, they collapse."[76] So disaster will strike, or it may not.

Actually, most empires take a long time to collapse, like the Roman, Ottoman, or Habsburg versions, whose demise unfolded over centuries. They collapse abruptly only in war, as did the tsa-rist, Austrian, Wilhelmine, and Turkish empires in World War I, and Japan's in World War II. Even in these cases, only Habsburg and the Porte literally disintegrated. Japan lost its short-lived war-time conquests, but the nation as such remained intact, turning into a commercial giant twenty-five years later. Russia just changed colors, from "White" to "Red," and then went on to expand into the heart of Europe. It would take another great war, the Cold War, to dismantle the Soviet empire seventy-four years later.

Yet this kind of war is not in America's future. There is no mean-ingful way in which others could destroy the United States, except at the price of self-immolation. In contrast to other empires, the United States will not be felled by war. Only the United States can do in the United States—as it almost did 150 years ago in the Civil War, in an attempt that is so deeply etched in the American memory that it does not invite repetition. In this century, sloth, hubris, or profligacy might gnaw at the vitality of the nation, as Declinists have prophe-sied for decades. But when and whether this would come to pass is indeed "unknowable," to recall Ferguson's key disclaimer. No such hesitation befell the Cassandras of Decline 5.0.

Some of their lore was again simply generic, that is, divorced from time and circumstance and thus achingly familiar to those who remember fifty years of similar wisdom. Two weeks after the fall of the house of Lehman in 2008, the Oxford don John Gray stressed a well-wrought theme: "The era of American global leadership . . . is over."[77] Actually, generic Declinism needs nei-ther date nor trigger. If it isn't repeated by the same prophet ten, twenty years down the lane, it is generational. So a few months before the Crash of 2008, the youngish Parag Khanna, of the New America Foundation in Washington, intoned, "America's standing in the world remains in steady decline." The disease was "imperial overstretch," and the price was the weakening of "America's armed forces" through overuse.[78] That had a familiar ring—recall Paul Kennedy's dirge twenty years earlier—and so did the report that "American power is in decline around the world." These obiter dicta could have been penned in 1958, 1968, 1978. So could this one: "We are competing—and losing—in a geopolitical marketplace alongside the world's other superpowers."[79]

Who were they? It used to be Russia in the 1950s and 1970s, and Japan in the 1980s. Now it was "the European Union and China." For Europe, it was the second time around the block. Twenty years earlier, an older generation of doomsters had touted the "rejuvenation of Europe and Japan," hence the "relative diminishing of the enormous American superiority."[80] A fact check: During those two decades, the EU-27's share of the global economy had dropped by 5 percentage points, and Japan's by three, while the United States take had remained the same. In the "competitive decadence" race, gold and silver were actually going to the EU and Japan.

And yet, claimed Khanna in 2008, "America is isolated while Europe and China occupy the two ends of the great Eurasian landmass that is the perennial center of gravity of geopolitics." Gone was not only the United States but also that colossus between Berlin and Beijing known as Russia and occupying eleven time zones. Europe was suddenly back again, perhaps because it had enjoyed a short-lived uptick in growth just prior to the Crash of 2008. One and a half years later, the Old Continent's days in the sun were over, and so *Time* unveiled "The Incredible Shrinking Europe."[81] Up or down—pushing the story is punditry's best friend.

Another recycled classic of Declinism read, "Over the past decade, the United States seemed to have lost ground in almost every conceivable area—political, economic, social, and international—and . . . its bearing in terms of values and principles. Arrogance, belligerence, individualism, and violence were trumping the values of human rights, equality, participation. . . ." As just retribution, the "United States is headed for hard times."[82] Those were the just wages of sin. Cotton Mather, Boston's stern (and influential) Puritan minister, could not have put it more cruelly three hundred years earlier, in 1709.[83]

Finally, two foreign voices. One was Kishore Mahbubani's, Singapore's former UN ambassador, whose bid to succeed Secretary-General Kofi Annan had been thwarted by Washington. He chronicled not just the degeneration of America but the triumph of Asia, as celebrated in the subtitle of his book *The New Asian Hemisphere: The Irresistible Shift of Global Power to the East*. The tone was avuncular, shading off into the patronizing: "Sadly . . . , Western intellectual life continues to be dominated by those who continue to celebrate the supremacy of the West. . . ." So the "West"—read: the United States—was losing its grip not only on power but also on reality—go from Chapter 11 straight to the couch. By contrast, "the rest of the world has moved on. A steady delegitimization of Western power . . . is underway." Now "other nations are . . . more competent in managing global . . . challenges."[84]

And who would inherit the earth? Only "four real candidates [could] provide global leadership today: the United States, the European Union, China and India." Japan, with the world's second-largest GDP and a per capita income ten times larger than China's, did not make it into this fellow Asian's pantheon. The United States? As "victim of the neo-cons on the right and the neo-protectionists on the left," it cannot bridge a "gap" between itself and the world that has "never been wider." So America was beyond redemption, the blame falling on both Bush forty-three on the right and Barack Obama on the left, whose Democrats were bouncing around protectionist shibboleths during the 2008 campaign. Rich and populous, Europe didn't make the cut, since it "has not been able to extend its benign influence outside its territory." India? It is "by far the weakest of the four." That left China, which "should eventually take over the mantle of global leadership from America."[85]

This was the polite version of Atlantis Lost—wishful thinking wrapped in detached analysis. Let us complement this take with the dyspeptic, no-holds-barred version of a Russian who had seen the Soviet empire disembowel itself and, in an act of psychic revenge, projected the same fate onto the United States. The Soviet Union had succumbed to its terminal economic incompetence, and so will the United States: "At some point during the coming years . . . , the economic system of the United States will teeter and fall. . . . America's economy will evaporate like the morning mist."[86] The author then meticulously tallied all the similarities, as he saw them, between the Soviet Union and the United States. Both were bastions of militarism, the "world's jailers," and deadly failures in education, ethnic integration, and health care. They were "evil empires" both.

Near the end of naughts, even before the Crash of 2008, the new Declinist consensus had settled on Asia—on China first and foremost, on India second, and on Russia and Brazil somewhere down the line. These were the fabled BRIC countries, the quartet that would inherit the world. The driver of the new dispensation was an old one. The United States was losing the growth race to those who were forging ahead at double-digit speed. In mid-decade, a former Japan booster like Clyde Prestowitz merely changed the names of the candidates in his *Three Billion New Capitalists: The Great Shift of Wealth and Power to the East.*[87] The chapter headings tell the tale. In this new world, things would be "Made in China" and "Serviced in India." And America was on the "Road to Ruin."

A former editor of the *Economist*, Bill Emmott, saw geopolitics following economics, with power growing not from the barrel of a gun but from GDP and trade statistics. Wasn't the World Bank predicting that China and India might triple their output in a matter of years? By the late 2020s, China would overtake the United States. And so, good-bye, America. *How the Power Struggle between China, India and Japan Will Shape Our Next Decade*, proclaimed the subtitle of his book *Rivals*.[88] Japan, stuck in real decline, was in again, and the United States was out.

The *Newsweek International* editor Fareed Zakaria, born in India and trained at Yale and Harvard, put an original gloss on an old story in 2008. It wasn't that America was decrepit and declining, as many previous authors had argued. America still had many assets on the ledger. Others were simply growing faster—at an awesome, unbreakable speed. A billion people in India, 1.3 billion in China—how could so much mass and momentum be stopped? Hence it was the "rise of the rest" that would dwarf the United States. And the future would belong to the "post-American world."[89] Two years later, the historian Niall Ferguson classified the United States as a "departing" power, up against the "arriving" power that was China.[90] Exit Gulliver, enter the Middle Kingdom. Finally for good?

Not yet. Four years after the Crash of 2008, the *Economist* put a strapping Uncle Sam on its cover, cheering him as "The Comeback Kid." Inside, the weekly announced, "Led by its inventive private sector, the economy is remaking itself. Old weaknesses are being remedied and new strengths discovered, with an agility that has much to teach to stagnant Europe and dirigiste Asia."[91] The United States was on the up; Europe and Asia were treading water. Earlier in the year, the *American Interest*, showing Uncle Sam punching with an oversized boxing glove, had put the same title—"The Comeback Kid"—on its cover. Inside, the journal presented articles like "How America Is Poised to Retake the Lead in the World Economy," "The Once and Future Dollar," and "The Population Boon."[92] *Foreign Affairs* put the "Demise of the Rest" on its cover. Inside, the title of the lead piece read, "Broken BRICs: Why the Rest Stopped Rising." Highlighting the tumbling growth rates of the quartet, the author added, "None of this should be surprising because it is hard to sustain rapid growth for more than a decade.[93]

Usually, Declinists just come back; they never repent. One did: Roger Altman, the former deputy treasury secretary turned business consultant. A prophet of decline in 2008, he celebrated America the Beautiful four years later.[94] The U.S. banking system had recovered faster "than anyone could have imagined. Capital and liquidity have been rebuilt to levels unseen in decades." The United States had made a "huge leap in industrial competitiveness" and could look forward to bringing back jobs from the rising rest. And the "breathtaking increase in oil and gas production" would "add more than one percentage point to annual GDP growth" within five years. Declinism, it seems, is a flexible device. In this case, it took four years to transition from Jeremiah to Pollyanna.[95] Through Declines 1.0 and 4.0, the American Phoenix had risen at comparable speeds.

Four years after *Rivals* had given the nod to China and India, its author thought that the "American century was *not* over." This might be the moment to "rethink all the fashionable assumptions about America's decline."[96] Another reformed Declinist, who had cheered Japan, China, and India in succession, now bet against them: "We are told again and again how China has enjoyed three decades of economic growth in excess of 10 percent annually, and how India and now others" were scoring in similar ways. But remember all previous economic miracles in Europe and Asia. "The truth is" that they all became unsustainable.[97]

In his presidential campaign of 2012, the Republican Mitt Romney sounded the trumpet for the "greatness of this country." Whereas President Obama had deflated the notion of "American exceptionalism," by noting that everybody else believed in his or her own country's exceptionalism,[98] Romney presented himself as "an unapologetic believer in the greatness of this country" who proclaimed, "This century must be an American century."[99] So, in fact, did the president. "America is back," he exulted in his 2012 State of the Union address. "Anyone who tells you otherwise, who tells you that America is in decline or that our influence has waned, doesn't know what they're talking about." Then he sounded a key theme of the Clinton administration: "America remains the one indispensable nation in world affairs."[100]

This sanguine portrayal of the country nicely shows that Declinism is a matter of dates, just like treason, as Talleyrand quipped. The night is always darkest during a presidential campaign. In office, especially as a second-term election is looming, it is "morning again in America," to recall Ronald Reagan's famous TV spot. So no more "decline" for Obama, as he prepared for his second run. This not-so-exceptional country was again the "indispensable nation."

A new cycle was unfolding, but trends, as this chapter has shown, are made up in the minds of beholders, and then for a purpose—be it political or pedagogical. Only time can tell what was a blip or a new pattern. Before we look at longer-term forces and numbers in chapter 3, let us ask why Declinism is such an evergreen. What are the functions of gloom and doom in the political discourse?

CHAPTER TWO

Politics and Prophecy, or the Uses of Declinism

History records five waves of American—let's call it— "hasbeenism" in as many decades. What is the moral of this oft-told tale? There are many, as the preceding chapter showed, but all of them share a common theme. "Decline Time in America" is never just a disinterested tally of trends and numbers. It is not about truth but about consequences, as in any morality tale. Declinism tells a story to shape belief and change behavior. The universal technique is dramatization and hyperbole. Since good news is no news, bad news is best in the marketplace of ideas. The winning vendor is not Pollyanna, the young girl who cheers the silver lining in every cloud, but Henny Penny, also known as Chicken Little, who always sees the sky falling.[1] But why does alarmism work so well, whether on the pulpit or on the hustings, whatever the inconvenient facts?

Since biblical times, prophets have never gone to town on rosy oratory, and politicos only rarely. Fire and brimstone are usually the best USP, "unique selling proposition" in marketing-speak. In our days, the looming-disaster strategy carries even more heft. For there was a time when the opposite—historical optimism—ran rampant in the West, roughly from the Enlightenment of the eighteenth century to the eve of World War I. Adam Smith and Karl Marx—one the father of liberalism, the other of communism—were historical optimists, and so were the French philosophes like Condorcet and Turgot.

History was the march out of misery, its end point a secular version of Eden. Yesterday was the vale of tears and oppression; tomorrow the age of reason and freedom would dawn; that was the promise of history. The Crystal Palace (1851) and the Eiffel Tower (1889) were built as soaring cathedrals to the faith in bigger and better, and forever more. Young America actually enshrined the triumph of progress in the Great Seal: "*novus ordo seclorum*." Now on every dollar bill, the motto was taken from a poem by Virgil: "The *great order of the ages* is born afresh / And now justice returns, honored rules return."

Reason, a shorthand for science, technology, and man's mastery over nature, did indeed triumph along with industrialization and explosive growth. Freedom took a few falls along the road, but the revolutions of the nineteenth century, even if they failed, showed that freedom would never stop banging on tyranny's door. The massacre that was World War I marked the turning point, revealing the evil face of technology triumphant.[2] The knowledge that raised the Eiffel Tower also gave the machine gun to the West, allowing one man to mow down a hundred without having to slow down for reloading. Nineteenth-century chemistry revolutionized industry, churning out those blessings, from petroleum to plastics and pharmacology, that made the modern world. But the same labs also invented poison gas. The hand that delivered good also created evil.

Worse, freedom's march was not only stopped but reversed. Democracy was flattened by the totalitarians of the twentieth century—Stalin, Mussolini, Hitler, Mao—and their fascist brothers in Iberia and Eastern Europe. Utopia in the here and now, as promised by the Enlightenment's faith in earthly redemption, died in the process. "What is the use of Utopia?" asked the Harvard political theorist Judith Shklar.[3] How to reason about the perfectibility of men and politics once the totalitarians had twisted hope into hell on earth? Their utopia, it turned out, was the universe of the Gulag and the death camp, and the road to salvation in the here and now led into a war that claimed 55 million lives.

And so, optimism as reigning creed of the West was pushed aside by pessimism. After World War I, Oswald Spengler, the German high priest of doom, ranted in his best-selling *The Decline of the West* against an "unbridled optimism that sets at naught all historical experience." It was sheer folly to try to "discover in the accidental present" a "striking progression-series" based not on "scientific proof, but on predilection."[4] It didn't get much better after the rubble of World War II had been cleared. The irony is quite thick. Flat or modest for millennia, economic growth rebounded in the middle of the twentieth century, yet pessimism actually increased, as well. Or more accurately: "Surveys consistently reveal individuals to be personally optimistic yet socially pessimistic."[5]

One by one, the great heroes of the eighteenth and nineteenth centuries ended up on Western culture's "Most Wanted" list: industry, technology, science—indeed, the very idea of progress itself. Suddenly progress had "become a lethal idée fixe, irreversibly destroying the very planet" mankind needed for its survival, growled *The Death of Progress*, a book that typified the tone of the 1970s.[6] Another killer app was Paul Ehrlich's *Population Bomb*, a twentieth-century remake of Malthus, predicting hundreds of million dead because food production could not keep up with the teeming masses about to inundate the globe. Material plenty, the dream of the ages, suddenly turned from friend to fiend. According to the Club of Rome, whose *Limits to Growth* (1972) sold 12 million copies, growth was the Faustian deceiver who would send the world to hell by devouring its resources, energy first (though the soothsayers did not set a fixed date).

In the 1980s, the nuclear bargain with the devil moved to the fore. In his best-selling *The Fate of the Earth*, Jonathan Schell predicted, that the only "class of animals" that would survive nuclear war was the "insect class."[7] Another curse of Faustian Man was "nuclear winter." Following a nuclear exchange, a smoke- and particle-laden atmosphere would thrust the world into a new ice age. As of the 1990s, nature would inflict the opposite revenge on the children of Prometheus. Having unleashed the fossil-fueled fire of industry, they were now reaping global warming. Their punishment would be the environmental apocalypse—melting ice caps, drowning coastal cities—that would dwarf the Flood. Grossing $125 million, *The Day after Tomorrow*, Hollywood's 2004 take on the end of the world, had it both ways: Global warming would first inundate the globe and then deep-freeze it. There was no way out; it was death by fire, water, and ice—and the demise of logic, as well.

THE STRUCTURE OF DOOMISM

The "death of progress" has pierced the historical optimism that is a pillar of the American creed. The country's founding ideology was the liberalism of the eighteenth century, the belief in the perfectibility of man, state, and culture. Conservatism, which holds to a tragic view of history, was always liberalism's sickly little brother in America. This ideological tradition could never grow strong enough to overshadow the mental landscape as it did in Europe, and no wonder: Wasn't America progress incarnate? The historical twist is that left and right have linked up on the common ground of pessimism. Twentieth-century American liberalism, social democratic rather than Lockean, now shares the dour weltanschauung of conservatism.

A weighty element of the liberal left's pessimism is a direct import from Europe: the Frankfurt School, transplanted during the Nazi era to the United States. There it was represented during the war by Theodor Adorno and Max Horkheimer[8] and in the 1960s by Herbert Marcuse. The *Kritische Schule* injected the deeply pessimistic views of Sigmund Freud into Marx, and gone was the classic Enlightenment optimist who saw man and society ascend to ever higher levels of well-being and freedom. Technology and plenty, the critics of the Enlightenment argued, would not liberate the common man, but enslave him anew in the prison of "false consciousness" built by the ruling elites. The new despair of the former torchbearers of progress may well be the reason why Declinism flourishes on both left and right. This new ideological kinship does not by itself explain the five waves of Declinism, but has certainly broadened its appeal.

Actually, "the sky is falling" should not be a very lucrative pitch. Such alarms stoke fear and panic; why invest in the future if the clock is running down? But the message has worked wonders since time immemorial because doom, in biblical as well as political prophecy, always comes with a shiny flip side, which is redemption. Darkness is the prelude to dawn. The gloomy forecast reviles past and present in order to promise the brightest of futures. Start with fire and brimstone, then jump to grace and deliverance in the here and now. Listen to Jeremiah as he thunders, "Turn from your wicked ways and reform your actions; then you will live in the [promised] land." Jeremiah may have been the father of modern campaign politics.

Preachers and politicos take naturally to this one-two punch because ruin followed by renewal is the oldest narrative in the mental data bank of mankind. The device is even older than the verdict of doom—the *Mene, Tekel* on the palace wall—revealed by Daniel. Start with the Flood, a universal theme played out over four chapters in Genesis, but found much earlier in Sumerian and Babylonian myth, as related in the *Gilgamesh Epic* dated 2700 BCE. Genesis, written in the fifth or sixth century BCE, expands and embellishes the original. It relates how "the Lord saw that the wickedness of man was great in the earth." So He decides to "blot out man whom I have created from the face of the land, for I am grieved that I have made them." The end is nigh, but don't despair. Mankind will be spared after all, because the Lord selects Noah, who has "found favor in His eyes," and commands him to build an ark that will save mankind.

So after death by Deluge, it will be rebirth for the righteous led by an ordinary mortal who knows the future, and how to act on it. This story never ends. The Children of Israel were punished for the Golden Calf, the idol that embodied a wicked past, with forty years in the wilderness. Yet if true to the Law and to God's messenger Moses, they will be rewarded with the Promised Land. As the Resurrection follows the Crucifixion, so misery will segue into salvation, but there has to be a leader, spiritual or political, to show the way: Moses or Jesus, John F. Kennedy or Ronald Reagan or Barack ("Yes, we can") Obama. The pairing of doom and deliverance defines the eternal archetype.

Here is a modern-day version of the classic. At the end of the 1970s, at the height of Jimmy Carter's "malaise," the American social critic Christopher Lasch published a generic lament, requiring only minor editing to make it timeless:

> Hardly more than a quarter-century after Henry Luce proclaimed the "American Century," American confidence has fallen to a low ebb. Those who recently dreamed of world power now despair of governing the city of New York. Defeat in Vietnam, economic stagnation, and the impending exhaustion of natural resources have produced a mood of pessimism in higher circles, which spreads through the rest of society as people lose faith in their leaders. [America] has lost both the capacity and the will to confront the difficulties that threaten to overwhelm it.[9]

Substitute "Afghanistan and Iraq" for "Vietnam" and "global financial crisis" for "economic stagnation" to bring the indictment up to date. "Exhaustion of natural resources," "pessimism," and "loss of faith in leaders" need no refurbishing; these themes are timeless. But hold the despair! This is merely the first paragraph of the book. True to the ancient model, the book ends in the last paragraph with the second part of the prophetic paradigm—the promise of redemption: "The will to build a better society . . . survives, along with traditions of localism, self-help and community action that only need the vision of a new society . . . to give them new vigor."[10] In all instances of Declinism, there is this double whammy of damnation and deliverance—if only we repented and reverted to the best traditions we have betrayed.

In all these narratives, ruin is the means, and rescue the end.

Terror is the teaching device that will change the course of history. For all his tirades, every Jeremiah actually *wants* to be disproved by making his errant flock atone and amend. "Declinism is a theory that has to be believed to be invalidated," explains Samuel Huntington.[11] It is the opposite of the familiar "self-fulfilling prophecy," a term coined by the sociologist Robert Merton. The alarm starts out with a "*false* definition of the situation" and then triggers "new behavior which makes the original false conception come 'true.' "[12] To predict a bank failure is to unleash a run that will actually cause the collapse.

Declinism markets a "self-*defeating* prophecy." Since these predictions deal with humans, and not planets or protozoans, they are designed to trigger reactions that lift the curse. Merton puts it thus: Evil does not come true "precisely because the prediction has become a new element" that changes the "initial course of developments."[13] So to foretell is to forestall—that is the very purpose of Declinism. Take the "impending exhaustion of natural resources" from Malthus to the Club of Rome, which foresaw the end of global growth some forty years ago, especially because of dwindling oil reserves. Myriad changes in behavior—from conservation to exploration—followed, causing oil gluts on the market in the 1980s and a gas glut in the 2010s. The world economy grew twentyfold in this period (nominally). Would that all catastrophes had such a short shelf life!

None of America's Declinists over the past half century, as presented in the preceding chapter, actually *wanted* the country to suffer its foreordained fate. The prophecy is *designed* to be self-defeating, and the structure of augury is always the same: This will happen unless . . . Holding up another nation as a model is to correct one's own, not to condemn it—from the Sputnik Shock of the

1950s to Obama's "Sputnik moment" in the 2010s. To praise others is to prod America. Russia, Europe, Japan, et al. *will* overtake us, unless we labor hard to change our self-inflicted destiny. The basic diagnosis remains constant; only the prescription will vary according to the ideological preferences of the seer.

In politics, "the sky is falling" has yet another purpose. It is no accident that the figure of the prophet, in the legend or on the stump, stands at the center of the narrative. We have to believe in the messenger so that he can rise above us and guide us to a better tomorrow. Hence dramatization and exaggeration, fibbing or even outright falsehood, are part and parcel of the prophecy. To hype is to win. Never mind that the Missile Gap and the Window of Vulnerability were mere myths. Expediency beats veracity in campaigning and sermonizing. And so, hyperbole paves the road from the vale of tears—or to the White House. "Follow me, and ye shall be saved!" is the eternal message. Or in Kennedy's words, borrowed from Churchill, "Come then—let us to the task, to the battle and the toil. . . ."[14]

Prophet or politico, the strategy is to paint the nation in hellish colors and then to offer oneself as a guide to heaven. The country is on the skids, but tomorrow it will rise again—if only you, the people, will anoint me as your leader. It worked for both John F. Kennedy and Ronald Reagan, who rode all the way to the White House on nonexisting Soviet missiles. Shakespeare wrote the original script. To "busy giddy minds with foreign quarrels" was Henry IV's advice to his son and successor. The democratic equivalent is to scare up votes with foreign threats.

After the election, dawn always follows doom—as when Kennedy called out, "Let the word go forth that the torch has been passed to a new generation of Americans."[15] Gone was the Soviet bear that had grown to monstrous size in the 1950s. And so again, twenty years later. At the end of Ronald Reagan's first term, his fabled campaign commercial exulted, "It's morning again in America. And under the leadership of President Reagan, our country is prouder and stronger and better."[16] In the fourth year of Barack Obama's first term, America was "back" and again on top. Collapse was yesterday, today it is resurrection. This miraculous turnaround might explain why Declinism usually blossoms at the end of an administration—and wilts quickly after victory.

THE FUNCTIONS OF DOOMISM

Declinism has served many objectives in American politics, as the first chapter shows. It has helped to turn elections in 1960 and 1980. It has made careers. It has changed defense policy three times, triggering massive rearmament in the early and late 1950s as well as in the early 1980s. It has galvanized the nation to launch great undertakings intended to undo the curse.

Winning the White House. John F. Kennedy was the first in modern times to ride a self-made wave of doom all the way into the Oval Office in 1960. The moment the Gaither Report appeared in 1957, Kennedy decided that he had found a winning issue in the tale of Moscow's looming victory in the nuclear arms race. The trial run was his senatorial campaign in 1958, when he painted "great danger within the next few years"[17] on the American wall. Two years later, then aiming for the White House, he accused the outgoing Eisenhower administration of betraying the national interest by allowing the Soviets to forge ahead. Once they had built up a larger and mightier arsenal, the very survival of America would hang in the balance.

It wasn't just a matter of numbers, for to lose the arms race was to lose America. The greatest power on earth was fated to shrink to a has-been. And so Kennedy oracled as Declinists have through the ages: "Maybe our brightest days were earlier, and . . . now we are going into the long, slow afternoon."[18] Thirty years later, it was the Soviet Union that slunk off into the darkness, never to reappear again. When the red hammer-and-sickle flag flying over the Kremlin came down for the last time on Christmas Day 1991, the Soviet empire expired. From its corpse rose fifteen independent republics.

Kennedy's feverish rhetoric helped him keep his Senate seat in 1958 and surely turned the cliff-hanger election of 1960 in his favor. JFK scored just 100,000 votes more than his Republican rival Richard Nixon did. (Cynics will say that the miracle was due to Mayor Richard J. Daley of Chicago, who made the dead rise from the graves in Cook County so that they could cast their votes and make Kennedy carry Illinois.) A margin that could have gone either way propelled Kennedy into the White House. Afterward, the Missile Gap miraculously disappeared.[19] Kennedy had invented the winning recipe, and exactly twenty years later, another presidential candidate, this time from the other side of the aisle, used practically the same ingredients to cook up victory for the Republicans.

Only the labels had changed in the run-up to Ronald Reagan's rout of Jimmy Carter. The Missile Gap was now called Window of Vulnerability. The language also echoed Kennedy's. Driving toward strategic superiority, the Soviets would not merely overtake the United States but pose a threat the United States had never faced. With their heavier and more accurate missiles, the Soviets might soon be able to launch a first strike that would all but disarm the United States, leaving it with only two choices: abject surrender or complete annihilation. Short of the apocalypse, the Soviets could intimidate and coerce the West, hence win the Cold War without unleashing a hot one.

Again, hyperbole—in truth, willful misrepresentation—carried the day. In the late 1970s, the United States was actually ahead by almost three to one in strategic warheads. In his campaign, Ronald Reagan blithely invoked Armageddon as Kennedy had done in 1960: "America's defense strength is at its lowest ebb in a generation, while the Soviet Union is vastly outspending us in both strategic and conventional arms."[20] The Soviets weren't outspending and never would outrace the United States. But whereas Kennedy had won with the narrowest of margins in 1960, Ronald Reagan was swept into the White House by a landslide twenty years later (with 489 to 89 Electoral College votes).

Incumbents are not so lucky, because they have to run against themselves. Amid a sinking economy and rising inflation, Jimmy Carter's "malaise" rhetoric of 1979 served up the classic one-two punch of prophets throughout the ages: We are falling, but we shall rise again—if you listen to me. The "very heart and soul and spirit of our national will" were at stake, he intoned. But fear not, he added in so many words, for I am here to save you. He had "decided to reach out and listen to the voices of America." And this is what he heard: "If you lead, Mr. President, we will follow." I am your prophet, and ye shall prosper if ye anoint me. The nation did not and sent Carter back to Georgia on Inauguration Day 1981.[21]

Doom as Career Builder. A close relative of the "Go Straight to the White House Gambit" is the "Piggy-Back Polka." This strategy is nicely exemplified by the Committee on the Present Danger in the waning Carter days. This group—drawn from academia, think tanks, and media—wrote the ideological software for Reagan's victory machine. The candidate himself had joined the executive committee in 1979. It laid out America's coming demise and then managed to spread the horror scenario to the public at large. A favorite outlet was *Commentary* magazine, which would gain influence as house organ of the neoconservative creed. As always, *Time* and *Newsweek* added their voices to popularize the grim tale of *America Perdita*.

The committee helped launch Reagan to the presidency; once in office, he returned the favor by bringing thirty-three of its members into his government. (In 1953, various members of an earlier CDP incarnation were offered positions in the Eisenhower administration.) George Shultz became secretary of state, and Jeanne Kirkpatrick, one of the committee's most gifted writers, went to the UN as U.S. ambassador. Richard Allen moved to the White House as national security adviser. William Casey was appointed director of the CIA, and Richard Perle, the new assistant secretary, came to occupy a powerful position in the Defense Department. Paul Nitze would lead the negotiations on Theater Nuclear Forces in Europe. Thus did prophecy, false as it turned out to be, act as a nifty career builder for Reagan as well as his intellectual allies.

Changing Policy I. Though they draw a straight line to hell, doomsayers *want* to be wrong; that is the name of the game. The prophecy must disprove itself. Especially when it came to defense spending and procurement, the mechanism functioned like clockwork, and so it was wound up again and again. As the stock drama—call it "Down Today, Out Tomorrow"—was restaged once per decade, yesterday's props and personages reappeared as well. Here, too, the Committee on the Present Danger played a starring role—and did so thrice in the past fifty seasons.

The committee was originally established in 1950 as a "citizen's lobby" to alert the country to the "present danger" posed by the Soviet Union and to publicize the National Security Council's top-secret NSC-68 Report. It did not take much lobbying. Once the Soviets had exploded their first nuclear bomb in 1949, grim forebodings spread through the entire policy establishment and thence to the nation. Wouldn't the Soviet Union pulverize the United States next, now that the American nuclear monopoly was broken? The nation, then good for one-half of the global economy, began to shudder.

Treasured by Cold War historians as a turning point, NSC-68 was a call to arms against an enemy "unlike previous aspirants to hegemony . . . animated by a new fanatic faith, anti-thetical to our own."[22] There was only one way: to outarm it, which the United States did in spades. Not only nuclear but also conventional forces expanded dramatically, for instance, when the United States, reversing years of demobilization, committed four additional divisions to Western Europe. The North Korean attack on the South acted as a catalyst. Military spending tripled during that period, "but only a small fraction of this was due to the Korean campaign as such."[23]

In 1976, the CPD was back, hawking the Window of Vulnerability as a threat that would deliver final victory to the Children of Darkness. The CPD came onstage for the third time in 2004 to steel the nation for the "Global War on Terror." Yet Terror International, lacking the punch to inflict strategic damage on the United States, wasn't quite the Soviet behemoth that had oppressed the American imagination all the way into the 1980s. Hence CDP III remained on the margin of the public's consciousness

In the Soviet case, the specter of Armageddon came to naught each time. Following each round of "The Russians Are Coming," policy shifted dramatically to erase the handwriting on America's wall. In 1950, the U.S. nuclear arsenal measured in the hundreds. Toward the end of the 1950s, the stockpile had grown to 5,000. By the time John ("Missile Gap") Kennedy was inaugurated, it had shot up to 25,000 (tactical and strategic) warheads. In the 1980s, the heyday of CDP II, the United States fielded a new class of nuclear weapons in Europe—572 cruise missiles and Pershing II— while adding a new generation of sophisticated strategic weapons to the arsenal. For its prophets, doom was never as sweet as in the decades of the nuclear buildup that thrust America's nuclear numbers from the low 100s to the mid-30,000s.

Changing Policy II. The mildest variant of Declinism was Richard Nixon's—not down today and out tomorrow, but downsizing. Beset by a war in Vietnam that America could no longer sustain, the president painted a new five-power world on American's wall; yesterday's global duopoly would soon expand into a balance-of-power system as in the eighteenth and nineteenth centuries. The tectonic change would require a new grand strategy: the shift from containment to détente with both Soviet Russia and "Red China," as it was known in those days. The suggestive message was this: If we are sinking, and they are rising, let's deal while the dealing is good.

The new strategy signaled realism as well as good realpolitik. The realism reflected the dire state of the nation, squeezed as it was by the revolt against the Vietnam War and the overspending legacy bequeathed by the preceding administration. Devaluation and inflation, wage and price controls were hammering the American economy. The "domestics" of decline need to be stressed.

The real problem was less the "rise of the rest" than the "unraveling of America."[24] Yet neither Nixon nor Kissinger was planning for self-demotion, which is something great powers never do. The repositioning was to place the United States at center stage in hard times. By opening up to China and courting Soviet Russia, America should still be able to orchestrate great-power diplomacy—and more economically than ever before. That was good realpolitik with a weak domestic hand.

Yet the shift from Cold War to cooperation required an ideological shift as well. Hence, a nation weaned on decades of anticommunism was suddenly treated to Nixon's tireless efforts at reeducation.[25] Communism was no longer "monolithic"; its unity had been "shattered." (Make that: We can deal with them one by one, and play one against the other.) Once we had a "monopoly or overwhelming superiority of nuclear weapons," but now that edge is gone. (Read: We have to talk to them.) Both the Soviet Union and the United States "have recognized a vital mutual interest in halting the dangerous momentum of the nuclear arms race." (Read: There is no shame in cooperation.) Ideological enmity was yesterday because "today, the 'isms' have lost their vitality." (So let's ditch the ideological baggage.) All told, "peace requires partnership," and that "requires a willingness to negotiate."[26]

Decline was the diagnosis, and modesty the medicine. Beset by war at home and abroad, Nixon rearranged the world's power map in order to change the mental map of America. The point of the exercise was to prepare the nation for a deal with yesterday's sworn enemies, Soviet Russia and Red China, so that Washington could extract leverage from either and pit both against Hanoi. Apparent decline was thus forged into a handy tool. The rhetoric was exaggerated, but its purpose was American power. The French have a term for this: *reculer pour mieux sauter.* Take a few steps backward to gather speed and jump all the farther.

The Nixon administration did not clear the Vietnam hurdle. Instead of serving as force multipliers of U.S. grand strategy, Moscow and Beijing were happy to let Hanoi inflict defeat on America. Still, the Cassandras who predicted America's bow-out were not vindicated, even though under Jimmy Carter the country seemed to sink into terminal decay. Phoenix rose under Reagan and soared under Clinton. And the Soviet Union disappeared from history. Fifteen years after the American retreat from Vietnam, the world was neither bi- nor multipolar but unipolar. America was the last man standing, towering over the world.

Rousing the Nation. Sputnik wasn't just a Soviet satellite, but a *Mene, Tekel* of biblical heft. In happy contrast to Babylon, though, the days of the American kingdom were not numbered, as the soothsayers of the 1950s had been shouting. The handwriting was a call to arms that galvanized the nation. One fruit of the alarmism was the National Defense Education Act less than one year later, financing an all-out campaign to improve American education. In the next ten years, federal expenditures on education grew almost fivefold.[27] This is what "Johnny can't read" wrought.

Another fruit of post-Sputnik agitation was a huge investment in missile development that would catapult the United States all the way to the moon in 1969. At that point, the country had around five strategic warheads for every Soviet one. The "military-industrial complex," as Eisenhower had called it, profited handsomely. "It is vital to the national interest that we increase the output of scientific and technical personnel," argued Wernher von Braun, the director of the Army Ballistic Missile Agency, in

1958.[28] Congress was happy to oblige, plowing billions not only into strategic rearmament but also into research and development. One year after Sputnik, Congress established the National Aeronautics and Space Administration in 1958. NASA's budget request for fiscal year 2013, approved by President Obama, was $18 billion.

Prophecy, to repeat, is not about truth but about consequences— all of them instrumental. Declinism spells out "repent and reform" in a secular vernacular. If Johnny can't read and Mary can't do her math, then America must revamp its educational system. If the Soviets are first in space, then the United States must catch up and propel a man to the moon. If the Soviets sprint ahead in the nuclear race (which they never did), then the country must outspend and outarm them. Declinism is not about diagnosis, but about the deluge that must not come. The prophet *wants* to be wrong.

Why Glee, Why Gloom?

What shall we conclude from half a century of American has-beenism? First, doom comes in cycles, as it has done since the birth of the Republic, not just since Sputnik.[29] As early as 1797, the French thinker Joseph de Maistre found grievous "symptoms of weakness and decay" in a country still in infancy.[30] If so, this sickly child made up for his measly health with sheer insolence. As an adolescent, the United States launched its very first war—against the Barbary pirates—in 1801. Eleven years later, it unleashed another against Britain, the world's naval superpower; luckily the War of 1812 ended in a draw, though the British burned down the White House in the process. Barely into adulthood in 1823, the United States ordered all the then great powers to lay off the Western Hemisphere; this was known as the Monroe Doctrine:

"the Americas for the Americans!" In between, Thomas Jefferson grabbed half a continent from Spain and France without firing a single shot. The largest chunk was known as the Louisiana Purchase, a steal at $15 million, today about $230 million. Expansion all the way to the Pacific followed. Decay, as diagnosed by Dr. de Maistre, has never been so lively.

Decay and rebirth followed a roller-coaster pattern. The Civil War almost tore the Union asunder. When it was over, the United States was one again. The transcontinental railroad and the telegraph turned the continent into a vast single market that drove rapid industrialization and attracted immigrants by the tens of millions. Hardly eight years after the Confederacy's surrender, decline was back. Its name was the "Long Depression," and it lasted from 1873 to 1896—a series of bubbles, panics, and busts. At the end of that period, a newly muscular (and brash) America bestrode the global stage, pocketing Cuba and the Philippines. From World War I, the United States emerged as arbiter of the international economy. The Roaring Twenties followed.

The United States was back on top again, but not for long. At the beginning of the 1930s, the sky was truly falling as the Great Depression brought the country to its knees. Before it was over, the Japanese attack on Pearl Harbor added military humiliation to economic tragedy. Yet in 1945 the United States found itself at the pinnacle of the global hierarchy. Five years later, another plunge into panic followed. Having broken America's nuclear monopoly, the Soviets might do in one fell swoop what Hitler and Hirohito couldn't even imagine; they might literally obliterate "America the Beautiful." This was the overture to the five acts of modern American Declinism, beginning with the Sputnik Shock.

The periodic rise and demise of Decline all the way into the twenty-first century ought to be good news, for what comes and goes cannot lead straight to the eighth circle of geopolitical hell. Cycles, by definition, do not a trend make. Nor does the swelling tide announce the deluge; it is in the nature of the tide to recede as regularly as it rises. But this is just a logical point. More interesting is the psychology of Declinism. Transcending the many ups and downs, it drives an enduring narrative about America, abroad as well as at home.

Ever since America was discovered, as this author has noted elsewhere, it "has been an object of the imagination. Long before the thirteen colonies coalesced into union, America was a construct more than a country—a canvas onto which [the world] would end-lessly project its fondest dreams and fiercest nightmares."[31]

America has remained a split screen for the mind, a frightful dystopia like *Brave New World* or a heavenly place on earth like Thomas More's *Utopia*. For the rest of the world, it has been either a magnet or a monster. Projection, be it fear or fantasy, guides the hand that holds the brush. On the canvas that is America, two motifs have always predominated, call them Babylon and New Jerusalem. One stands for decrepitude and abomination, the other for boundless energy and hope. More recently, "hope" and "yes, we can" were the mantras of Barack Obama's 2008 campaign, a vision cheered around the world.

Finis Americae also comes in two varieties: glee and gloom. Glee is mostly celebrated abroad, and for good reason. Wanting America to falter comes naturally to smaller nations that must coexist with this real-life Gulliver, for he irks by just being there, and terrifies when he throws his weight around. To find solace, the lesser play-ers will magnify the giant's warts and count each new one as proof of a terminal malady. And why not? It is hard to share the global neighborhood with Mr. Big. So every decade, hope springs anew that he will be cut down to size by a mightier rival, be it Russia or Japan, Europe or China.

Such unkind wishes are actually a perverse way of paying homage to the giant's fearsome strength. Small powers are never diagnosed with debility; nor do they provoke schadenfreude when they take a fall. The rise-and-fall literature on Rome fills a small library, and so do the tomes on the decline of Britain, the preeminent power of the nineteenth century. The output is definitely on the small side for present-day France, Germany, or Canada. These may stumble at times—recall the "Eurosclerosis" of the 1990s and the euro crisis that erupted in 2010—but they never threaten.

So it is reassuring to see Gulliver stumble. But there is more. For Declinists abroad, the American canvas also offers a chance to paint a dystopia for home consumption. It is a morality tale with a pedagogical message: Do not fall for the siren that is America. She may be seductive, but beware. The Swiss historian Jakob Burckhardt, who was much admired by Nietzsche, pointed specifically to the United States while praising the fruits of democracy and modernity in the last third of the nineteenth century: "equality before the law," "mobility," "freedom of industry," "enormous material growth," the "beginning of absolute political equality." But then he switched to the dark side of the canvas. "It is doubtful whether the world . . . has thus become a happier place." For "money has become the measure of all things." Life in Europe was somehow better in the Middle Ages—an era "without deadly competition, without credit and capitalism."[32] (This is an old trope that leaves out pestilence and poverty, short lives and long wars.) Capitalism is the threat and America its vanguard. This motif has been a classic of anti-modernism for two centuries in Europe.

Naturally, it was painted in the gloomiest colors in the aftermath of the Crash of 2008.

Go back twenty years for this piece of generic Declinism by the British pundit-philosopher John Gray. For him, the drivers of America's decay are the "free market" and the "religious right" that lords it over the Congress. The European left does not treasure either; so to unmask the seductress, the critics will be delighted to turn any crisis symptom into proof of pathology.[33] According to Gray, writing two years into the longest American expansion, the country was degenerating into a melee of "warring cultural and ethnic groups," with "ungovernability" just around the corner. It all added up to a "spectacle of American decline." But this dismal verdict was just the first half of a one-two punch. The second was an appeal to his country: Break the Special Relationship! Britain should finally choose its "real destiny as a European nation."[34] The point is to hold up decrepit America as a warning to the seer's gullible compatriots: Don't go there, the American road leads to ruin.

The recurring counsel for fellow Europeans boils down to a single injunction: "Discard America, it is dystopia." In 2010, a German piece of political pedagogy carried the headline "Good Night, America." Running on for ten pages, the cover story of *Der Spiegel* dwelled on the nation's economic plight two years after the fall of the house of Lehman. The moral read, in so many words, "America is utopia no more." In the past, the United States had been "a radical, free, forward-looking and bold country—a triumphant country, or so it appeared." It used to be "a country of limitless possibility." Now look again. The "dream" had degenerated into a "nightmare," terms that replicated Hannah Arendt's penned sixty years earlier.[35] At "some point, everything comes to an end. The United States is a confused and fearful country in 2010." Worse, it "is a hate-filled country." And "once decline has gotten underway, it isn't easy to change direction."[36] So, at last, the United States was finished.

If glee is generally produced abroad, the gloom is basically Made in U.S.A., and then with a very different thrust. The purpose is not to gloat but to lament in the way of the prophet Obadiah: "Behold I have made you small among the nations; you are much despised." The prophet Amos quotes God: "The virgin of Israel has fallen." (Put in America here.) Then, in a striking contemporary analogy: "I will raise up against you a nation, says the Lord." (Insert Russia, Europe, Japan, China.) But those who atone will be richly rewarded: "And I will return the captivity of My people Israel, and they shall rebuild desolate cities and inhabit [them], and they shall plant vineyards and drink their wine." Finally, the central role of the prophet—Obadiah—as redeemer: "And saviors shall ascend Mt. Zion."

Biblical prophets used to invoke the wrath of God to discipline the wayward. Latter-day seers deploy the vernacular of international politics. Disgrace among the nations is the prod that will restore righteousness where backsliding or hubris has reigned. Repent and return to building the New Jerusalem, runs the standard tale of woe. The ways vary according to ideological coloration, be it liberal or libertarian, isolationist or exemplarist.

John Winthrop's "Cittie uppon a Hill"[37] has been many things in American history. For Alexander Hamilton, Theodore Roosevelt, or John F. Kennedy, this City was a nationalist project—an exceptional America with exceptional power. At the very birth of the Republic, Hamilton invoked a Declinist motif to make his point. "Poverty and disgrace" would descend on the young nation unless it established "one great American system" so "superior" to the rest that it would be "able to dictate the terms of the connection between the old and the new world."[38] How to make the nation rally around this "great system"? Raise the specter of American frailty or fall from power. So Hamilton got his strong executive, and Kennedy the White House, followed by the imperial temptation of the 1960s. The "survival of liberty," JFK famously orated, could be assured only if the nation stood ready to "pay any price" and "bear any burden." This City would not just sit on its Hill but venture forth to fulfill its mission. It would vindicate American exceptionalism.

These words echoed Theodore Roosevelt's seventy-five years earlier. "Is America a weakling, to shrink from the work of the great world powers?" he famously asked in a letter to John Hay in 1897. "No! The young giant of the West stands on a continent and clasps the crest of an ocean in either hand."[39] As secretary of the navy, Roosevelt got the ships, the money, and the guns to launch the Spanish-American War and the country's colonial career. For the nationalist school, America's greatness demanded unity and exertion—assertiveness abroad and a muscular state at home.

The opposite blueprint was drawn by the Jeffersonians, the opponents of Hamilton and the strong-state Federalists. For them, the "survival of liberty" called not for empire but for humility. The nation's freedom was as fragile as it was precious, and the search for grandeur would poison freedom by bringing forth a "man on a horseback," Jefferson feared. So the prescription was for small government and isolation from the world. The contemporary syllogism, repeated a hundredfold, runs like this: We must not play policeman to the world. The price is imperial overstretch, unbearable military expenditures, high taxes, and big government. If we do, we risk peril and perdition. To reverse the downward spiral, we must get out of harm's way and "walk humbly with our God," as John Winthrop counseled nearly four hundred years ago.

Jefferson picked up on this theme in his first inaugural address: "Kindly separated by nature and a wide ocean from the exterminating havoc of one quarter of the globe; too high minded to endure the degradations of the others, possessing a chosen country," he pledged "honest friendship with all nations, entangling alliances with none."[40] To avoid the "havoc," which would contaminate it, the nation had to stay at home—where, one should add, there was much to do, like conquering an entire continent.

John Quincy Adams is another exemplar of this American classic. For him America's "glory" was not "dominion, but liberty." If she enlisted "under other banners than her own," he orated, "she would involve herself, beyond the power of extrication, in all the wars of interest and intrigue, of individual avarice, envy, and ambition." America would "no longer be the ruler of her own spirit" if she became "the dictatress of the world."[41] Ambition and empire, reads this morality tale, pave the road to ruin.

Folly goeth before the fall, runs the Jeffersonian conviction. This stance might be called anticipatory Declinism. Decline is not yet, as the contemporary variant has it. But beware. Unless the nation abjures grandstanding and power mongering, its body and soul will suffer. This theme is also part of the modern liberal faith, which is represented by the Democratic left and its intellectual *confrères*. "Come home, America," was George McGovern's battle cry in the 1972 campaign against Richard Nixon—and retroactively against the expansionist tradition represented by old-style Democratic presidents like Truman, Kennedy, and Johnson.

For Jeffersonians, old-style liberals, self-corruption and decline flow from overcommitment and imperial arrogance. But the new story line of the liberal left comes with a different twist and purpose. In contrast to that of Jefferson and John Quincy Adams, its antidote is not small but interventionist government at home. Genuine strength demands less warfare for the sake of more welfare. The New Jerusalem of the Democratic left is not the bristling armory but the laboratory of an exemplary society. "Imperial overstretch," which suffuses so much of liberal thinking, is at heart not a diagnosis but a device—as is the case with all variants of Declinism. The specter of America's fall from grace is summoned for a grand political design. It is the transformation of America in the name of equality and social justice. Retrenchment and self-containment, disarmament and withdrawal from distant wars of choice, as most recently practiced by the Obama administration, is the first step toward America as it should be: ever stronger because it cares (and pays) for the weak. "Nation-building right here at home" was the president's motto.[42]

Whether on the left or on the right, "The sky is falling!" is the call of the righteous that will make goodness triumph. Whatever the ideological impetus, Declinism is about prophecies that must not come true so that America's real greatness (and exceptionalism) may triumph. Hence, Declinism is a political program even though it comes in the guise of an empirical exercise such as counting guns and measuring growth. The nice part is that these predictions cannot be empirically refuted, because they come without a date.

Or the date keeps receding into the future. While Sputnik was still careening through the American mind, the great economist Paul Samuelson, who would receive the Nobel Prize in 1970, predicted that Soviet national income might overtake the American one by 1984, but surely by 1997. In the 1980 edition of *Economics*, the dates of doom were pushed back to 2010, respectively 2012.[43]

How to gainsay those who either cheer or fear America's demise? No soothsayer has ever been silenced by facts because prophecy is inherently unfalsifiable. If disaster does not strike tomorrow, it will next week or next year.

So, the doomsters always come back. They are often the same people, repeating what they predicted twenty or forty years before.[44] During the Crash of 2008, a *New Yorker* cartoon gently poked fun at such recidivists. It shows a penitent with a placard proclaiming, "The End Is *Still* Coming," and has a passerby ask, "Wasn't that Paul Krugman?"—the economist and perennial Cassandra of the *New York Times* op-ed page?[45] The sellers of doom usually do not yield to obstreperous facts; they choose only those that fit their plea. And these will always be found in a welter of fractious detail. This is the difference between human affairs and the orbits of electrons and planets.

Nor are prophets ever held to account; this is another nice part of the job. "Arch-pessimists," muses Matt Ridley in his *The Rational Optimist*, "are feted, showered with honors and rarely challenged, let alone confronted with their past mistakes."[46] It helps to attach distant dates to predictions, as did the Club of Rome in 1972 when it gave the apocalypse a hundred years to come true. Dennis Meadows, the author of *The Limits to Growth*, keeps jetting around the world where he pitches his rolling prophecies to rapturous audiences. "The other day," he reported, "I reached one million frequent-flyer miles at a single airline."[47] As we observed in the beginning of this chapter, the rosy view of history celebrated from the Enlightenment to the early part of the twentieth century has yielded to a dim outlook on the future—first in Europe and then in America. Among the commentariat, Chicken Little routinely does better than Pollyanna, and with no penalties attached.

Why is business so good? "The wonderful thing" about prophecy, notes Tim Harford tongue in cheek, "is that both the forecaster and his audience feel that something profound has been expressed. And nobody will remember the forecast anyway."[48] Has our foresight improved with the explosion of scientific knowledge and the computer-driven revolution in data gathering and processing? Modern-day prophets, be they gloomsters or hypesters, still are not very effective, concludes the psychologist Philip Tetlock after an exhaustive review of 82,000 predictions by 284 policy experts over twenty years. Whatever their political coloration, the vast majority performed worse than if they had blindly pulled their forecasts out of a hat. A reviewer of Tetlock's *Expert Political Judgment* adds, "These experts never lose their reputations, or their jobs, because long shots are their business"—just like the ventures of their biblical ancestors.[49]

"Decline Time in America" is also a long-shot business; above all, though, it is didactic repertoire theater, played out left, right, and center not in order to analyze but to agitate. It is like Brechtian drama, which is performance with a purpose—or the stage as classroom. Unfortunately, to invoke cycles and unearth agendas, let alone to skewer the bloopers of yesterday's Cassandras, does not dispose of the larger issue.

That not all past prophecies of America's decline have come true obviously does not mean they never will. To believe that tomorrow will be like today, hence as good or better, is to fall for the same fallacy as do the Declinists who also project the present into the future.[50] There are neither logical nor historical reasons to assume that the tide will recede forever when it comes to human rather than lunar affairs. History is full of empires and nations whose debility was terminal: Egypt, Babylon, Persia, Rome, the Mogul and Ottoman Empires, Britain, Soviet Russia . . .

In 1897, Britain celebrated Queen Victoria's Diamond Jubilee. Yet at the peak of British power, Rudyard Kipling penned this little elegy to empire in his oft-quoted poem "Recessional":

> *Far-called, our navies melt away;*
> *On dune and headland sinks the fire;*
> *Lo, all our pomp of yesterday*
> *Is one with Nineveh and Tyre!*

He was off by a generation only. German and American growth rates were already outstripping Britain's, and the nation would never recover from the bloodletting of the Great War. In the next forty years, Britain would lose its entire empire. Even a country of English settlement, Canada, dropped the Union Jack in favor of the maple leaf. Britain survived the Hitlerian onslaught only by grace of American power. Afterward, Britannia no longer ruled the waves; its American offspring did. Sometimes, prophets *are* proven right. So as we peer into the twenty-first century, the question remains: What *is* America's standing in the world, and what might topple No. 1 from its towering perch?

CHAPTER THREE

The Powers and Their Power: Measuring What Matters

THE FACTS AND THE FIGURES

In all instances of Declinism, economic failure serves as exhibit A. But the numbers for 2012 show the U.S. economy at $16 trillion, almost three times the size of Japan's and more than twice the size of China's. These are the world's two next-biggest economies. It takes the third heavyweight, Germany, to even out the scales.

What about the great risers of the twenty-first century? These are the fabled BRICs—Brazil, Russia, India, and China—which are said to inherit the earth. Their main claim to collective fame is an acronym that was invented by a Goldman Sachs economist. Apart from growth and size, they share no other feature, let alone purpose that would go beyond a habit of opposing the West on humanitarian intervention and sanctions against the villains of the day. BRIC stands for interference, not involvement, in the travails of the world. The acronym is not like "NATO" or "Scandinavia"; it designates neither a political nor a cultural community. Russia, India, and China are in fact strategic rivals, each tied by interest to the United States.

Brazil is the odd man out because it is located half a world away. Its ambitions are vague, its grand strategy even hazier.

How do the BRICs compare with the rest in "The World's Top Twelve" (figure 4)? Two of them, Russia and India, are in ninth and tenth place, in the same neighborhood as Spain. Together, the quartet weighs in at $12 trillion. So even if they had a common agenda, they are nowhere near trumping the U.S. economy, let alone America's vast array of other power assets, hard and soft. The scales tip in favor of the risers only when Japan is thrown in, the defrocked giant of *Rising Sun* fame. J-BRIC is good for $17 trillion, but as a geoeconomic grouping it is as meaningful as FIFA, the world soccer organization.

As figure 4 shows, the gap between the United States and the

4. GDP of the World's Top Twelve Economies, 2011 (Billions of USD, current)

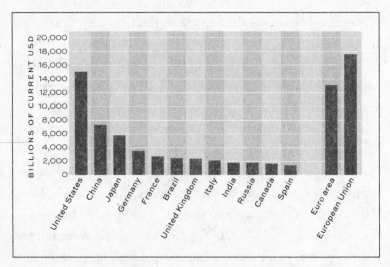

SOURCE: World Bank, national accounts data (2011).

next three remains enormous. Of course, these numbers will tilt against the United States as—and if—the rising rest proceed forevermore along the straight upward line all Declinists take for granted. How long might it take? To put this twenty-first-century snapshot in perspective, let us consult history for a glimpse of previous great-power dynamics. A useful baseline is 1870 because it marks the slow resumption of the "struggle for mastery in Europe," to recall the title of A. J. P. Taylor's majestic treatise on the traditional balance of power. The calm in the aftermath of the Napoleonic Wars was fading, and rivalry was returning. As France fell back, Prussia-Germany forged ahead. The ranking of economic power in Europe began to wobble. The Reich's steady growth might soon put Britain's place at the top in jeopardy.

Why invoke this distant past? The duel between Germany and Britain in the late nineteenth century bears an uncanny resemblance to the Chinese-American contest in our time: land power vs. sea power, upstart vs. top dog, and authoritarian modernization vs. liberal capitalism. Yet this is where the similarity ends. The United States is an XXL version of Britain, an economic giant without precedent in the modern state system, and so the contrast between the two cases could not be starker. During the heyday of the multipower world, the economies of the greats were closely bunched together, as the left column in table I indicates. The right-hand column, "Percentage of Britain," makes the same point in a different way. Compared with the leading nation of the nineteenth century, the others in the lineup were not much weaker (or stronger). In the power game of the period, the key players were in the same league.

Today, No. 1 and the rest are separated not by percentages but by factors, as table II shows. The U.S. economy leads China's and Japan's, which occupy the No. 2 and No. 3 spots, by multiples, not by percentages. The American economy is about as big as the next three together—two of which, Japan and Germany, are allies of over sixty years' standing. In the five-power world of the nineteenth century, when there were no such permanent alliances, the ranking was exactly reversed. The foremost power of the day, Britain, faced a foursome whose combined weight was *three times larger* than its own. Britain was at that point the biggest empire in history, but among the powers, it was not even first among equals, as table I shows.

I. Economic Power in the Nineteenth Century

	GNP 1870 (Billions of 1960 USD)	% of Britain
Russia	22.9	117%
Britain	19.6	100%
France	16.8	86%
Germany	16.6	85%
Habsburg	11.3	58%

Calculated from Paul Bairoch, "Europe's Gross National Product, 1800–1975," *Journal of European Economic History* 5 (1976): 273–340.

By way of metaphor, yesterday's great powers all lived in similar-sized apartments and on the same floor. In the twenty-first century, the United States occupies the penthouse across the entire sixteenth floor, while China and Japan dwell in a much more modest place on the seventh and sixth floors. On the third resides Germany; France and Britain are on the second. India has just moved up one flight from the basement. There is only one exception to this vast disparity: the European Union with a GDP of $17 trillion, which does overshadow the American GDP.

Alas, the EU is neither a state nor a strategic actor. It is a collection of twenty-seven nations living side by side, yet in separate residences. The EU finally did acquire a "president" and a "foreign minister" in 2010, but the quotation marks around these titles are deliberate. Real decision-making power continues to reside in the European Council, which represents not "Europe" but twenty-seven national governments. The answer to Henry Kissinger's apocryphal quip "When I want to call Europe, what number do I use?" has not become any easier.[1] There were nine numbers when Kissinger was secretary of state, and there are twenty-seven that must be dialed today when high politics is at stake. The current high representative for foreign affairs, Catherine Ashton, likes to jest, "Yes, I have a number. When you dial it, you hear a computer voice saying: For Germany, press 1, for France, press 2 . . ."

The more appropriate comparison is with the seventeen-member euro-zone. It has a common currency and a rudimentary economic government—more precisely, a common monetary policy that also sets limits to fiscal policy (which are routinely honored in the breach, and were so most brazenly after the Crash of 2008). That grouping commands a collective GDP of $12 trillion, still three floors below the United States'. Either way, a set of seventeen or twenty-seven states does not a strategic player make. A decade into its existence, the deadly crisis of the common currency demonstrated that Euroland was not even an "optimal currency area." How could it be, given the clash of cultures that pitted the big spenders of "Club Med" from Greece to Portugal against the more frugal members of "Club North," centered on Germany?

How about per capita income? Though slightly ahead, the United States dwells in the same neighborhood as its Western allies and Japan, its protégé in the Pacific. Compare this with

II. Economic Power in the Twenty-First Century
(Billions of USD, current)

World	70,020	% of United States
1. United States	14,991	100
2. China	7,318	49
3. Japan	5,867	39
4. Germany	3,601	24
5. France	2,773	18
6. Brazil	2,477	16
7. United Kingdom	2,445	16
8. Italy	2,194	15
9. India	1,873	12
10. Russia	1,858	12
11. Canada	1,736	12
12. Spain	1,4771	10
European Union	*17,584*	*117*
Euro zone	*13,080*	*87*

SOURCE: World Bank, national accounts data (2011).

the rising rest. The BRICs—Brazil, Russia, India, and China—are strung out along a range from $1,400 to $10,000 per person, whereas the United States is good for close to $50,000. It is not clear how China could soon best a nation like the United States that weighs in with a per-person income ten times larger. A nation becomes neither rich nor powerful by adding up 1.3 billion very poor people—unless riches are falsely measured by current account surpluses, where China leads the world, followed by Germany and Japan. Do their currency hoards make them the mightiest nations on earth? Power is more than cash; so their impressive financial weight does not presage America's early eviction from the penthouse of global power.

FRAMES VS. FILMS

The preceding section presented snapshots. What about evolution over time? The central argument of Declinism since the Sputnik Shock of half a century ago is not about the here and now but about tomorrow—about rates of change. It is not about the fall of the United States but about the "rise of the rest."[2] The rest has been a motley bunch. It used to be the Soviet Union, Japan, and Europe that would eventually overtake the United States; now it is China et al. When? Sometime between 2025

5. Per Capita GDP (USD, 2011)

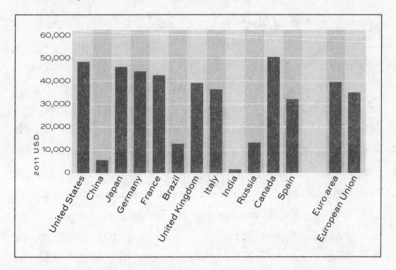

SOURCE: World Bank, national accounts data (2011).

and 2050, the predictions run; whatever the date, doom is the destiny of No. 1.

This is the accepted wisdom. Yet the data (figure 6 and table III) tell a different tale; this is the first surprise. Taking the longer view, one would expect that the American share of the global economy had been shrinking as the various upstarts kept rising. Over the past forty years, though, the U.S. share has remained remarkably constant.[3] It was 27 percent in 1970 and 25.4 percent in 2012. So somebody else must be contracting faster than the United States in order to make room for the expanding rest, which leads to the next surprise: The losers in the GDP race are the two great risers of the past, Europe and Japan.

Russia was America's nemesis all the way into the 1980s, apparently always poised to overtake the United States. Yet its share of the global economy has come down from 3 percent to 2 percent, which puts it behind Italy and on a par with Spain, neither of which is exactly a threat to American primacy. Europe (EU-27) has done worst, shedding almost ten percentage points from 1970 to 2012. Japan, the scourge of the 1980s, has been declining slowly for the past twenty years—from 10 to 9 percent of the global take. The winners, of course, are China and India, but their growth rates are no surprise at all. Countries that start out at the bottom rung of the ladder, say at $1 trillion, and then climb to the next, which is $2 trillion, double their take and thus boast 100 percent growth. But in absolute terms, they still have a way to go. Take the great riser India. Its economy took off once it ditched the Soviet model in favor of capitalist development, but its share of the world total is still minuscule. Its slice is not much bigger than Scandinavia's, though its population is forty times larger. The record holder is China, leaping up from .8 percent to 8 percent.[4]

6. Share of GDP, 1970–2012

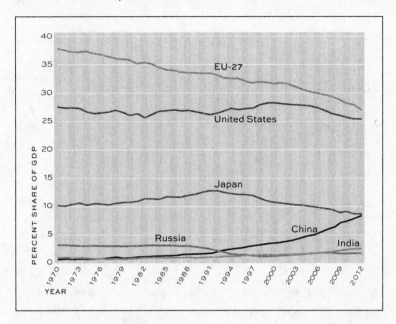

SOURCE: U.S. Department of Agriculture, Economic Research Service, "Real Historical Shares Values," http://www.ers.usda.gov/data-products/international-macro economic-data-set.aspx#.UagMvpymU-w.

Caveat 1. To dwell on these statistics is not to minimize China's and India's "great leap forward," to borrow from Mao. These are impressive by any standard, but there are three caveats. The first emerges from history, which whispers that it takes a while to outrace No. 1 even when the gap is far narrower than the one between China and the United States today. The economy of Germany, "China" to Britain in the nineteenth century, was two-thirds of Albion's when the Reich's steep rise began after unification in 1871.[5] Over the next decades, it would boast the highest growth in Europe. Yet it took forty years, until the eve of World War I, for

III. Risers and Losers, 1970–2012: Percent of World GDP

	1970	2012
United States	27.63	25.37
EU-27	37.64	27.08
Russia	3.27	1.83
Japan	10.07	8.76
India	.97	2.64
China	.76	8.41

SOURCE: U.S. Department of Agriculture, Economic Research Service, "Real Historical Shares Values," http://www.ers.usda.gov/data-products/international-macro economic-data-set.aspx#.UagMvpymU-w.

the Reich to draw merely even with Britain, and this from a starting position much closer to Britain's than China's was to America's at the beginning of the race. China will have to leap a lot farther to close the distance to the United States, whose economy is bigger not by one-third (as Britain's was vis-à-vis Germany in 1871) but by more than a factor of two.

Caveat 2. Declinists would not be impressed by such historical reminiscences. China has been growing more than twice as fast as the Bismarckian Reich, hasn't it?[6] Correct, but this is where the second counsel of caution claims its due. Growth is always spectacular when it starts from a low base. India and China have mesmerized the world with their 10 percent, but Ghana grew by 13 percent in 2011. Indigents like Mongolia and Turkmenistan grew at double-digit rates. Even war-torn Afghanistan clocked in with 7 percent. When it comes to amazing growth, small, that is, humble beginnings, is truly beautiful.

These nations are not generally regarded as future masters of the universe; their economies are *too* small. But they do deliver a sense of perspective by highlighting the baseline fallacy. It all depends on when the tally begins. To caricature the point, let us go way back in time. Asia minus Japan, fabulously rich by the standards of the era, was good for almost two-thirds of the world economy in 1500; half a millennium later, its share had dwindled to less than one-third.[7] By that yardstick, Asia ascendant shows rampant decline. These are the games people play with baselines, but there is a more serious point. As the baseline goes higher, as economies mature, growth slows. This is a law of economic history that even China and India cannot endlessly defy—more about this in the next two chapters.

Certainly, the previous batch of risers has not unhinged that law. Japan, the wunderkind of the 1960s and 1970s, began to falter in the 1980s and to stagnate in the 1990s. Europe, also much celebrated a generation ago, has taken the hardest hit. Its slice of the world product has shrunk by almost ten percentage points. In the 1970s, it boasted above 3 percent growth. The rate fell steadily decade after decade. By the naughts it had dropped to a bit more than 1 percent.[8] In this perspective, "decline" as applied to the United States should be replaced by *déclin*, *declino*, and *decadencia*. The share of Russia has fallen behind India's. And yet the heir of the Soviet empire gets to wear the BRIC badge as one of the world's new big four.

Caveat 3. The third counsel of caution is so counterintuitive that it needs to be made in visual terms, as presented in figure 7. This graph goes to the heart of the matter. Declinism, to repeat, is not about a single frame but about a film. It is about change over time, about growth rates over the longer haul. In this perspective, the Soviet Union, Japan, and Europe morph into yesterday's faux risers. But this time, so the claim goes, the Chinese and Indian hares *will* win over the tortoise and so reverse the moral of Aesop's fable, where it is the plodding tortoise that beats the overconfident mammal. Take the stubble-footed American turtle, shuffling along at its historical growth rate of 3 percent, and set it against those Asian long-legs sprinting three times faster. No matter how far ahead the American reptile was at the start, it is only a matter of time until it is left in the dust. That is the dictate of logic; eventually, the fast will outrun the slow.

At a minimum, the distance should be shrinking. Alas, the growth figures of the last twenty years do not hold out the gold medal to Beijing anytime soon. More startling still, it does not matter much whether GDP is measured in current dollars or in PPP (purchasing power parity). PPP is so beloved by Declinists because it inflates the size of emerging economies. Instead of measuring GDP in current dollars, PPP multiplies it by a factor X, which reflects lower prices and wages in the home market as well as undervalued currencies. Hence a dollar goes much farther in these countries than in the United States; hence the "real" economy is a lot larger than GDP at official exchange rates. And thus the hares look a lot more muscular than the tortoise.

Yet no matter whether it is real dollars or purchasing power, and contrary to widespread belief, these lithe lagomorphs are not outracing the lumbering leatherneck. Figure 7 compares the progress of the U.S. and the Chinese economies over the last twenty years—after the hare had shifted into steady fast-paced growth. (The author is indebted to Michael Beckley who published similar graphs in a pathbreaking analysis in *International Security*.)[9] These curves represent not speed but size. They show that China, though racing much faster than Uncle Sam, is not gaining on the United States when size of GDP is measured. The gap is not closing.

7. United States vs. China: GDP, 1990–2012
(Billions of USD, current and PPP)

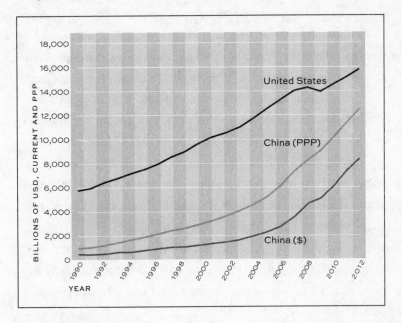

SOURCE: IMF World Economic Outlook Database, April 2013.

The data in figure 7 deflate an optical illusion that so often afflicts the Declinist literature as it focuses on the speeding hare while ignoring the steady pace of the turtle. To add to the surprise: When measured in current dollars, the distance between China and the United States actually widened in the first decade of the race. Today, it is still a bit wider than it was twenty years ago. In PPP, the gap has been narrowing ever so slowly, but purchasing-power parity is a tricky, if not misleading, gauge in the contest of nations. Exaggerating the prowess of the new entrants, PPP invariably undercounts the strength of the advanced nations.*

How to explain an optical illusion that informs so much Declinist thinking? The short answer is: wrong yardstick. Speed does not measure what truly matters in comparing national economies. It is size and weight that count; so the more appropriate metaphor should be deer vs. elephant. If the leading economy is as huge as the American one, a small growth rate still adds a lot of weight every year. If the other economies—those of China, India, and Russia— are much smaller, then even more rapid growth adds less body mass. Let's put this in numbers. In the middle of the 1990s, when China's growth had accelerated to a steady 10 percent, it added $200 billion to its GDP in one year. At that point, however, the United States stood at $12 billion. Growing at a mere 3 percent, the American economy added $360 billion per annum. What the pachyderm lacks in speed, it makes up in for mass. And though speed fascinates, mass counts for more when calculating relative economic power.

---

*Theoretically, PPP is a useful tool, which evens out exchange-rate fluctuations and measures what a dollar actually buys in various countries. It takes into account that a dollar spent in the United States, where great wealth makes for high factor prices (for labor and land, including raw materials and rents), buys less than a dollar converted into RMB and spent in China. In a poor country, labor and land are cheap. Hence a dollar is "worth more," especially in China, where its buying power is inflated by an artificially low exchange rate that is to fuel export-led growth. In PPP, China's GDP jumps from $7 trillion to $11 trillion (2011). Naturally, PPP is the favorite yardstick of the rise-of-the-rest school because it magnifies the economic weight of less developed countries and so buttresses the Declinist case. But in the arena of geopolitics and geoeconomics, it is not the low wage of a migrant worker that counts, or the pittance paid for a haircut or a bowl of rice. It is the price of sophisticated military hardware that China and India buy from Russia, the EU, or Israel. High technology, licenses, and oil and other raw materials must also be bought at exchange-rate prices. When the Chinese invest abroad to secure markets, resources, and political allegiance, they must also spend "real" dollars. So GDP measured in exchange-rate dollars is a more realistic yardstick of national economic power.

True, higher growth will eventually beat lower growth if China's economy keeps up its pace in perpetuity. When will the deer finally leave the elephant in the dust? Not so soon. Let's do a little arithmetic. Assume China grows at 7.5 percent (2012 rate).[10] That adds $450 billion to a $7 trillion economy. Now multiply America's $16 billion by 3 percent (2012 estimate). This adds $480 billion, representing a larger weight gain for the elephant and a slightly widening gap between the United States and China. Now give China the benefit of the doubt and assume that its post-2008 slowdown was merely cyclical. At, say, 9 percent it might add $540 billion to a $7 trillion economy, $60 billion more than the United States. Whichever way one plays the numbers, the upshot is that it will take many, many years for China to best the United States.

When progress is calculated by per capita rather than national income, as in figure 8, the tusker does even better, whether the yardstick is current dollars or PPP. And why? Because in that race, the weight difference at the start was even more lopsided. Again, take the middle of the last decade. China's per-person income was then around $2,000, but America's was $40,000. That is like being twenty laps ahead. Nor does the margin shrink. Figure 8 in fact shows that the deer has actually slowed a bit relative to the elephant over the past twenty years, the current gap being significantly larger than it was twenty-odd years ago. All together, these numbers should shake firmly held beliefs and thus correct standard perceptions about who is shrinking and who is bulging.

What about the other great risers? When the lumbering red-white-and-blue creature is matched against the Indian and the Russian deer, there is practically no contest. India is about forty-five laps behind the United States. Though Russia boasted extraordinary

8. United States vs. China: GDP Per Capita, 1991–2012 (USD, current and PPP)

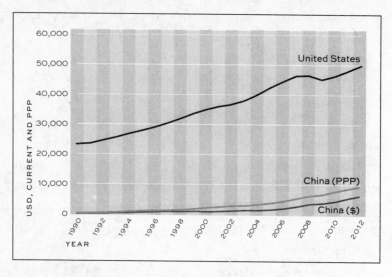

SOURCE: IMF World Economic Outlook Database, April 2012.

growth during the Putin reign (nearly 5 percent in the naughts), the gap between Kremlin capitalism and the real thing in America is as wide as ever, as figure 9 shows. In the case of Russia and India, as in that of China, an optical illusion feeds the saga of the "Rest Routs the West."

Western authors and pundits naturally focus on the breathtaking rise of the happy few—oligarchs, family corporations, and state enterprises. Won't they shoulder aside yesterday's giants like GM, BP, Siemens, General Electric, Gaz de France, and Toyota? They could. But companies are not countries, and the fortunes of the few do not make up for the misery of the many who number in the hundreds of millions. By that measure, a nation's true strength

9. United States vs. Russia and India: GDP Per Capita, 1991–2012 (USD, 2010)

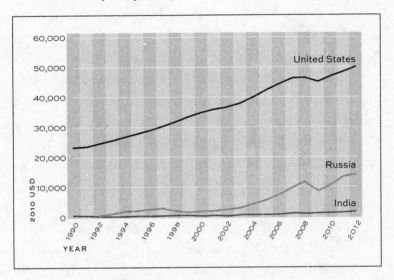

SOURCE: IMF World Economic Outlook Database, April 2013.

springs not from the volume of its GDP, or from its growth rates, but from the lot of its citizens. In this race, the rest has to run even faster to catch up with the West.

Does per capita income, where 313 million Americans and 500 million Europeans are way ahead of the rest, matter more than GDP? It all depends on how much China, with its great strategic ambitions, can extract from 1.3 billion very poor people. For the sake of grandeur, the regime could certainly keep more for itself in order to invest in state enterprises and modernize its military arsenal. This was the basic choice of the *ancien régime* in eighteenth-century Europe and twentieth-century Russia. But neither the Bourbons nor the Bolsheviks could forever defang the oldest dilemma of all potentates, the warfare vs. welfare squeeze. Nor can China's authoritarian modernizers shrug off this dilemma when it comes to lifting a billion people from abject poverty—more about this in chapter 6.

Paradoxically, the task will not become any easier as the Chinese masses grow richer and older, hence more demanding. In PPP per person, China is anything but a great power. It dwells in a poor global neighborhood, just above Albania and El Salvador and below Bosnia and Ecuador. And so does India. In current dollars, China lives next to Algeria, Angola, Jordan, and Tunisia. Its per-person income is separated from the wealth of the rich West by a factor of ten to twelve.

Of course, population size and landmass do matter, and so Luxembourg, the world's champion in per capita income, which is twenty-five times richer than China, is a minnow when it comes to geopolitical and geoeconomic clout. So are the next three, Norway, Qatar, and Switzerland, which are also dwarfs on the world stage. So what other weights and measures are relevant?

What Is Power?

Power is the central and yet trickiest concept of political science, and that is why the global ranking game is such a free-for-all, with as many yardsticks as players. The best take on power is this classic: the "capacity to make others do what they would otherwise not want to do." Is it sheer muscle? Not quite, for the ability to break a man's arm is not the same as to make him a violin virtuoso. Sheer strength does not correlate with the achievements of power. "You can lead a horse to water, but you can't make him drink," goes the saying. The schoolyard bully is never elected class president. And a pounding jackhammer is useless where a dentist's drill must whine. Frequently, power even resides in weakness, as America's routine failure to impose its will on smaller allies demonstrates. For it is not in the interest of the leader to punish, hence to undermine, his wards.

Al-Qaeda's career since 2001 provides the most spectacular illustration of the power of the weak. With a platoon of operatives armed with nothing more sophisticated than box cutters, al-Qaeda managed to launch the first attack on U.S. territory since Pearl Harbor. In addition to inflicting thousandfold death, the terror group triggered two wars—directly in Afghanistan and indirectly in Iraq—which turned into America's longest. In the course of a decade, the United States was forced to spend $1.3 trillion on these inconclusive campaigns. Saddam Hussein is dead, but Iraq is neither a healthy nor a stable democracy. The Taliban were driven out of Afghanistan; a decade later, they were back. And terror has imposed a terrible burden on the United States: countless tens of billions of dollars lost on surveillance, policing, and work hours wasted standing in airport security lines. On the part of Terror International, a tiny investment generated a huge return in terms of economic damage wrought. This is jujitsu in international politics, where the weak use the weight of the strong to throw them off balance.

In other words, there is a critical difference between the *assets* of power and its *achievements*. Raw muscle does not trump all. Britain, as the historical snapshot (table I) shows, was not even first in GDP during the nineteenth century. And yet it was the dominant player in the classical balance-of-power game. As it had in previous centuries, Britain masterminded the coalitions that brought down its most dangerous rivals—from Habsburg-Spain to the France of Louis XIV and Napoleon I. All the while, it was amassing an empire that would blanket half the globe.

There is a lot more to power than the "stuff"—guns and butter, demography and geography—a nation can throw into the scales: agenda setting, diplomatic skills, reputation, cultural attraction. Difficult to count and weigh, these assets will be analyzed in the concluding chapter. This chapter tries to gauge what can be expressed in numbers. These physical advantages are at the core of the Declinist argument, which revolves around the question "Who has what today, and who will have more of it tomorrow?" Ever since modern Declinism arose some sixty years ago, two types of national resources have always dominated the debate. Exhibit A is the economy. Exhibit B is the military.

Guns, Reach, and Power. Economically, the United States remains in a class of its own, as the data just presented show, even as its rivals began to speed up at the end of the twentieth century. Let us now look at exhibit B, the military. Does power grow out of a barrel of a gun? If it does, the United States again plays in a league of its own—and will continue to do so for a long time. With defense outlays of $660 billion in 2012,[11] the United States as top spender accounted for close to 40 percent of the world's military total. America's presumptive challengers China, India, and Russia *together* devoted $200 billion to their militaries; so this trio weighed in with less than one-third of the American total. With the end of the war in Afghanistan, the American figure will be reduced by $100 billion by 2012, but this cut will not unhinge the global ranking.

The numbers for China and Russia are very rough and not very realistic estimates; so let's double their official defense budgets, and throw in India, as well. The total of the trio then comes to $400 billion in 2012, still way short of U.S. outlays, even as these fall to

IV.   World's Top Ten Military Spenders, 2012

Country	Spending ($billion)	World Share (%)
1. United States	660	38
2. China	102	5.8
3. United Kingdom	61	3.4
4. Russia	60	3.4
5. Japan	59	3.3
6. Saudi Arabia	52.5	3.0
7. France	48	2.7
8. Germany	40	2.3
9. India	38.5	2.2
10. Brazil	35	2.0
World Total:	1735	

SOURCE: Total U.S. defense spending in FY2013 was $856 billion; subtracting veterans benefits and foreign military/economic aid leaves $660 billion for the military (http://www.usgovernmentspending.com/us_defense_spending_30.html). Other national figures are from IISS, *The Military Balance 2013*, p. 41; world total is from Sipri Military Expenditure Database 2012.

$680 billion by 2016. The official budget of China, touted as the next ruler of the roost is less than one-seventh of the American one, so let's double it to $200 billion (2012). Even at this generous estimate, China's military expenditure amounts to less than one-third of the American total. The disparity in nuclear weapons is even starker. The U.S. (and the Russian) arsenal is measured by the thousands, that of the others—China, India, Pakistan, Israel—is measured by the tens or hundreds.

Yet military superiority is not just a matter of numbers, just as a bank account is not the same as productive capital. China's land army is the world's largest, but size by itself says little about usability. The critical variable is projection capabilities, how to "git thar fustest with the mostest," according to the oft-cited, but apocryphal, maxim of the Civil War general Nathan Bedford Forrest. Add to mass and speed a third item: "how to git thar farthest." Navies remain the classic tool of power projection. They are not as fast as combat planes, but a lot more agile than land armies. They do not need bases in friendly territory. Ships carry more heft and firepower than aircraft, and they do not depend on treacherous refueling maneuvers in the air. What they lack in speed, they make up for in sustainability; they can roam the oceans for months. And in versatility: Since almost three-quarters of mankind now live within two hundred miles of the sea, navies can project power on land as well as across the sea.

This is where the United States boasts another superlative no other great power can match: naval tonnage, as a rough-and-ready measure of reach and muscle. At the end of the naughts, the U.S. Navy weighed in with 3.1 million tons.[12] Let us put this number in perspective. It exceeds the total tonnage of the world's next thirteen navies combined. At the height of its dominance, Britain was much more modest in its reach, trying to hold to a two-navy standard. Today, the United States enjoys a *thirteen-navy standard*.[13] Nor does this exhaust the American advantage. Besides that of the United States, there are only twenty significant navies in the world, that is, with a tonnage (displacement) of 50,000 tons or more. Out of these, eighteen belong to formal allies or friendlies—to nations that will either support the United States in a confrontation or stay out of the fray. That count leaves only China and Russia as worthy opponents.[14]

Both are rearming, especially Russia, which let its navy go to

V. Naval Tonnage: Great Powers, 1900 (in millions)

Britain	1,065
Total of Next Seven Nations	2,019
France	499
Russia	383
United States	333
Germany	285
Italy	245
Japan	187
Austria-Hungary	87

Calculated from Quincy Wright, *A Study of War* (Chicago: University of Chicago Press, 1942), pp. 670–71.

rot in the 1990s. So, again, let us take the longer view by placing this lineup in historical perspective and going back more than a century, to 1900. This was three years after Queen Victoria's Diamond Jubilee, when Britannia ruled the waves with the world's largest navy. Yet for all its might, it still did not tower over the rest as today's U.S. Navy does. In fact, the Royal Navy was clearly outclassed by the next seven navies, which had a combined advantage of almost twice the tonnage of Britain's.

Now go back to the early twentieth century, to the 1922 Washington Naval Conference, which tried to decree a balance of power at sea. The three top contestants—the United States, Britain, and Japan—were allowed navies in the ratios of 5:5:3, which was a reasonably balanced distribution. At that time, the world's greatest maritime power, Britain, boasted a total tonnage of 525,000. Compare that with America's fleet today, which is five times larger. With its nuclear-powered carriers and submarines, the USN commands a projection capability the world has never seen. China, Russia, India, Japan, or the EU could not conduct a major war eight thousand miles from their shores, as the United States did twice in Iraq and once in Afghanistan. A hundred years ago, only the Royal Navy could operate across the Seven Seas; the navies of Germany, France, Russia, and Japan would not venture beyond their "home oceans"—the Atlantic or the Pacific.

Today, the aircraft carrier is the premier vehicle of force projection. Russia has one, China has none, though one, a former Soviet vessel, is in the works, and another is in planning. The United States has ten, all nuclear-powered and in a class of their own, their displacement exceeding the tonnage of the world's other carriers by factors ranging from two to seven. Three more will go to sea in this decade. These behemoths, carrying three times as many planes as China's single carrier, give the United States an "overwhelming lead in sea-based tactical aviation," as measured by a seaborne air force that outstrips any other navy's by at least nine hundred aircraft.[15] Paul Kennedy, the most famous Declinist, notes in admiration, "No equivalent concentration of power to a US carrier task force exists in the world."[16]

What goes for the U.S. Navy, goes as well for the U.S. Air Force, the swiftest arm of power projection. It is by far the world's largest and most sophisticated, given its advanced stealth technology, its drones and 168 fifth-generation tactical aircraft owned by none of its presumptive rivals, though China and Russia are developing them. "By 2020," predicted Secretary of Defense Robert Gates in 2010, "the United States will have . . . 20 times more advanced stealth fighters than China."[17] The following table offers a rough-and-ready count of airpower, which includes naval aviation as well.

VI.   Combat-Capable Aircraft (fixed wing)

United States	3,591
China	2,004
Russia	1,909
India	829
Japan	466

SOURCE: IISS, *The Military Balance 2012*, pp. 59–65, 197, 238, 246, 253–54.

Tactical aviation is a very simplified measure of airpower, because these numbers do not distinguish between short-range and long-range. Nor do they reveal much about projection capabilities. So let us break down these totals and look at naval aviation, which provides a rough measure of projection forces. Here the gap widens dramatically, as table VII shows:

A more interesting measure of force projection has nothing to do with bombs and bullets, be they sea-based or land-based. What matters in long-range fighting is the enablers, that is, refueling and transport aircraft. Tankers extend the range of bombers, fighters, and cargo planes. Transporters carry matériel and forces from here

VII.   Naval Aviation

United States	1,429
China	311
Russia	116
Japan	95
India	31

SOURCE: IISS, *The Military Balance 2012*. The U.S. number is the sum of Navy and Marines aircraft.

VIII.   Tankers and Transport Aircraft (fixed wing)

United States	1,318
NATO Europe	411
Russia	208
France	72
China	77
United Kingdom	55
Japan	34
India	30

SOURCE: IISS, *The Military Balance 2013*, p. 45. Figures for NATO Europe and Japan taken from *The Military Balance 2011*.

to there. Again, the United States comes out on top, dwarfing the next strongest—Russia—by a factor of almost seven. Only one player looks like a worthy competitor, with a total of 411. This is "NATO Europe," and it happens to be part of an alliance led by the United States since 1949. Russia comes in third, with more than 200. China's potential is one-third of the Russian one. Japan and India bring up the rear. The United States beats all the BRICs by almost four to one.

The largest and best-prepared forces in the world become worthless as a means of warfare if they cannot "git thar fustest and farthest with the mostest," to recall General Forrest. That is why the Europeans had to rely on the global U.S. network—transports, tankers, bombers, and space-based surveillance—when they intervened in the Balkans in the 1990s and again in Libya in 2011.[18] That is why Israel's military options against Iran's nuclear weapons program are limited. Pilot for pilot, Israel's air force may well be world's best, but to conduct a decisive air campaign over a thousand miles takes more than one of the largest tactical forces in the world. With just a handful of tankers and no blue-water navy, distance is Israel's worst enemy and Iran's best friend.

America faces no such enemy with its 150 strategic bombers of the B-1, B-2, and B-52 type. They are backed up by some 200 long-distance jet tankers that can set up a string of fuel stations around the globe. Thus a B–2 stealth bomber can rise in Missouri, drop its load anywhere in the Middle East, and return home in one trip. China has some 80 heavy bombers (H–6, copied from the Soviet Tu-16) with a combat radius of one thousand nautical miles that could be extended by some 20 tankers of the same type. Still, these bombers are a regional, not a global, weapon. Russia has some 80 long-range bombers, but they are configured for nuclear mission—not very useful for warfare in the twenty-first century.

Such number games can go on forever, but they all end up with similar scores: This American empire, doomed as it is said to be, is far out on any scale of military power one may choose—save for the number of men under arms, where China beats the United States by two to one. There are no latter-day Germanic tribes on the horizon that finally did in the Roman Empire, but even that took three hundred years, as Edward Gibbon—the ur-Declinist—is supposed to have said. One reason why Rome's fate will not be America's is a critical difference in the nature of these two empires.

An Empire of Bases. Rome's was an empire of possession; America's is one of bases.[19] The difference between the two is the cost of control. Rome ruled, the United States rents (though the leases are sometimes canceled by landlords whose interests change). Rome conquered, America co-opts. Rome imposed itself on the weak; America invites them in, or is invited by them. Rome had to govern and suppress in an arc from Britannia to Basra. But the American empire has the lightest footprint in history, lighter even than the British one, which could never take a rest from fighting rebellious natives. To lease is cheaper than to own.

Compared with Rome's, America's empire of bases is both economical and useful in the pursuit of primacy. Here, too, the United States plays in a league of its own. The number of U.S. installations is unclear since some status of forces agreements (SOFA) are classified. But two experts who should know have spoken of "more than 115."[20] Britain and France have a few bases. China has none, but is thinking about them.[21] Russia used to have many in the Soviet days, in places ranging from Cuba to Vietnam, from Somalia to Yemen, and of course throughout Eastern Europe. Today, it has about two dozen, but all of them close-by in the "Near Abroad," from Belarus via Ukraine to Tajikistan. None of these powers has a globe-circling network like that of the United States. The list of the more important ones runs on for four pages (small print) in *The Military Balance 2011*, published by the International Institute for Strategic Studies.

Bases abroad spell out a simple message: "global reach." They harbor forces ready to use, and the matériel that goes with them. No other candidate for first place in the "post-American world" has this kind of toolbox, which undoes the curse of all previous empires: distance and the time needed to bridge it. According to the Department of Defense, close to 300,000 U.S. military personnel were stationed on foreign soil at the turn of 2011 (including troops in Iraq and Afghanistan slated for withdrawal).[22]

Isn't this "imperial overstretch," as so many Declinists have argued for half a century? Certainly, a homebody the United States has not been. Just consider the 300,000 troops it had stationed in Europe during the Cold War (which have now dwindled to 30,000). Then survey the long string of wars the United States has fought, from Korea to Vietnam, from Iraq and Serbia to Afghanistan and, indirectly, Libya. Doesn't the tally add up to overextension, the deadly disease of empire? Again, history counsels caution. The American empire flies first class, but pays economy. Defense spending since World War II looks like a hockey stick lying on its side—blade left, shaft right. In the peak year of the war, the United States spent two-fifths of GDP on its military. During the Vietnam years, it was one-tenth. Then defense outlays trended down to 5 percent. Take the war decade of the naughts, from the attack on the Twin Towers in 2001 to the departure of U.S. troops from Iraq in 2011. Never has imperial warfare been so cheap: an average of 4.5 percent of GDP per year. Defense spending in the 2010s will stay roughly at that level.[23]

Still, "global overstretch"—the curse of empires through the ages—remains a classic of Declinism. The historical data do not seem to support the verdict. By comparison with previous empires, the United States is a miser, staying far below the military expenditures previous hegemons had to carry. These did indeed sink under an insufferable military burden, as shown in table IX.

By historical standards, the U.S. defense burden is extraordinarily low, hence sustainable over the long haul. In the lineup of greats, only Britain, another sea power, was able to match America's empire on the cheap. But didn't overstretch finally do in Britannia by tearing its economic fabric at the end of the nineteenth century, once the "struggle for mastery in Europe" had resumed? After reviewing mountains of statistics, the historian John M. Hobson concluded, first, that Britain "remained the least burdened of the Great Powers" from 1870 to the eve of World War I, and,

IX.   Defense Burdens and Military Expenditures

State	Military Expenditure as % of GDP
Rome (1st–2nd c.)	~45–70%
Habsburg Empire (17th c.)	50–90%
USSR (1981–90)	15.65%
Great Britain (1900)	3.6%
France (end of 17th c.)	~70%

SOURCES: Rome—*The Cambridge Economic History of the Greco-Roman World*, ed. Walter Scheidel, Ian Morris, and Richard P. Saller (2007), p. 611. Military expenditure was estimated at 400–500 million sesterces, compared with 700–800 million for total national expenditure (as a proxy for national income). Habsburg—*The Fiscal-Military State in Eighteenth-Century Europe*, ed. Christopher Storrs (2009), pp. 63–64. USSR—*Soviet Defense Spending: A History of CIA Estimates, 1950–90*, by Noel E. Firth and James H. Noren (1998), p. 130. Ten-year average using current levels of GDP. Great Britain—*A Study of War*, by Quincy Wright, 2nd ed. (1965), p. 670. France—*The Fiscal-Military State in Eighteenth-Century Europe*, p. 155.

second, that the theory that "military expenditures reduce economic growth" has "no foundation."[24] Britain's slide in the twentieth century was due to a myriad of reasons rooted in the economy itself, from declining innovation to rising welfare spending.

Nor does imperial overload explain America's deadly economic crises in the twentieth and twenty-first centuries, one following on the Crash of 1929 and the other on the Crash of 2008. If there is a link, it works in the opposite direction of the one posited by the imperial-overload school. The Great Depression ended for good during World War II when defense spending rocketed past the 40 percent mark of GDP. War, as it were, was good for the economy, with the state delivering the aggregate demand the economy would not generate on its own.

The long recession of 2008 has not been defense related, either.

The culprits were a real estate bubble pumped up by easy money and government-backed "subprime" mortgages lavished on tens of millions of risky customers. At any rate, constant military spending in the 4 percent range of GDP cannot explain both the Crash of 2008 and the recovery in 2010. The extravagance of past empires was indeed driven by war as a royal routine. In the United States, as the record of the last half century shows, it wasn't war that weighed down the economy, but the steady growth of civilian expenditures, above all for publicly financed health care and income transfers. The Vietnam War was the great exception, as the federal deficit climbed to 10 percent of GDP. But even in war, social outlays—remember Lyndon B. Johnson's Great Society—exploded, as well. And the trend kept heading north, no matter which party occupied the White House. While the Pentagon's take has been trending down, the government's total share has been rising. Half a century ago, total government spending in the United States was 30 percent of GDP; at 40 percent at the beginning of the 2010s, it was creeping up to the European average.

If unbridled deficits are bad for the economy, hence the cause of long-term decay, history will finger welfare rather than warfare in the case of the United States. In the past fifty years, defense spending has undulated down from a high of 10 percent to around 4 percent. So the fate of Rome and Habsburg will not be America's. Nonetheless, the wolf is finally said to be at the door and destined to stay; Decline 5.0, the latest iteration, is for real, claim the prophets of doom. It isn't that the United States is sinking; the rest is simply rising faster and thus slated to dislodge America.

Before we get to China, let us look at East Asia's earlier fast risers. These are Taiwan, South Korea, and Japan, which all followed a growth model similar to China's. Let us label it "modernitarianism," a neologism that bundles terms such as "authoritarian modernization," "guided capitalism," and "centralized capitalism." In the 1980s, Japan—the largest of the trio—began to oppress the American imagination as China has been doing in our time. How far did the "Dragons" and "Tigers" get, how long did their "economic miracles" last? The answers should tell us something about the future of China's spectacular career.

CHAPTER FOUR

Hype and History: Why Tomorrow Is Not Like Yesterday

The High Rollers of the Twentieth Century

The rise-of-the-rest school assumes that tomorrow will be a remake of yesterday—that it is up, up, and away for China, India, and all the other fast climbers of the twenty-first century. Yet history bids us to be wary. Rapid growth characterized every "economic miracle" in the past. It started with Britain, the United States, and Germany in the nineteenth century, and it continued with Japan, Taiwan, Korea, and West Germany after World War II. Yet none of them managed to sustain the wondrous pace of the early decades, and all of them eventually slowed down. They all declined to a "normal" rate as youthful exuberance gave way to maturity. What is "normal"? For the United States, the average of the three decades before the Crash of 2008 was well above 3 percent. Germany came down from 3 percent to less than 2 percent. Japan declined from 4.5 percent to 1.2 percent.[1]

What rises comes down and levels out as countries progress from agriculture and crafts to manufacturing and thence to a service and knowledge economy. In the process, the countryside empties out and no longer provides a seemingly limitless reservoir of cheap labor. As fixed investment rises, its marginal return declines, and each new unit of capital generates less output than the preceding one. This is one of the oldest laws of economics: the law of diminishing returns.

The leveling-out effect also applies to industrialized economies that emerged from a catch-up phase in the aftermath of war and destruction, as did Japan and West Germany after World War II. In either case, the pattern is the same. Think of a sharply rising plane that overshoots as it climbs skyward, then descends and straightens out into the horizontal of a normal flight pattern. The trend line, it should be stressed, is never smooth. In the shorter run, it is twisted by the ups and downs of the business cycle or by shocks from beyond the economy such as civil strife or war. The swings can be quite dramatic, but Declinists beware: What is now is not necessarily forever. Only hindsight reveals what has endured.

In the middle of the "Surging Seventies," Japanese growth flip-flopped from 8 percent to below zero in the space of two years. South Korea, another wunderkind of the 1970s, gyrated between +12 percent and –1.5 percent. As the Cultural Revolution burned through China in the same decade, growth plunged from a historical onetime high of 19 percent to below zero. Recent Chinese history perfectly illustrates the role of "exogenous" shocks, whose ravages are far worse than those wrought by a cyclical downturn. Next to war, domestic turmoil is the most brutal brake on growth. In the first two years of the Cultural Revolution, growth shrank by eight, then by seven, percentage points. After the Tiananmen Square massacre of 1989, double-digit growth dropped to a measly 2.5 percent for two years in a row.

The Cultural Revolution and Tiananmen hint at a curse that

may return to haunt China down the line: The stronger the state's grip, the more vulnerable the economy to political shocks. This is why the Chinese authorities obsessively look at every civic disturbance through the prism of Tiananmen, though that revolt occurred a generation ago. "Chinese leaders are haunted by the fear that their days in power are numbered," writes the China scholar Susan Shirk. "They watched with foreboding as communist governments in the Soviet Union and Eastern Europe collapsed almost overnight beginning in 1989, the same year in which massive prodemocracy protests in Beijing's Tiananmen Square and more than one hundred other cities nearly toppled communist rule in China."[2]

Hence the big question of the twenty-first century that is often shrugged off by the rise-of-the-rest school as it praises authoritarian modernization—what we're calling modernitarianism—over the messy ways of liberal democracy: Can a despotic regime keep managing a feat that history says is impossible? Can it keep the people in check while unshackling one market after another according to the unspoken slogan "Enrich yourselves, but leave the driving to us?"[3]

Just as political chaos is poison for the economy, tranquillity or unity restored fuels the engine of growth. The best examples are the United States after the Civil War and Germany after unification in 1871. As authority was recentralized in Washington and Berlin, these splintered nations were fused into vast single markets that broke down internal barriers such as customs walls and separate currencies. No less important was the single "political market" that reunited South and North in the United States and hammered twenty-five German states into the Bismarckian Reich.

Now a national legal system would enforce contracts and protect property, reassuring investors and consumers. A mighty state laid down a nationwide infrastructure of canals, ports, and rail-roads, as China is doing today. As a result, growth soared in the United States and in Imperial Germany. In Japan, it was the Meiji Restoration that fused some three hundred feudal domains into a single state under the emperor. And so modern Japan became the first Asian nation to join the Industrial Revolution, which until 1868 had been a strictly Western affair. By 1905, the country was a major military power that won the Russo-Japanese War.

Ever since the emergence of the first risers, the basic histori-cal pattern has been a snaking curve, which spells out the same old warning: Look at the entire film, not just at individual frames. Growth surges during the takeoff, then drops to a high plateau of private wealth and public welfare. Such is the long-run destiny of nations, though the underlying trend is routinely obscured by wild gyrations in the short run. This is the reason instant Declin-ism is such a treacherous business. Japan offers the most dramatic case in point. When Japan reached its last peak, in 1988, which it hasn't scaled again, so did the adulation of the soothsayers, be they professors or pundits. "The American century is over," trumpeted one of them."[4] Accordingly, the United States was a Japanese "col-ony in the making."[5] The irony couldn't be thicker. In fact, 1988 marked not the end of the American century but the beginning of the long good-bye to Japan's economic miracle. To add to the irony, the United States at this point was a mere four years away from the longest expansion in its history.

Let's go back farther in time to get a better grip on the "snake" of economic growth. After the Civil War, the United States bestrode the global stage as the second riser of the nineteenth cen-tury—as the upstart that would eventually dislodge the first one, Great Britain. From the end of the Civil War in 1865 to the end of the century, the size of the U.S. economy *quadrupled* in real terms.[6] That makes for Chinese-style growth—300 percent in thirty-five years. Yet a few years after "reunification," the United States plunged into the Long Depression. Lasting from 1873 to 1896, a string of bursts and busts bounced back and forth across the Atlantic, the contagion spreading through markets far and wide. Altogether, the United States was in recession for 161 months, for a total of almost fourteen years. Still, in the last quarter of the nineteenth century, U.S. GDP more than tripled. Western Europe's almost doubled amid wild swings of the growth curve. The United States and Europe were the West's Tigers and Dragons in the heyday of industrialization, but at various points during the Long Depression they looked more like scrawny cats and weakly lizards.

Depending on the time frame, it was therefore either rampant decay or stunning expansion. In the Great Depression, the U.S. economy contracted by one-third.[7] In the first three years of World War II, it shot up by 70 percent! Today, the U.S. economy is down to a "normal" average of 3 percent (not counting the Crash of 2008 and its recessionary aftermath). Germany's economy shrank by 16 percent in the first three years of the *Weltwirtschaftskrise*, as the Great Depression is known in German. Then, after defeat and destruction in World War II, West Germany grew at close to 8 percent during the decade of its *Wirtschaftswunder* ("economic miracle") in the 1950s. Yet in the 1990s, the average for reunified Germany would plummet to 2 percent, in the next decade to 1 percent. South Korea boasted double-digit annual growth in the 1960s and 1970s. In the 1990s, it was down to between 2 percent and 4 percent. Emerging from the devastation of World War II, Japan grew at a double-digit rate in the 1950s and 1960s; in the 1990s, it oscillated between +2 percent and –2 percent.

Once the long run irons out the cyclical kinks, it spells out an enduring message: There is no endless double-digit growth in economic history; what goes up, eventually comes down to "normal." Amazing growth, taking off from desolation or backwardness, flattens out, interspersed with boom and bust. Yesterday, the world looked with awe and envy at South Korea, Taiwan, and especially Japan. So in 1988, starstruck *Time* magazine ran a piece under the headline "Japan: From Superrich to Superpower."[8] Today, the world is mesmerized by awesome growth in China and India (while ignoring the breathtaking record of sub-Saharan Africa). Why should China et al. defy the verdict of economic history from here to eternity? No other country has escaped from this history since the Industrial Revolution unleashed the West's spectacular expansion in the middle of the nineteenth century.

Why has the law of diminishing growth held up so well? Let us look at the Asian Dragons and Tigers, which rose from abject poverty to double-digit growth after World War II: South Korea, Taiwan, Japan. They share with China not only a common geography—East Asia—but also a similar model of development. Though each followed a distinct national path, the short formula was this equation: "Overinvestment plus underconsumption plus undervalued currency plus protection equals rampant export-led growth."

Protection, by the way, was also part of the American model in the high-growth era of the late nineteenth century, when the average tariff rate stood at 30 percent. Nor is protection just a matter of customs barriers. An artificially undervalued currency has the same effect, stimulating exports and holding down imports. Take the West German example: In the era of the

Wirtschaftswunder, until the mid-1960s, the exchange rate was cast in concrete at 4.2 deutsche marks to the greenback. In subsequent decades, the value of the deutsche mark (later folded into the euro) would almost triple versus the dollar. And the German growth rate was cut in three, compared with the golden days of the postwar recovery.[9]

None of these economic miracles lasted, as figure 10 shows. What goes up, must come down, whether it is balloons, airplanes, or economies. The career of the world's previous risers whispers: Beware of the short run; do not mistake a particular twist of the "snake" for destiny unveiled, whether it bends up or down at any given moment.

10.   GDP Growth by Decade: First Up, Then Down

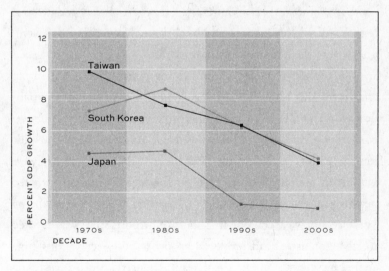

SOURCE: U.S. Department of Agriculture, Economic Research Service, "Real Historical Shares Values," http://www.ers.usda.gov/Data/Macroeconomics/Data/HistoricalGDPSharesValues.xls.

A Tale of Tigers and Dragons

South Korea's Growth Model

South Korea makes for an instructive comparison with China. When South Korea's takeoff began in the early 1960s, it was one of the poorest countries in the world.[10] It is now No. 15 in the global GDP ranking, up there with the richest countries of the West. The political model was "authoritarian modernization," as in China and Taiwan. Syngman Rhee, a dictator in all but name, ruled in the 1950s; for the next twenty years, the iron-fisted general Park Chung Hee occupied the Blue House, followed by various military regimes all the way into the 1990s.

The propellant that catapulted the war-torn, poorly endowed economy into the ranks of the newly industrialized countries (NICs)—"emerging economies," as they are called today—was "exports first" or "nation building through export promotion." Those were the national slogans of the day.

This strategy entailed enormous investment outlays, rising to almost two-fifths of GDP. (The current U.S. investment rate, public and private, is less than 10 percent.) The flip side was underconsumption at home. Workers were sucked from the countryside into the cities, as they would later be in China (and as they were in Britain and the United States). The steady flow of uprooted peasants helped keep wages down, as it had in the industrializing West a century earlier. The first stage of "exports first" was devoted to labor-intensive stuff produced at low wages—echoes of China again. First it was light, then heavy, industry. Since investment regularly exceeded savings until the late 1980s, vast quantities of capital had to be imported from abroad. Capital imports are a classic of rapid development, as the experience of the United States in the nineteenth century also shows—and China's early phase does in spades.

"Exports first" was managed authoritarian-style. "The country's initial export expansion was effectively 'forced' by the . . . government."[11] How so? In a manner reminiscent of Gosplan, the Soviet planning authority, firms were handed ambitious export targets by the Ministry of Trade and Industry, and these were orders rather than mere guidelines. If the companies succeeded, they reaped rich rewards such as tax breaks, ample credit, and political favors. Only in the 1980s were domestic markets opened bit by bit while export subsidies came down.

As the economy moved from labor-intensive light industry to capital-intensive heavy industry, concentration of ownership proceeded apace, strengthening the hands of very large companies and conglomerates. These *chaebol* provided the prequel to the story of China's state-owned enterprises. With capital accumulating by leaps and bounds, monopolies and oligopolies flourished, but economic efficiency did not. The country was soon beset by overcapacity. The stress on heavy industry, fed by generous credit from government-controlled banks, led to an overheated economy in the late 1970s and to rapid wage increases that overtook productivity growth. Naturally, the price was runaway inflation (almost 30 percent) and massive real estate speculation, as in Japan.

This is where economics began to collide with politics, as it usually does when a rising middle class begins to rub up against dictatorial rule. A classic law of political unrest, usually attributed to the French thinker Alexis de Tocqueville, predicts that despotic governance runs the greatest risk when life gets better and when rising expectations are rudely interrupted by economic calamity. At the cusp of the 1980s, consumption fell while unemployment rose. Thus, economic misfortune triggered political disaster in the 1980s.

In May 1980, student and labor unrest erupted, followed by the imposition of martial law. A week later, the notorious Gwangju Massacre claimed two hundred lives. In June, the National Assembly was dissolved. But repression no longer worked, as it did on Beijing's Tiananmen Square. Later in the year, the president was forced to resign in favor of yet another military strongman. Timid political reforms could not still the student protests. Reenergized growth merely widened the gap between rich and poor, country and city—presaging the pattern that now afflicts China. In 1987, a million students marched throughout the country. The opposition to the military was not to be mollified, as happens so often when concessions merely whet the appetite for more. It took another five years for the first civilian president in a generation to be installed, in 1992, marking the birth of the "New Korea." Parliamentary elections were held in 1995.

That was the end of thirty-five years of modernitarianism. As that era petered out, trade and market liberalization gained the upper hand. Consumption as share of GDP, suppressed for the sake of "exports first," began to rise at the turn of the millennium. But the double-digit growth of the 1970s and 1980s is a thing of the past. South Korea's "normal" rate now hovers around 4 percent, the persistent slowdown have begun in 2003. Why?

The most compelling answer is offered by the Korean scholar Jeong-Yeon Lee. He explains South Korea's stunning high-growth career with the "massive mobilization of fixed-capital investment," which underlies every East Asian economic miracle. Tersely, he adds, "This type of economic growth is not sustainable due to diminishing marginal returns on capital"[12]—which is also a classic of economic history formulated first by the French philosopher and economist Turgot. The more capital a nation injects in order to force growth, the less output it extracts from each additional shot. Add one power plow to the farm, and its yield will surge; add the fifth, and the extra return on capital dwindles.[13] Hence, as a nation's capital stock piles up, fabulous growth must flatten out, and so it did in South Korea as elsewhere in the East Asian world where the Tigers and Dragons roamed.

Taiwan's Growth Model

The war-torn and backward economy of Taiwan approached its takeoff point with a per-person income that had remained flat for almost a generation. The level of prosperity the island had enjoyed just before World War II was reattained only in 1960. In the 1960s, per capita income grew just minimally, by less than 2 percent. Supercharged growth took off in the 1970s when the economy expanded at an average rate of almost 10 percent. The 1970s were the golden age of the Taiwanese economy, spawning yet another Asian economic miracle. In the 1980s, growth remained awesome by Western standards—a bit less than 8 percent on average—but softly the trend line began to tilt down. In the 1990s, the average was a bit more than 6 percent; in the naughts, it was down to a bit more than 4 percent.[14]

Low beginnings, spectacular growth, rising prosperity, the new normal—this is the typical pattern. The ingredients of Taiwan's success story were typical, as well: authoritarian rule, forced capital accumulation, infant-industry protection, high walls against imports, export *über alles*, a very high saving rate, and an undervalued currency.

The artificial cheapness of the Taiwanese dollar was euphemistically defined as "maintenance of a single, competitive but stable, equilibrium exchange rate that facilitates exports."[15] At the start of the 1960s, the currency was pegged to the dollar for two decades, as it had been in West Germany during its *Wirtschaftswunder* years. The Chinese have done the same to the dollar. The currency rose to a realistic market rate only when the New Taiwan dollar was cut loose to float, soaring by as much as 60 percent in the 1980s. Naturally, an undervalued currency is good not only for exports (and bad for imports). Undervaluation also keeps money at home, where it is saved and turned into domestic capital rather than being flung outward for travel and foreign investments. Money spent at home was worth more, so to speak, than money spent abroad.

Add to this the downside of "Asian values," though corruption and cronyism were less egregious than in Japan or South Korea. It was the not-so-invisible hand of government, bureaucracy, and business networks that parceled out privileges and power—China enthusiasts take note. Benefits came in the form of closed markets, cheap loans, gifts, and bribes, which was a far cry from the idealized version of the neutral state as celebrated by Adam Smith in his *Wealth of Nations*. Its mainstay, Smith insisted, was an "equal and impartial administration of justice . . . which . . . by securing to every man the fruits of his own industry, gives the greatest and most effectual encouragement to every sort of industry."[16] In other words, the rule of law is the best promoter of innovation and growth.

Yet Asia by no means has a historical monopoly on this type of Asian values. Indeed, lavish rent seeking, as granted by the state to favored groups, has worked its insidious ways in the West, as well. The two rapid risers of the late nineteenth century—the United States and Imperial Germany—enjoyed myriad kindness as from the cornucopia of the state, be they monopolies, cartels, franchises, subsidies, import barriers, or the suppression of labor unrest. With the notable exception of Britain, which enjoyed the competitive blessings of the "first industrializer" and so opted for free trade until 1914, the magnificent success story of the West unfolded behind the high walls of the nation-state, with the quite visible hand of the government bestowing succor and privilege. China didn't invent this model.

Recall also the first decades after World War II when "globalization" was a term yet to be invented. Recall government monopolies like "Ma Bell" or the airline oligopoly in the United States. In Europe, professions, utilities, and financial markets were sheltered until the EU Commission took the ax to them in the 1990s. The key difference between the West and the East was the extent of state intervention. In postwar East Asia, it was first and foremost the iron fist of authoritarianism that drove the shift from Agraria to Industria.

In Taiwan, the story begins with a man whom President Harry S. Truman once denounced as "dictator" and "usurper." That gentleman was Chiang Kai-shek, who set up government in Taipei in 1949 after he had lost the long-running civil war against the Chinese Communists on the mainland. He ruled at the head of a one-party state until his death in 1975. Though the Republic of China was blessed with a proper democratic constitution, inconveniences such as free elections were postponed sine die. After all, how could they be held when totalitarian communism was about to pounce from across the Straits? Every member of the National Assembly held his post indefinitely. Naturally, it reelected Chiang four times, never mind constitutional term limits.

After the tyrant's death, continuity was assured by "dynastic dictatorship," a commoner's version of inherited power, when Chiang fils succeeded his father, ruling until 1988. Under Chiang Ching-kuo, the iron grip of the Kuomintang, the one and only legal party, relaxed a bit, but military supremacy endured. The son's economic policy was a classic of modernitarianism. Its drivers were called "Fourteen" and "Ten Major Construction Projects," or "Twelve New Development Projects." They added up to a gigantic infrastructure program of highways, ports, airports, and power plants, whose vast expenditures unleashed the "Taiwan miracle." In the United States, a democratic president like Dwight D. Eisenhower never managed to launch more than one such grand project, the Interstate Highway System.

As in Korea, though, wealth bestowed from above eventually brought about middle-class discontent from below. In 1987, Chiang ended martial law. Opposition parties, though still illegal, were now tolerated. After his death, his successor Lee Teng-hui yielded the biggest prize: Lifetime tenure in the National Assembly went out the window, and in came free elections in 1991. Three years later, the lifetime presidency also became history. By 1996, Taiwan had its first popularly elected president. In 2000, the one-party state was buried for good when Chen Shui-bian narrowly defeated the Kuomintang candidate for the presidency.

Correlation is never causation, but the link between rising democracy and falling growth bears an uncanny resemblance to the Korean experience. Nor is this just an accident. As power trickles down from the top, it spreads from the one to the many, who claim not only a louder voice but also a larger slice of the economic pie. Newly enfranchised citizens want more private and public wealth. Hence, forced capital accumulation—the lodestar of modernitarianism—necessarily suffers as consumption rises. But this is only half of the story.

The other half is an old acquaintance of economic history. As the Korean example shows, capital exploitation runs up against its own limits in a maturing economy. Each new chunk of fixed investment generates less output than in a takeoff economy. In Taiwan, gross capital formation (in real terms) rose fourteen-fold between 1970 and 2000. Yet growth fell as the capital stock rose. In the 1970s, Taiwan's golden age, average growth was just a shade below 10 percent. By the last decade of the twentieth century, it had declined to 6.5 percent, by the first decade of the twenty-first to 4 percent.[17] So far, none of the previous rapid risers has overturned the cruel law of diminishing returns. Can China and India do so, as the rise-of-the-rest camp presumes? In that case, the miracle economies of the twenty-first century would not be from this world.

Japan's Growth Model

Japan was the "China" of the 1960s and 1970s, the world's super-star and the source of endless angst attacks roiling the American soul. Nobody could stop this steamroller, its economy forging ahead at double-digit speed that threatened to wipe out competing industries around the globe. "The time will never again come when America will regain its strength in industry," crowed Sony's chairman Akio Morita in 1989, one year after Japanese growth had passed its peak. He predicted a "totally new configuration in the balance of power in the world"—power growing out of the assembly line. Actually, "there is no hope for the U.S.," pronounced Shintaro Ishihara, a former cabinet minister and author of *The Japan That Can Say No*, a nationalist tract that further stoked American angst.[18]

If they had been gifted with true foresight, the doctors of Decline—in Japan as well as in America—would have reserved the no-hope diagnosis for the Japanese patient. At the turn of the millennium, Japanese growth had collapsed to almost zero; for the rest of the twenty-first century's first decade, the economy sputtered along at an average of less than 1 percent. Nor was this a mere blip. The "dismal naughts" limned the "new normal," following on the "Lost Decade" of the 1990s, when growth averaged out at 1.5 percent.

Recalling Japan's fall from its perch as No. 1,[19] a former high official in the country's Economic Planning Agency lamented, "All of our long-cherished assumptions—that the Japanese economy will always grow, that asset prices always rise, that full employment is virtually guaranteed, that financial institutions are invulnerable . . . are now being overturned."[20] Standard fare of the 1990s, these cast-in-concrete convictions had given Americans the shivers. In 1991, *The Coming War with Japan* came out, the title saying it all.[21] Running for the presidency in 1992, the year of *Rising Sun*, the former Democratic senator from Massachusetts Paul Tsongas announced, "The cold war is over; Japan has won."[22] Why did this unstoppable behemoth stumble and stay down? Wasn't Japan, like China today, destined to leave the United States in the dust within a couple of decades?

At first sight, Japan doesn't fit into the East Asian model of modernitarianism that used to characterize South Korea and Taiwan, and continues to typify China's red-flag version today. Japan's spectacular rise from the ashes of World War II was not masterminded by a tyrannical regime. The new Japan began as an American-imposed democracy with all the formal trappings, including a many-hued party spectrum. On closer inspection, however, Japan was de facto a one-party state, with the Liberal Democrats essentially running the country (with a three-year break) until 2009 when the party lost its seemingly eternal majority.

Japan was by no means a dictatorship, be it the Kuomintang or the Communist kind. But its skyrocketing growth did follow an authoritarian trajectory—call it "controlled" or "organized" capitalism. Or a system of "interlocking oligopolies." At the center of the web sat the one-and-only Liberal Democratic Party (LDP). Next to it towered a mighty bureaucracy, at its core the vaunted MITI, the Ministry of International Trade and Industry. Big business and big banking completed the trio. Only big labor was missing in this cathedral of collusion. Instead, there was small labor—company unions presiding over workers bought off by lifetime tenure and modest profit sharing. Just as elsewhere in East Asia, the system favored exports over imports, investment over consumption, producers over consumers, bank loans over equity capital.[23]

This is how William Overholt, an old Asia hand based at Harvard, dissects "Japan, Inc.," a top-down system designed for war in the 1940s, but carried forward into Japan's democratic future:

Among the changes introduced by the Japanese government were lifetime employment, seniority pay, company unions, firms that gave priority to employees over shareholders, government policies that put banks before capital markets, and . . . policy coordination between government and corporations . . . The new system squeezed individual consumption to a minimum, channeled savings into the government and thence into favored industries, allowed banks to focus their lending on affiliated companies . . . and gave bureaucrats vast financial and economic power with limited political accountability. [The arrangement also] encouraged domestic cartels and international protectionism . . . [24]

With a few strokes of the pen, this description would also fit South Korea, Taiwan, and China. The first commandment was "export *über alles*," hence "fixed-capital investment above all," hence depressed consumption as well as held-down exchange rates and wages. Like the other Dragons, Tokyo flooded favored firms with tsunamis of cheap capital. While the Japanese miracle was breaking one record after another, the political system—a one-party state in all but name—began to ossify. Power was being concentrated in the hands of (often unelected) party leaders, whose factions had their own ties to the bureaucracy and to deep-pocketed corporations. Absent were transparency and accountability, and so was "Throw the rascals out," as the traditional battle cry of American politics has it.

This hardening web of collusion and corruption served all kinds of useful purposes, like predictability, trade surpluses, and, of course, patronage for the loyal minions of Japan's "organized capitalism." Not served were free and fair markets. Those are characterized by easy entry and harsh competition, the efficient allocation of resources and the speedy demise of failing firms. By the end of the 1970s, the oldest law of economics—of supply and demand—began to bite. If a good is too cheap, it will be overused, never mind profitability. Underpriced capital will be flung about, pumping up stock market and real estate bubbles, especially when capital controls, as elsewhere among East Asia's rapid risers, stop money from flowing into direct investments abroad. At the height of the market, as the famous story goes, the land under the emperor's palace in Tokyo was said to be worth as much as all of California. This story is impossible to confirm, but it makes the point very nicely.

The bubble burst on 29 December 1989, when the Nikkei reached an all-time high. Some forty years later, the index was still down to one-quarter of the record set in 1989. But the central moral of this tale is not about bursting bubbles, not even about "lost decades." It reaches deeply into the fabric of the wider East Asian economic miracle, delivering a larger lesson. A collusive system lacks transparency, accountability, and checks and balances. Equating the national interest with "exports first," such a system will

- reduce the cost and risk of investment
- generate overinvestment
- spawn overcapacity and
- lead to diminishing returns on capital.

Roughly, this is the story of East Asia as a whole: extravagant growth segueing into normalcy or even long-term decline as in Japan. Why does this model, fabulously successful at first, turn on itself? In the language of academic economics, the answer runs like this: "The performance of the Japanese economy was very good in the 1980s," recall two Japan experts. It seemed "poised to catch up with the United States. However, the trend reversed itself subsequent to 1991. . . ." How to explain the sudden downturn? "We note a significant capital deepening, with the capital-output ratio increasing by nearly 30 percent . . . from 1990 to 2000." In other words, too much capital produces too little extra output, hence a "low rate of return" and "low productivity growth." Both could be explained by a "policy that subsidizes inefficient firms and declining industries."[25] This is the academic short take on a "collusive capitalism" that worked beautifully during the takeoff, but failed miserably in maturity.

China is by no means a mature economy, but the telltale signs of the Japanese experience abound already. Even years before the Crash of 2008, Beijing had to bail out some of its largest banks, riddled as they were with bad debt. Japan's murderous real estate bubble shows up China's empty skyscrapers and ghost cities. As in the case of the East Asians, wages keep rising at a rapid rate, leveling the cost advantage that made Japan, then China "factories of the world" (see figure 13 in chapter 5). History—the history of all rapid risers—is catching up with the twenty-first-century juggernaut that is China.

Politics vs. Economics

How East Asia's Dragons fared in the longer run is not just an academic exercise in growth theory, let alone a seminar in economic history. It is about the big question of the twentieth century, thrust forward into the twenty-first. The classic formulation, setting the democracies against the totalitarians, has always been: Who is on the right side of history? Is it liberal democracy, with power growing from the bottom up, hedged in by free markets, the rule of law, accountability, and the separation of powers? Or is it despotic centralism in the ways of Stalin and Hitler, the most recent, though far less cruel, variant being the Chinese one: state capitalism plus one-party rule?

The demise of communism did not dispatch the big question; it only laid it to rest for a couple of decades. Now the spectacular rise of China and the crises of the democratic economies—bubbles and busts, overspending and astronomical debt—have disinterred what seemed safely buried in a graveyard called "The End of History," when liberal democracy would triumph everywhere. Now the dead have risen from their graves, strutting and crowing. And many in the West are asking: Isn't top-down or *dirigiste* capitalism, as practiced in the past by the Dragons and currently by China, the better road to riches and global muscle than the muddled, self-stultifying ways of liberal democracy?[26]

Western intellectuals of all shades have always had a soft spot for strongmen, just think of Jean-Paul Sartre's adulation of Stalin or the German professoriat's early defection to Hitler. The French Nobelist André Gide saw the "promise of salvation for mankind" embodied in Stalin's Russia. And no wonder: These tyrants promised not only earthly redemption but also economic rebirth; they were the hands-on engineers, while thinkers dream and debate, craving power, but being too timorous to go for it. Too bad that the price was untold human suffering, but as Bertolt Brecht, the poet laureate of German communism, famously lectured, "First the grub, then the morals."[27] Today's Declinists succumb to a similar temptation. They survey the crises of Western capitalism and look at China's thirty-year miracle. Then they conclude once more that state supremacy, especially when flanked by markets and profits, can do better than liberal democracy. Power does breed growth initially, but in the longer run, it falters, as the pockmarked history of the twentieth century reveals.

The fascination never dies, but the object of reverence does, as the sorry end of the Soviet Union demonstrates. The Muscovite empire wasn't even felled by war, as was Nazi Germany. The supreme leader does well in whipping his people into frenzied industrialization, achieving in years what took the democracies decades in the past two centuries. Under Hitler, the Flying Hamburger train covered the distance between Berlin and Hamburg in 138 minutes; in democratic Germany, it took the German Railroad sixty-six years to match that record. The reasons are simple. The Nazis didn't have to worry about local resistance and environmental-impact statements. A German-designed maglev train now whizzes back and forth between Shanghai airport and the city; at home, it was derailed by a cantankerous democracy rallying against the noise and the subsidies.

Top-down economics succeeds at first, but fails later, as the Soviet model shows. Or it doesn't even reach the takeoff point, as a long list of imitators, from Nasser's Egypt to Castro's Cuba, demonstrates. Nor are twenty-first century populist caudillos doing better, as Argentina, Ecuador, and Venezuela illustrate. Authoritarian or "guided" modernization, as the three Asian Dragons show, plants the seeds of its own demise. The system moves mountains in its youth, but eventually hardens into a mountain range itself—stony, impenetrable, and immovable. It empowers vested interests that, like privileged players throughout history, first ignore and then resist change because it poses a mortal threat to their status and income. This is in the nature of every such society, which Francis Fukuyama, reflecting on the French *ancien régime*, labels "rent seeking."

He explains: "In such a society, the elites spend all of their time trying to capture public office in order to secure a rent for themselves"—that is, more riches than a free market would grant. In the French case, the "rent" was a "legal claim to a specific revenue stream that could be appropriated for private use."[28] In other words, the game of the mighty is to convert public power into personal profit—damn markets and competition. The French example easily extends to twentieth-century East Asia, where the game was played by both state and society, be it openly or by underhanded give-and-take. Raising the banner of national advantage, the state favors industries and organized interests; in turn, these seek more power in order to gain monopolies, subsidies, tax breaks, and protection so as to increase their "rents"—wealth and status above and beyond what a competitive system would deliver.

The larger the state, the richer the rents. If the state rather than the market determines economic outcomes, politics beats profitability as allocator of resources. Licenses, building permits, capital, import barriers, and anticompetitive regulations go to the state's own or to favored players, breeding corruption and inefficiency. Nor is such a system easily repaired. The state depends on its clients, as these do on their mighty benefactor. This widening web of collusion breeds either stagnation or revolt.

What can the little Dragons tell us about the big one, China? The model followed by all of them is virtually the same. But some differences are glaring. One is sheer size, and thus China will be a heavyweight in the world economy no matter what. Another is demography. The little Dragons have completed the classic course. Along that route, toilers of the land, just as in the West, thronged the cities in search of a better life. This "industrial reserve army" held down wages, driving up the profit rate and the capital stock. And so, South Korea, Taiwan, and Japan turned into mighty "factories of the world," whose textiles, tools, cars, and electronics threatened to overwhelm Western industry, as China's export juggernaut does today. Once it empties out, the countryside can no longer feed the industrial machine with cheap labor. Yet China still has hundreds of millions poised to leave rural poverty behind.

So do not confuse China with Japan, whose shrinking and aging population will not be replenished soon by immigration or procreation; Japan ranks at the very bottom of the world fertility table, one notch above Taiwan and one below South Korea. Call it East Asia's "death wish." China's "reserve army" still has a long way to go. Nor has this very poor country exhausted the classical advantages of state capitalism, such as forced capital accumulation, sup- pressed consumption, and a cavalier disregard for the environment.

Discontent, as measured by the frequency of "public distur- bances," is rising, but it is about local corruption and elite rent seek- ing, not about cracking the power monopoly of the Communist Party. One Tiananmen demonstration does not a revolution make, and so there is no shortcut to the mass-based protest that dispatched the tyrants of Taipei and Seoul. Nor is there an imminent ballot-box revolution in China's future. It took Japan's voters half a century to dismantle the informal one-party state run by the LDP, and this in a land of free elections. The CCP need not fear such calamity; it is the one and only party in a land of make-believe elections.

And yet. History does not bode well for authoritarian modern- ization, be it "controlled, "guided," or plain state capitalism. Either the system freezes up and then turns upon itself, devouring the seeds of spectacular growth and finally producing stagnation. This is the Japanese "model" that began to falter twenty years before the de facto monopoly of the LDP was broken. Or the country follows the "Western route" where growth first spawned wealth, then a middle class, then democratization cum welfare state and slowing growth. This is the road traveled by Taiwan and South Korea—the oriental version of Westernization.

The irony is that *both* despotism and democracy, though for very different reasons, are incompatible with dazzling growth over the long haul. So far, China has been able to steer past either shoal; it is rising riches without slowdown or revolt—a political miracle without precedent. The strategy is to unleash markets and to fetter politics, "make money, not trouble." Can China continue to defy history? This is the question of the next chapter.

CHAPTER FIVE

The Next Number One: China and Yesterday's Highfliers

A Superstar Is Born

Soviet Russia in the 1960s, Europe in the 1970s, Japan in the 1980s—these were yesterday's superstars. Now it is China, with three lesser contenders in tow: India, Russia, and Brazil. Perhaps as precise a date as any for China's anointment as coming master of the universe is 2003, when a team of Goldman Sachs economists published a paper entitled *Dreaming with BRICs: The Path to 2050.*[1] By midcentury, the report pronounced, the Chinese economy would be No. 1, nine trillion ahead of America's in 2003 dollars. India would come in third. But doom would strike even earlier, as China would draw even with the United States in 2041.[2]

"No idea has done more to muddle thinking about the global economy than that of the BRICs," wrote the Morgan Stanley economist Ruchir Sharma a decade after *Dreaming* had come out. They had nothing in common save great size and a catchy acronym, and by the early 2010s, their fantastic growth rates were dropping like, well, bricks. Brazil's and Russia's tempos had halved, while China's was down to a bit more than 7 percent, a long slide from the double-digit peaks that had so awed the Goldman Sachs team.[3]

Economists would not be economists if they didn't hedge such a bold bet. Hence the old joke: Why are there no one-handed economists? Because they always need two—for saying "on the one hand" and "on the other." So the Goldman team pedaled back: "For our projections to be close to the truth," the BRICs need to "remain on a steady growth track and keep the conditions in place that will allow that to happen." Thus, the prediction slid off into a tautology: China will keep running if the fuel does. But "that is harder than it sounds." Hence there is a "good chance that the projections might not be realized."[4] So for the next two pages, the authors did what smart prophets always do: never soothsay without covering your posterior.

For one, the economic policies had to be right, like low inflation and sound public finances. The politics, not exactly a minor variable, had to be right as well for the next fifty years. Hence beware of "political uncertainty and instability"—historical jokers econometrists cannot squeeze into their equations. Of course, these miracle economies had to remain open, so that investment and trade could continue to feed growth. Moreover, education would have to turn hundreds of millions of the very poor into "human capital." Finally, the "demographic assumptions may also turn out to be incorrect." An excellent caveat, for even a decade ago, the demographics of two of the BRICs were heading down, with Russia dying and China rapidly aging.

Such cautionary asides did not dampen the enthusiasm of the media, which often gloss over the finer print. For the pundits, no hedging. China would dethrone the United States by midcentury, period! If Goldman Sachs, the Midas among the investment banks, said so, then it had to be true. Not to be outdone, other soothsayers quickly fingered 2025 or even 2020 as annus horribilis, when China would leave the United States in the dust. Why even stop with America as a has-been? In 2009, a British prophet went whole hog, proclaiming "the end of the Western world" as such.[5]

One year later, prominent academics had waded into the next-master-of-the-universe sweepstakes. His eyes on China, the economics Nobel laureate Robert Fogel of the University of Chicago sounded like his eponymous Harvard colleague Ezra Vogel back in 1979. (Both names hark back to the German word for "bird," a creature that loves to soar off into the sky.) Ezra Vogel's *Japan as Number One* had launched a decade of hyperbole, trumpeting that Japan would overtake the United States by 1990. It didn't.

Vogel was thirty years ago, an eon in augury. But in prophecy, memories are short. So Robert Fogel doubled down on the Goldman Sachs bet, cutting the date of doom by ten years.[6] In 2040, he trumpeted, the Chinese economy will reach $123 trillion, or "nearly *three times the economic output of the entire globe in 2000*. . . . This is what economic hegemony will look like." (According to Goldman Sachs, China would have barely drawn even with the United States in 2040, with $26 trillion.) Why no hedging, as would befit a two-handed economist? Because the more modest predictions, Fogel divulged, "grossly underestimate the extent of the rise—and how fast it's coming." For China had everything "going so right for it."

How would China educate hundred of millions for work in an advancing economy? Just project recent trends forward. And so Fogel prophesied that China would "increase its high school enrollment rate to the neighborhood of 100 percent and the college rate to about 50 percent over the next generation." In other words, the Chinese rate would exceed the current American college rate by about ten percentage points, while the United States is spending roughly twice as much as share of GDP on a population a quarter as big. What about the rural half of China's 1.3 billion people? Would those 700 million crowd into the cities with their better schools? It doesn't matter, Fogel claimed. "Productivity is increasing even for those who remain in rural areas." What about the politics tagged as the great unknown in Goldman's celebration of the BRIC dream team? Not to worry. "The Chinese political system is likely not what you think." For Fogel, the one-party state was well on the way to a democracy of sorts.

Though China is no "open democracy, there's more criticism and debate in upper echelons of policymaking than many realize," the economist reported. True enough; compared with the Soviet Politburo, the debate within the Chinese Communist Party does indeed sound like a free-for-all. But elite contest, as historians recall, has roiled every top-down system in the past and should not be confused with the real thing. If history is a guide, totalitarian systems do not ripen into democracy. They are broken by war, as was Nazi Germany. Or they implode like the Soviet Union. Or they degenerate into sheer tyranny like France's infant democracy under the Jacobins.

Yet neither collapse nor radicalization is good for a country's economic health. Postcommunist Russia slid into two decades of economic catastrophe; today, Russia remains basically an extraction economy whose fate hangs on the price of raw materials like gas, oil, and ore. China's Cultural Revolution—Maoism to the max— brought growth to a standstill. Even the speedy repression of the Tiananmen revolt came with a hefty price, as growth dropped by seven percentage points from its 1988 peak. When China's politics go wrong, these numbers suggest, "great leaps" go backward. Unfortunately, political earthquakes cannot be fitted into straight-line projections.

If the future cannot be known, what about the past? At this point in the argument, members of the rising-rest school like to trundle out China's glorious history. So does Fogel, who is being cited here at length because his $123 trillion miracle forecast is but the extreme version of the hero worship accorded to China Superstar. "While Europe was fumbling in the Dark Ages," Fogel enthuses, "China cultivated the highest standards of living in the world." This is true, but not as dramatic as it sounds when held up against the actual numbers.

China and Western Europe were about even in per capita income when Christ was born. A thousand years later, the Chinese were indeed ahead, but not the Eighth Wonder of the World. Their per-person income topped the West's by a mere 12 percent. This happy state lasted until the fourteenth century. By the fifteenth, the West Europeans were pulling ahead, while the Chinese went into centuries of decline. By mid-twentieth century, Western Europe's per capita was ten times larger than China's.[7]

So the Middle Kingdom had its day in the sun during the first millennium, but wandered off into the sunset, so to speak, in the second. Meanwhile, Western Europe went on to conquer the four corners of the earth, propelled forward by the three R's of the Renaissance, Reformation, and Industrial Revolution. Why this reversal of fortunes? The trite answer is: What goes up must come down. But this platitude raises a more interesting question: Why did China fall off its perch just then?[8]

The reasons are familiar. Traditional Chinese culture churned out inventions like clocks, printing, and gunpowder (it did *not* invent spaghetti) before the West got there, but it missed out on science and its parent, freedom of inquiry. Science is the rational, systematic search for knowledge that doesn't just produce paper or porcelain, two other Chinese firsts, but also unlocks the laws of the universe. The West went from gunpowder to chemistry and from clocks to physics. Both produced inventions by the millions. The Chinese did not manage to bridge the gap between science and invention, because the institutions were wrong. The imperial state was miraculously efficient in expanding its sway and wealth, conquering enemies and nature, building ports and fleets, roads and canals. But it could not deliver what would make the West the master of the modern world.[9]

How could the emperor, a godlike figure, countenance freedom of inquiry, participation, accountability, and the rule of law? Or the separation of the private and the public spheres? Christianity deserves some credit here for Luther's doctrine of the "two king-doms," which harks back to Jesus' "render unto Caesar . . ." Out of this duality emerged a typically Western idea: the separation of church and state, hence of faith and reason. The much-maligned Roman Church deserves credit, too. While busily burning here-tics on the stake, it opened its monasteries to learning, turning its cathedral schools, such as those in Bologna, Paris, and Oxford, into universities after 1100.

The *Una Sancta* found no imitators in China. No dualism, no demarcation between the spheres of God and governance, or between society and state, public and private. Hence no space for the kind of autonomy that breeds diversity and breaks intellec-tual molds. The single-sphere, rigidly governed imperial system of China was bound to ossify, accepting no other legitimate authority than the ruler's. Or doomed to explode.

The French scholar Etienne Balazs calls this system the "Moloch-State," another word for totalitarianism: "No private initiative, no expression of public life that can escape official control. There is . . . a whole array of state monopolies, which comprise the great consumption staples: salt, iron, tea, alcohol, foreign trade. There is a monopoly of education, jealously guarded. There is practically a monopoly of letters. . . ."[10]

In his book *What Went Wrong?*, Bernard Lewis muses about the "clash between Islam and modernity"—thus the subtitle. In crisis, he writes, a culture can ask two questions. One is "What did we do wrong?" The other is "Who did this to us?" The former leads to "How can we do it right?," which is a central feature of Western modernity. "Who did this?" is the trait of a closed culture like Imperial China's. It leads not to reform but to scapegoating, paranoia, and revolt.[11] Hence, the ancient Middle Kingdom was a breeding ground for conspiracy and rebellion. Its counterpart was repression. So next to porcelain and gun powder, China boasts another first. In the fourteenth century, the Ming dynasty invented an early version of the modern police state, followed by several deadly purges. Such a spiral of revolt and repression has been a constant companion of Chinese history, all the way to the civil war of the twentieth century.

Admiral Zheng He's "Treasure Fleet," actually seven that sailed the seas in as many expeditions from 1405 to 1433, is regularly cited as an illustration of China's superpower status during the Ming dynasty. The first expedition involved some 250 ships; all told, the Chinese fleet probably dwarfed any other in its days. It roamed the oceans from Java to Jeddah and East Africa, bringing back booty and prisoners, but without leaving any traces. It was armed tourism, not empire building in the European way. After a string of bloody power struggles at home, a new emperor and his successors proceeded to scuttle the fleet.

Large, oceangoing vessels were outlawed, and so was foreign trade. Just as the Age of Discovery was dawning in Europe, sailing the high seas became a capital offense. Beset by Mongolian hordes from the north, China closed up. As the fleet went down, the Great Wall in all its isolationist splendor kept going up. In the seventeenth century, the coastal population was forcibly removed inland. In the eighteenth century, Britain tried to establish a permanent embassy, as was the custom in the West, in Beijing. The envoy was told that "it was otherwise in China which never sends ambassadors to foreign countries." The Europeans were the "outer barbarians." The civilized world was East Asia, made up of subservient states acknowledging the primacy of the Middle Kingdom and its emperor as "Son of Heaven."[12] And China went into centuries of decline and "intellectual xenophobia," as the Harvard historian David Landes called it.[13] It was stagnation, but not stability.

Endless revolt finally brought down the last dynasty, the Qing, at the beginning of the twentieth century. The Taiping Rebellion in the middle of the nineteenth was "one of the largest and most devastating uprisings in world history," recalls the historian Charles Horner. "Tens of millions were engaged on both sides" of the civil war, and "casualties ran into the tens of millions."[14] In 1911, the Qings simply abdicated, but peace was not to be China's future. Mao Zedong is reputed to have killed close to 200,000 "class enemies" in the purges of the early 1930s. His Great Leap Forward ended in the Great Chinese Famine, which claimed the lives of 30 million.[15]

Present-day China, of course, will scuttle neither science nor globalization, nor build, even metaphorically, a new Great Wall, but other mainstays of imperial rule persist in a modern guise. For all of its experiments in market liberalization, the Communist Party remains paramount, obsessively guarding its supremacy. As in ancient China, rising wealth makes for rising inequality, especially between coast and inland, spawning corruption and unrest. China is brilliant at appropriating foreign technology, but the Internet remains tightly controlled, and the free exchange of knowledge is rigorously rationed.

What made Silicon Valley, that twenty-first-century entrepôt of cyber technology, the envy of the world—the constant babble, sharing, and job hopping between competing firms—is not a Chinese cultural trait.[16] For its admirers, China's glorious past is not tainted by the bitter aftermath. Accordingly, China is merely returning to its rightful place in history. Or, as Fogel puts it, the ascent of China is "merely a return to [an earlier] status quo." For the rise-of-the-rest school, it is either back to the fifteenth or forward into the twenty-first. China, like Parker Lewis, the hero of a wildly popular U.S. sitcom in the 1990s, just "can't lose."[17]

Another American China expert thinks so, too. Albert Keidel, a former Treasury Department official, advances Goldman Sachs' date of doom to 2035 (GDP equality with the United States) and predicts for 2050 a Chinese economy twice the size of America's. Like Fogel, he echoes the Japan rapture of the 1980s—different countries, similar language. It is forward forever, and the Chinese, like yesterday's Japanese, will deftly clear whatever hurdle might rise up on their way.

Would mounting inequality derail the Chinese boom? Not really, because rapidly dropping poverty "may be [the] more significant" countertrend. The prospect of social unrest should not be exaggerated because Chinese officialdom is learning how to develop "more sophisticated crowd-control" and "more adequate systems of compensation for legitimate grievances." China's record on the environment is also improving, and "sooner or later, higher incomes and greater public concern will win out, despite China's reluctance to strengthen democratic politics." So the people will win, though democracy may not.

What about a banking system that, like Japan's at a similar stage, showers cheap loans on privileged players? This is actually a "strength of Chinese finance," as it is "a bank-based system for supplementing the budget resources needed for public investments." A different interpretation might see such a blessing as a curse, with the state giving unto itself under this dispensation. An inevitable consequence is the misallocation of capital; the other is corruption. A serious problem, Keidel concedes, but "corruption has clearly not prevented growth in the past and is unlikely to do so in the future."[18] Corruption is indeed compatible with high growth, as the case of India shows, a country that scores even higher on the sleaze index than China. Yet growing corruption it is not a harbinger of societal harmony down the line.[19] Finally, what about artificially low exchange rates said to be at the heart of China's "export first" model? A "secondary influence, at best," since the real growth engine is domestic demand. This explanation was penned before the Crash of 2008, one of those unforeseen events that scramble the most sophisticated econometrics. In 2009, when world trade—demand from the outside—contracted dramatically, Chinese growth dropped by almost three percentage points compared with 2007, the year before the house of Lehman fell.

As limned by Keidel and many other experts, visions of China's happy future recall an underlying purpose of Declinism, as laid out in chapter 2: diagnosis as pedagogy. America is doomed, but it shall rise again—or brake its fall—if it wakes up and mends its ways. In this case, the formula comes with a Liberal tinge. First, according to Keidel, the United States must invest a lot more in public infrastructure, health, social security, and education. Second, it should manage decline gracefully by engaging China across the board before it acquires military primacy: Don't contain, don't confront, but co-opt while you are still ahead. This is prophecy as a device.

MODERNITARIANISM: NEW DRAGON VS. OLD TIGERS

State capitalism, now back in fashion, is an old idea—recall the government-chartered East India Company, which ranged across the British Empire from the seventeenth century to the nineteenth, complete with its own army and fleet. In the twentieth century, as mentioned previously, it was Stalin and Hitler who drove their nations to new heights of industrialization. The modernitarianism model failed miserably in the decolonized Arab world, but "managed" or "organized" capitalism has been fabulously successful in lifting East Asian nations from poverty after World War II. The sterling record still comes with a warning. The advantages of "early capitalism," to apply a Marxist label to backward Taiwan and South Korea, do eventually wane. The same caveat holds for the "catch-up capitalism" of previously industrialized West Germany and Japan. Looking at China, the Chicago economist Raghuram Rajan cautions, "The experiences of Germany and Japan offer grim portents for the future."[20] He might have cited Asia's "early" or "start-up capitalists," as well.

What do the careers of the previous risers—Dragons, Tigers, and Teutons—forebode for China? Berlin is five thousand miles away from Beijing, Tokyo, Taipei, and Seoul, but in all cases, the strategies have been uncannily alike across civilizations. Above all, it was "exports first," and so China's export has grown faster than the economy for the past quarter century. This queen of growth was served by four handmaidens, also classics of economic history. These were underconsumption, oversaving, overinvestment, and deliberately depressed exchange rates. The pattern holds for all, but in China's case three differences stick out, which may explain why the Middle Kingdom's miracle has outperformed and, so far, outlasted East Asia's.

Pull Back the State. The first difference is the sweep of state power in the takeoff phase. Formally capitalist, the East Asian systems were de facto planned economies. Yet with its "Four Modernizations," China immediately went the other way, jumping out of the collectivist starting blocks by *loosening* Soviet-style centralization. To be sure, Deng's China also picked winners in the ways of Japan's MITI. It also coddled favorite entities as did South Korea with its *chaebol* conglomerates—and still does. The Plan was still the Plan, and state ownership still supreme. But the orthodoxy came with porous walls and new players.

For one, Deng did away with Mao's communes, and land tenure began to seep back to the peasants through long-term leases from the "collective." Like Europe's feudal tenants to their lords, they gave the prescribed share to the collective, selling the rest to the government at more generous prices than in the past or on newly formed free markets. Within the first decade of Deng's reforms, the output of cash crops like sugarcane and tobacco had doubled, just as free-market theory would have predicted.

Second, industry was freed in a peculiarly Chinese way. The

large combines of the Maoist economy continued to rule the roost. But suddenly they had to share the yard with a fuzzy new animal, belonging neither to the central state nor to private individuals. This was the TVE, the township and village enterprise. Taking over from Mao's commune and brigade enterprise, the TVE was managed and owned by the local "collective," with the emphasis on "local."

When Deng's reforms took hold after 1978, the TVEs still had to run on the leash of the Plan, but on a much longer one, which allowed them to roam their home grounds in search of opportunity. While title to the enterprises stayed with the local government, "use rights," as in the case of the newly freed peasants, successively devolved from apparatchiks to managers. Over the next two decades, the TVEs grew explosively, quintupling employment to 135 million and boosting turnover by an astounding multiple of twenty-five. This was the "free market" *à la chinoise*: Big Brother held the straps, his small siblings—public, not private, outfits—bought, sold, and invested. Beijing remained at a distance, geographically as well as administratively.

Bring in the World. Unlike its East Asian brethren, China plunged into the global market not just by pushing exports but by systematically pulling in foreign capital. By contrast, it was a while before outsiders could buy their way into Japan, Taiwan, and South Korea. An early Chinese tool of foreign-capital harvesting was the special economic zone. The first one was set up in Shenzhen in 1980. Now there are twenty, nourished by tax breaks, management autonomy, and easy profit repatriation.

Naturally, the Communist Church would stand untouched; reform would not ring in the Reformation. So, early on, China's officialdom took pains to dispel any impression of "right-wing deviationism," presenting these zones as "a minor change in state economic policy." They were "not in basic conflict with China's socialist economic system," since "state capitalism has the lion's share."[21] And has kept it.

Socialist in principle, the zones became hotbeds of profit making and globalization, with lower taxes and regulations for both joint and foreign-owned ventures. They inhaled overseas capital like a whale gobbling up krill by the thousands of gallons of seawater. Take the original four, strung out along the Pacific on either side of Hong Kong. In the next thirty years, they leapt from practically zero to the stars. In Shenzhen, the fastest-feeding whale, foreign direct investment (FDI) exploded from a measly $5.5 million in 1978 to almost $4 billion in 2008, which translates into a 700-fold increase. Shenzhen was also the first to set up a stock exchange. Gorging themselves on foreign monies, the first four boosted GDP by astronomical multiples. Again, Shenzhen held the galactic record, increasing GDP by a factor of 2,800![22] Yet these startling numbers come with a classic caveat. Taking off from a very low base, growth soars with mind-boggling speed, by factors rather than mere percentages. But it is a long way from close to zero to real riches. In 2008, the per capita income of Shenzhen, one of China's richest regions, was still only one-quarter of the United States' as a whole.

China sucked in the world's wealth from day one; the East Asians did not. On the other hand, China's capitalism remains "organized" and "controlled"; indeed, it is "state capitalism" plain and simple. For all its privatization, the Chinese economy remains heavily dominated by state-owned enterprises. So while East Asians and Germans have gone the other way by privatizing and deregulating, the state sector remains king, nay, emperor in China. While democracy and liberalization have swept East Asia's first risers, the Communist Party remains at the helm in China, and it does not intend to relinquish it, as Japan's LDP, Taiwan's Kuomintang, and South Korea's strongmen eventually had to do. So the earlier pathologies of the East Asian trio continue to beset China. These are the three C's—crony capitalism, corruption, and collusion—plus the F of favoritism, or *guanxi*, as an ancient tradition has it.

Keep the State in Charge. These enduring traits reflect a third difference between the Chinese Dragon and its East Asian brothers. Contrary to the expectations held by reverent China watchers, state capitalism is not a way station, as it was among the East Asian Dragons. The behemoth has just put on new capitalist garb. Gone is the drab apparatchik presiding over a bureaucratic production unit chained to the Plan; meet Mr. CEO decked out in tie and white shirt, whose children study in America's top schools. But even as the economy matures, the state will not vacate Lenin's "commanding heights of the economy," whence it rules the plains, dotted as they are with private preserves. The government will decide and dispose. Meet "Communist Capitalism" or "State Capitalism 2.0," touted both in China and in the West as the better-designed version of the models that failed in the twentieth century.

How would we know that the state remains triumphant, given myriad reforms since Deng's Four Modernizations? Take market capitalization. The share of the state-owned enterprises in the Chinese stock market has risen continuously: from 73 percent in 1995 to 83 percent in 2007.[23] The *Economist* puts the most recent (2011) figure at 80 percent, adding, "The Chinese state is the biggest shareholder in the country's 150 biggest companies and guides and goads thousands more. It shapes the overall market by managing its currency, directing money to favored industries and working closely with Chinese companies abroad."[24]

Richard McGregor, author of *The Party: The Secret World of China's Communist Rulers*, has captured the essence of the system in a poignant piece of reportage on the "red machine":

> On the desks of the heads of China's fifty-odd biggest state companies . . . sits a red phone. . . .
>
> The "red machine" is like no ordinary phone. Each one has just a four-digit number. It connects only to similar phones with four-digit numbers within the same encrypted system. . . .
>
> "Red machines" are dotted throughout Beijing in offices of officials of requisite rank, on the desks of ministers and vice-ministers, the chief editors of party newspapers, the chairmen and women of the elite state enterprises and the leaders of innumerable party-controlled bodies. . . .
>
> One vice-minister told me that more than half of the calls he received on his "red machine" were requests for favours from senior party officials, along the lines of: "Can you give my son, daughter, niece, nephew, cousin or good friend and so on, a job?"[25]

Nor is this just a story about insiders vs. outsiders. It is above all about boundless control. "The party," sums up McGregor elsewhere, "dictates all senior personnel appointments in ministries and companies, universities and the media, through a shadowy and little-known body called the Organization Department. Through the department, the party oversees just about every significant position in every field in the country." Mark Kitto, a Briton who has lived and worked in China for sixteen years, puts it just as harshly: "The country is ruled from behind closed doors, a building without an address or a telephone number."[26] Clearly, adds McGregor, "the Chinese remember Stalin's dictate that the cadres decide everything."[27] A free market this is not; it is rather a market free of interference from pesky rivals.

State Capitalism 2.0

The Party decides everything, but just how big is the state sector? Very big, though "the truth is that nobody knows for sure."[28] Applying a standard Western measure—government spending as share of GDP—might show a China that is a libertarian's dream. The take comes out to about one-fifth of total spending, whereas in the West, government is good for about one-half, the bulk being social transfers. Yet for all their spending, Western governments are not in the business of business. Where they used to be, they have pulled out over the last quarter century by privatizing entire industries, from aviation to utilities.

So let's look not at public expenditures but at the state-owned enterprises (SOEs). No longer slaves to the Plan, they are market participants, just like Western corporations. But the SOEs are a lot more "equal" than the private players. They thrive on favorable tax treatment and preferred access to bank financing at below-market interest rates—echoes of the Japanese *keiretsu* and the Korean *chaebol*. If those goodies are not good enough, the SOEs get straight capital injections. Naturally, they are first in line when it comes to government procurement. In turn, the "SOEs and their wholly-owned subsidiaries are likely to pursue the goals of the state."[29] Their number in 2010 was fifty thousand. Or twice as many. Nobody quite knows (see below for the reasons).

But hasn't their number declined precipitously? True enough, as the left side of figure 11 shows, but without leveling the playing field—quite the contrary. For the dominance of the SOEs, as measured by their assets, has risen much faster than their number has shrunk, as the right side demonstrates. So it is fewer SOEs, but the trend line reflects the famous slogan "Retain the large, release the small." In the process, the "large" have gained a lot more clout.

In the past decade, the proliferating nonstate enterprises have not added weight, as they might have in a free market where the small can feed on myriad capital sources and expand with com-

11. Role and Assets of State-Owned Enterprises in China's Economy

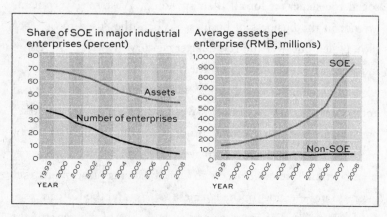

SOURCE: Gao Xu, "State-Owned Enterprises in China: How Big Are They?," 19 January 2010, http://blogs.worldbank.org/eastasiapacific/state-owned-enterprises-in-china-how-big-are-they.

mercial success. The SOEs, by contrast, are bulging, their average assets having grown sixfold. The trend continues. Average assets in the centrally administered SOEs rose by 31 percent in 2010.[30] Together, these numbers limn anything but an ever more perfect market economy, as China admirers believe. Indeed, these figures bespeak rising imperfection, revealing the surging market power of the SOEs and the steady concentration of capital in the hands of the state.

Or put it this way: The total profits earned by China's top 500 private companies in 2009 were less than the total revenue of two state-controlled firms, China Mobile and Sinopec. The government also controls the six big banks and three giant insurance companies. In 2010, 40 out of the 46 Chinese companies listed in Fortune's 500 were state owned.[31] The share of private companies among the 2,000-plus listed on China's stock exchanges is a tiny 5 percent. And, of course, those who run the SOEs are overwhelmingly senior members of the Party. So Beijing shows no sign of evacuating the "commanding heights." The marching order is to go from peak to peak. "National Champions," as they are called in the Western *dirigiste* tradition, are named "strategic emerging industries" in Chinese. The current Five-Year Plan (issued in 2011) picks up where the preceding one left off, pledging large-scale government investment and preferential funding for such sectors as IT, biotech, and high-end manufacturing.

What is private and public is like a Chinese puzzle—shapes within shapes, rings within rings. The usual estimates for the state sector range between 30 and 50 percent of GDP. These are fuzzy figures because the government has been restructuring the SOEs, particularly in industry. In the process, it has placed holding upon holding, freely mixing state and private capital. The official definition of an SOE is "wholly owned and fully controlled by the government," local or central. By that token, their share is inevitably undercounted.

Why would this be so? Excluded from the official designation is a vast army of close relatives: cooperatives with equity in SOEs, joint-operation enterprises, limited-liability corporations with shares held by the state, holdings where the majority stake belongs to the government.[32] To separate private from public is like unscrambling eggs. The color is a rich yellow—yellow like the large star in the upper left of the red Chinese flag that symbolizes the Communist Party and its supremacy over the four social classes, represented by the smaller stars.

Let's go beyond the crude (and misleading) categories of "public" and "private." If one takes listed nonfinancial firms and groups them by largest shareholder, then the private sector comes out to 26 percent, plus 1 percent for foreign companies—not insignificant, but decidedly on the small side. If the measure is gross industrial output, the private sector grows to 41 percent (2009)—better. Now let's apply the yardstick of fixed domestic investment, also for 2009. In this case, the sector labeled "private" shrinks to 22 percent, the huge lion's share being reserved for the state. Finally, go down to the local level. Here the share of fixed investments managed by the authorities is practically Soviet-sized: 95 percent in manufacturing, 98 percent in real estate, 99 percent in the wholesale and retail trade.[33] In other words, while most of the eggs are scrambled, the cook is always the state, high above or down below.

What do these omelets tell us about the downside of China's exalted future?

The Perils of Power. Caixin, an independent Chinese business magazine, reports numbers that depict an omnipotent state:

The vitality of the Chinese economy is being stifled by SOEs, especially central-level, or top, SOEs, and this is borne out by research. In October 2011, the State-Owned Assets Supervision and Administration Commission of the State Council released a breakdown of state-owned assets and earnings information for 102 for-profit SOEs. This showed that in 2010, the capital of 102 central-level SOEs was equivalent to 61.4 percent of GDP, and their earnings equaled 42.2 percent of GDP.[34]

So "Communist capitalism" is far more powerful than the "monopoly capitalism" Karl Marx decried in the nineteenth-century West, by which he meant government-decreed monopolies, as well as the capital concentration that bred oligopolies and cartels. These do wonders for their stockholders, but they also stymie competition and innovation. Recall "Ma Bell" in twentieth-century America, a government-sponsored monopoly that could hold back on new technology and keep long-distance rates sky-high. Or any of the government-controlled telecoms in Europe that relied on mechanical relays and copper cables all the way through the 1980s while computer-switching and fiberglass cables were already on the market. Only after the breakup of AT&T and the privatization of Europe's PTTs were their heirs forced to compete and innovate.

Where power beats markets, as these examples show, East and West do meet. The weight of the state behind them, Chinese SOEs have been famously successful in "acquiring" foreign technology, be it by exacting blueprints as the price of market entry, outright theft, or retroengineering. But to copy is not to invent and to innovate, which is what mature market economies do, especially as production moves up the value chain. The Politburo can hardly give birth to Apple, which started out with Steve Job's $1,750 and a garage.

This is where market capitalism beats state capitalism because the many small (or start-ups) make many small bets, whereas the state makes a few big ones—wrong bet, huge loss. One of the West's costliest white elephants in the innovation game was the Concorde supersonic aircraft, jointly financed by Britain and France to the tune of billions; it was grounded for good in 2003. Big is undoubtedly beautiful in an early phase of development, but it is competition and "creative destruction" that have turned genuine capitalism into the juggernaut of the world economy.

Familism and Favoritism. The children of state ownership are collusion, fraud, and corruption, the scourges of China past and present. Aside from the moral costs, the economic loss is enormous. Why compete and bring the best for least to the market if you can wheel and deal? Why would an official enforce impersonal rules, if he can bend them for his own gain? Why persuade a private bank to finance a project by pitching its merits? In 2009, reports the *Economist*, 85 percent of $1.4 trillion in bank loans went to state companies.[35] Capital hoarding plus collusion was also the hallmark of the East Asian model, and the flattening growth curves in chapter 4's figure 10 show how this model has fared in the longer run.

A duo of China boosters has put a pretty gloss on the rent-seeking combination "state on top, graft below." They write, "Officials at all levels possess the authority as well as the resources needed to promote local growth"—a heartening point. "They also have strong incentive to do so"—even better. And why? "Because their career prospects, as well as personal financial opportunities for themselves and their families, friends, and supporters, are closely tied to the economic trajectory of [their] jurisdictions."[36] In

the twenty-first-century Protestant West, they would call this nepotism and graft, the enemies of the market and the rule of law.

The more state, the more corruption; this is an iron law tra-
versing ideological boundaries. If the government allocates land,
capital, and franchises, then *guanxi* ("connections," "personal rela-
tionships") and straight payola trump economic excellence. Why
compete in an auction, if a phone call will do? Why build your
own franchise with an unbeatable brand like McDonald's or Apple
if you can get an exclusive corner of the market from the government? Corruption is easier than competition. Hence a glaring
recent instance of *guanxi* in high places. At the end of 2012, the
New York Times unearthed a web of family connections centered on
Prime Minister Wen Jiabao. All told, his son, mother, and wife,
various offspring, and cronies had amassed a fortune worth $2.7
billion. The regime was not amused and blocked a slew of search
terms in China's social media.[37]

The tale of the Wondrous Wens underlines the *endemic* problem of a system where power breeds wealth. Indeed, corruption
has grown with the nation's riches, as one would expect. The
more there is to get, the more the privileged will be on the take.
According to government sources, 106,000 officials were found
guilty of corruption in 2009, an increase of 2.5 percent over the
year before.[38] The smarter ones, some 16,000 SOE executives, have
taken the money and run, mainly to the United States, where their
offspring had already set up shop. The grand theft, stretched out
over a decade, runs to $120 billion, according to the People's Bank
of China.[39] Liberally inflicting the death penalty does not help,
as the 16,000 show who got away. The rule of law would, but that
would spell the end of Party supremacy.

Yet corruption, once exposed, is just the most dramatic symptom of system malfunction. The Party that runs the economy does

not promote "the best and the brightest." As the China scholar Susan Shirk notes, "patronage is the coin of the realm in Chinese elite politics."[40] The Brookings researcher Cheng Li observes that the "selection of leaders" suffers from "nepotism and patron-client ties."[41] These beat talent and achievement on the economic level, as well. After a sophisticated statistical analysis, a trio of China scholars concludes, "We find no relationship between growth performance and party ranking, and a strong relationship between factional ties and rank."[42] In other words, merit and competition lose out in the race to the top. In addition, they found what should not be in a communist system: the power of "dynastic succession." In modern China, this is known as the "princeling phenomenon," in which privilege and status are showered on the children of senior party officials. As in the *ancien régimes* of Europe, such features tend to pave the road to stagnation.

Market Power vs. Market Prowess. Efficiency does not blossom in a system where administrative power skews economic outcomes. China.org, a semiofficial news site, gingerly describes the problems: "The low efficiency of SOEs is an issue of international concern. It also exists in China. In the process of China's reform and opening up, the low efficiency of SOEs has stood out more prominently. This explains why SOEs use a majority of the State's fixed assets and bank loans while creating only one-third of the industrial output."[43]

To make the point more bluntly: The state uses capital less efficiently than private business, and its beneficiaries grow more slowly because ample and cheap funds push aside the classic calculus of market economics—how to extract the most from the least. China excels at building prestige projects like skyscrapers or the maglev train in Shanghai. Close calculation would have nixed the speeding wonder, as it did in Germany in 2010, where the Transrapid technology was prototyped. Instead, the Deutsche Bahn, the successor of the state-run railroads, keeps investing in a profitable high-speed rail system. As in Japan in the 1980s, cheap capital breeds overbuilding and asset inflation. The Chinese real estate bubble burst at the end of the preceding decade. By 2010, some 64 million apartments stood empty.[44]

A congressional study, authored by the Asian expert Wayne Morrison, sums it all up:

> State-owned enterprises . . . put a heavy strain on China's economy. By some estimates, over half lose money and must be supported by subsidies, mainly through state banks. Government support of unprofitable SOEs diverts resources away from potentially more efficient and profitable enterprises. In addition, the poor financial condition of many SOEs makes it difficult for the government to reduce trade barriers out of fear that doing so would lead to widespread bankruptcies . . . and unemployment.[45]

Yes, there is fierce competition in the state sector, and executives are rewarded for piling up revenue. But the ultimate yardstick of performance is "political rather than commercial interests."[46] And political clout does not translate into profitability. This is an old story, retold endlessly by the chroniclers of Gosplan-style management, from Moscow to East Berlin. Once the Wall came down, exposing state-run enterprises to the cruelties of the international market, death came swiftly.

How well are Chinese SOEs doing? As expected, their profitability lagged visibly behind the private sector's in the past decade, though return on assets in both sectors rose in tandem as the Chinese economy grew. Alas, this trend lasted only until the Crash of 2008, when SOE profitability dropped sharply, the gap almost tripling. The dreary performance in crisis times suggests more vulnerability down the line, echoing the troubles of East Asia's first risers.[47] One is overleverage, courtesy of state-owned banks. The other is overinvestment and its downside, which is shrinking profitability—just as the law of diminishing returns predicts.

Nor did blame fall only on the world economic crisis, which pushed China's growth rate as far down as 6 percent—a cyclical slump that must not (yet) be equated with a secular decline. Still, as global trade came back, overall SOE profitability kept tumbling. In 2011, the profits of all SOEs fell by nearly 11 percent. The centrally administered state enterprises were down even more. "These figures represent the second decline since 2009," the annus horribilis.[48]

Taking the longer view, Beijing's Unirule Institute of Economics reports that SOE assets and their book profits have come mainly from taxes, credit, and other hidden subsidies. From 2001 to 2008, these emoluments added up to 6 trillion yuan, while the profits totaled 4.9 trillion yuan. At the 2008 yuan–dollar exchange rate, the subsidies came to $820 billion, and the profits to $670 billion, which yields a negative return on the state's largesse to its own.

Wayne Morrison, the congressional researcher, notes that the government "has used the banking system to keep afloat money-losing SOEs by pressuring state banks to provide low-interest loans, without which a large number of SOEs would likely go bankrupt." He reckons that one-half of state-owned bank loans go to the SOEs, even though a large share of them won't be repaid. By contrast, "many private companies in China find it difficult to borrow from state banks."[49] Such are the bitter fruits of cheap money lavished by the state on itself. Just ask the East Asian Dragons and Tigers, which have been there before. What works wonders in the beginning falls and flattens as "organized capitalism" leaves the takeoff stage behind.

Overinvestment. All previous economic miracles in East Asia have sprung from overinvestment and underconsumption. The formula has made for astronomical growth from a low base. If a nation starts out on the road to development, it must sacrifice today in order to reap tomorrow. Don't eat the corn, sow it. But the law of diminishing returns warns: Don't keep doing it. More seed per acre doesn't produce ever more ears, and so yields per bushel of seed corn will flatten and fall.

A Chinese scholar has presented some telling numbers on what Marx belabored as "tendentially falling profit rate." In the first half of the 1990s, 100 million yuan in fixed investments yielded 66.2 million in additional GDP and 400 new jobs. In the naughts, the same 100 million added less than half as much to GDP while creating only 170 new jobs, again less than half of a decade earlier.[50] Turgot and Ricardo, who formulated the law of diminishing returns, would clap their hands in delight. If it had existed in their days, the Nobel Prize in Economics surely would have been theirs.

Nor have the macroeconomics improved. China now devotes nearly one-half of its GDP to fixed investment. Its twin is underconsumption—a ruthlessly suppressed standard of living. This ratio is unmatched around the globe. In the EU, for instance, the investment share of GDP stands at less than one-fifth. Worse, figure 12 shows that China's economy is by no means "maturing," as East Asia's did by raising consumption and cutting investment. Indeed,

China has been *regressing* since the turn of the millennium: Investment is up sharply, consumption has dropped just as harshly. If these trends are not reversed, they will deepen the four nastiest fault lines in China's future.

12.   A Chinese Curse: Investment Up,
       Consumption Down (Percent of GDP)

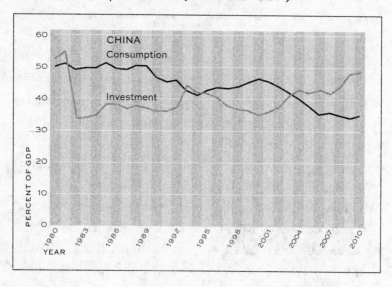

SOURCE: CEIC (via economywatch.com) and World Bank Databank.

THE FOUR FAULT LINES OF STATE CAPITALISM 2.0

1. More Is Less. One is the curse of overinvestment amply demonstrated by the careers of East Asia's previous risers, with more input yielding less output and growth. Call this the "Turgot/Ricardo trap." Let's take the two "early-capitalist" economies Taiwan and South Korea, which, like China, started out at the bottom. Overinvestment generated high growth, and growth pushed up per capita income. But then growth and income began to part ways.

As the East Asians became richer, growth began to falter. The tipping point in Taiwan was 1980, when per capita income topped $6,000. In the 1980s, average growth dropped by two percentage points and kept falling. In South Korea, the tipping point came in 1990, when income reached $12,000 (all figures in 2005 dollars). In the 1990s, growth shrank by two and a half points, now standing at around 4 percent. The classical economists would mumble about our old acquaintance "diminishing return on capital," while adding, "Past the tipping point, investment falls, and so does growth." A modern-day economist, Edward Chancellor, puts it thus: "Policies that have delivered in the past are losing their efficacy. Ever greater amounts of credit and investment are needed to help maintain the same level of GDP growth. . . . Beijing's vaunted policy makers may find that they have run out of options."[51]

Chancellor represents the "China gloom" school. Like its rivals in the Boom camp, he extrapolates from past to future. But more interesting is the mood change he embodied as China's growth rates sank below double-digit at the beginning of the 2010s. Suddenly, China looked like Japan, yesterday's champion. "China has all the earmarks of a classic mania that will end badly—a compelling growth story that seduces investors into ill-starred speculation, blind faith in the competence of Chinese authorities to manage through any cycle, and overinvestment in fixed assets with inadequate returns facilitated by an explosion in credit."[52]

2. Self-limiting Growth. The second fault line is also an old acquaintance: soaring wages that come with a larger pie and cut into profitability some more, if productivity does not increase pari passu. Wages, as figure 13 shows, rose only modestly in the early stages of Deng's reforms, when the economy had lots of slack in terms of underutilized factors like land and labor. Then they exploded, growing eightfold between the mid-1990s and 2010.

13.   The Wages of Success:
        Rising Wealth, Blunted Edge

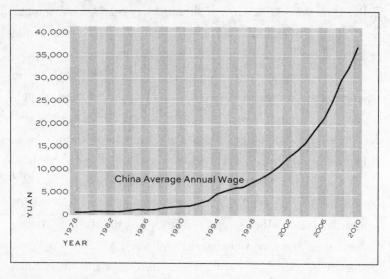

SOURCE: National Bureau of Statistics of China, China Statistical Database, http://219.235.129.58/welcome.do.

Soaring wages don't tell the real story. In fact, they mean little if productivity rises just as rapidly, keeping unit-labor costs, hence a nation's competitive edge, unchanged. Yet China, like the earlier Dragons, may have reached its own tipping point. In economic theory, this is the "Lewis turning point," named after Arthur Lewis, an economics Nobel laureate. He argues that a development model like China's is driven by a seemingly unlimited labor pool fed by the migration from subsistence agriculture to industry. Labor remains cheap, raising profits and delivering the capital for further investment. Yet invariably, the source of surplus labor dries up, and wages begin to rise while growth slows. In China, the turning point should not have come as a surprise. Although China can still tap into a vast human reservoir beyond the cities, the country's adverse demographics—the price of the one-child policy and rapid aging—seem to play a more powerful role (for the dire data, see chapter 6).

Rising productivity, which comes with an expanding capital stock, might have neutralized the demographics. Productivity is indeed rising in China, but apparently not fast enough to compensate for exponential wage gains, as illustrated by figure 13. A 2012 Boston Consulting Group study has looked at the recent past, comparing trends in the United States and China. The numbers are staggering, shaking a key assumption of Declinism: China's eternal cost-advantage in manufacturing. It may be coming to an end, having in the past fed frenzied export-led growth and streams of foreign capital while decimating American industry.

According to the report, the tally hardly favors the Chinese upstart. "In 2000, factory wages in China averaged just 52 cents an hour, or a mere 3 percent of what average U.S. factory workers earned. Since then, Chinese wages and benefits have been rising by double digits each year, averaging increases of 19 percent from 2005 to 2010. The fully loaded costs of U.S. production workers, in contrast, rose by less than 4 percent annually between 2005 and 2010." Furthermore, Chinese wages will keep soaring. The *Economist* forecast that Chinese manufacturing costs would reach the American level by 2015.[53]

Just as startling are the productivity trends. The long and the short of it is that China's productivity gains "will not compensate for wages likely to rise twice as fast."[54] The numbers are stark, confirming the insights of development economics. In 2005, the productivity-adjusted wage of an American worker was almost five times larger than the hourly pay of his Chinese counterpart. By 2010, the gap had shrunk to 3.2 times. By 2015, an American work hour will cost only a bit more than twice the Chinese one. If these trends persist, China is slated to go the way of Asia's previous wunderkinder. And an economy that seemed to defy the gravitational pull of the laws of economics will come back to earth, landing where the older Dragons have already settled.

BCG concludes on an upbeat note for the United States: "By around 2015, the total labor-cost savings of manufacturing many goods in China will be only 10 to 15 percent annually when actual labor content is factored in."[55] Subtract from this margin the cost of shipping and financing a global supply chain. The bottom line whispers that jobs will wander off to cheaper locales: Vietnam today, Africa tomorrow. Seemingly boundless growth slows as other regions vie with China as "factories of the world." Or they will come home to America, nourishing the country's "reindustrialization." Its first shoots emerged at the beginning of the 2010s. Karl Marx highlighted the reasons ages ago: In a globalized economy, capital knows neither roots nor loyalty.

3. The Tocqueville Trap. China's third and most dangerous fault line is Tocqueville's "revolution of rising expectations." In the *Old Regime and the French Revolution*, Tocqueville famously theorizes that such eruptions are triggered by improving, rather than worsening, conditions.[56] Even as GDP rises, making everybody richer, a shrinking consumption share spells out, "Less for the people, and

more for the almighty state," the biggest investor of them all by orders of magnitude. As the gap widens, GNH, "gross national happiness," does not rise. Discontent flows from disparities in relative gain, that is, rising inequality. In the midnaughts, the Gini coefficient, a standard measure of inequality, soared to .44 in China. At the beginning of the 2010s, the Gini had risen to .5.[57] Meanwhile, the income gap between urban and rural has been widening dramatically. When Deng's reforms began, the two sections of the country were even. Some forty years later, the disposable income in the cities was three times higher than that in the country. Relative deprivation ("both of us are getting richer, but you keep getting more") is a revolutionary classic.

There are only two solutions: either repression or democratization, neither of which is good for the health of State Capitalism 2.0, which has bequeathed such fabulous riches to China. Repression, as Tiananmen showed, immediately translates into nosediving growth, and so did the Mao-to-the-max version known as the Cultural Revolution. Democratization implies the end of Chinese state capitalism. As in Taiwan and South Korea, the empowered masses will demand more for themselves and grant less to the state, the engine of furious growth since Deng's Four Modernizations. They will want more consumption and welfare. They will claim a larger voice in economic policy, insisting on environmental protection over ruthless land use—a trend familiar in the West, where rising wealth has been driving environmentalism. In short, democratic governance does not harmonize with frantic industrialization, as the careers of the little Dragons show. Look at the trend lines in figure 10 (chapter 4). The historical correlation is perfect. Growth favors democratization, and as democracy expands, growth shrinks.

Revolution will not soon break out in China. The Communist Party remains on top, and it does so, presumably, because China has seen too many revolts in the twentieth century. Traumatized by Tiananmen, the CCP has proven a lot more nimble than its East European sisters in containing dissent. Indeed, tolerance of small-scale dissent, as the lively letters-to-the-editor columns show, is the safety valve that keeps steam from building a mighty head. So are prosperity and co-optation by which the young, ambitious, and restless are brought into the fold of the Party.

Yet this is not democracy, quite the opposite. The benign historical experience of the West—from wealth to liberty, though with murderous totalitarian lapses—has jelled into a kind of economic determinism: with development comes democracy. Running for the presidency, George W. Bush orated with respect to China, "Economic freedom creates habits of liberty. And [those] create expectations of democracy."[58] President Obama put it just as firmly: "History shows that . . . democracy and economic growth go hand in hand. And prosperity without freedom is just another form of poverty" because it "ignores the will of the people."[59]

This deterministic blend of Karl Marx and John Locke does hold for the West, as well as for East Asia's first risers, where it happened much faster. Yet the CCP is hounded not only by Tiananmen and the Cultural Revolution but also by centuries of Chinese history. Replete with revolt and repression, these spell out a bloody lesson: "Maintain state supremacy, or else." The Party remembers the history of the West as well, where markets ultimately did push aside the *ancien régimes*. Cutting this link is precisely the purpose of the CCP. Reform must never unleash the Reformation.

History confronts State Capitalism 2.0 with a sublime dilemma: Both democracy and despotism are bad for the Chinese model, as this analysis has tried to show. Democracy will slow growth, and statism *à la chinoise*, no matter how nimble, will do so as well. Like the *ancien régime* in France, the system cannot help parceling out privilege and profit to rent-seeking elites in order to bind them to the state and so bind the economy itself. This may be good for the system, but it will not allow the economy to live up to its potential. To be so enabled, a mature economy requires a level playing field and the rule of law, yet a supreme state allows for neither.

The next step, historically, has been democracy, but participation and the diffusion of power, shifting resources from the state to society, do not coexist with double-digit growth, as East Asia and Western Europe show. It is a double bind, no matter which way the Party turns. A slowdown lurks on either side. So good-bye to spectacular growth, whether it is revolt and repression or the vindication of the Liberal faith in a nation that has known only emperors and oligarchies, be they by divine, dynastic, or revolutionary right.

  4. Demography as Destiny. Predicting the fate of nations is as reliable a business as foretelling earthquakes and tsunamis. But there is a fourth fault line that is widening no matter how the economy fares or the Party maneuvers. Its name is "demography." Demography is about long-term forces unfolding over decades, not about blips or cycles. These forces are largely autonomous, hence removed from the grasp of the state. The Chinese regime might well decide to drop the one-child policy, but liberalization will take generations to bear fruit, so to speak. Cultural change is even harder to reverse, as Europe's desperate attempts to raise fertility rates suggest. Once women are educated and working, procreation is trumped by prosperity, independence, and career. Lavish family allowances and day care boost fertility only at the margin, if at all.

Dropping birthrates are the price of modernization; that is the gist of a very long story. The West has been paying it since the dawn of the twentieth century; it has risen steeply since World War II. Today, only the United States and Iceland come close to the steady-state rate of 2.1 children per woman of childbearing age. Even an authoritarian regime like China's will not be able to lift the curse of modernity. So demography is destiny. China's population dynamics, as the next chapter tries to show, will flummox the prophets who foresee the unstoppable rise of the Chinese behemoth.

CHAPTER SIX

Challengers and Champions: Why America's Edge Will Endure

DEMOGRAPHY AND DESTINY

Let us recall the small print in the Goldman Sachs 2050 scenario: The "demographic assumptions may turn out to be incorrect"; aging might take its toll on China's spectacular economic performance. First, to the upside, which reflects the single-most important difference between the new Dragon and the old ones. China has the largest population on earth, half of which is still living in the countryside—a vast "industrial reserve army" waiting to move. Growth theory has always revolved around plentiful labor, and so the West German economic miracle might have been a tepid tale had it not been for 6.5 million refugees from the amputated territories in Eastern Europe who ended up in the Federal Republic, plus another three million who fled the East German "Workers and Peasants State" before the Berlin Wall went up in 1961. Add to this migration millions of *Gastarbeiter* ("guest workers") who kept the West German machinery humming in the 1960s and 1970s.

Tiny by Chinese standards, Taiwan and South Korea soon used

up their reserves, and so did Japan. China still has a long way to go. Half the population remains poised to go urban and sell its labor at low wages; this is where the analogies between China and East Asia's first risers end. Time—more precisely, personal income—is also on China's side. Recall that the Taiwanese tipping point, after which growth began to flatten, was $6,000, and South Korea's $12,000. So China (2011) is still far behind at $3,200 (all figures in 2005 dollars). That said, there is a nasty problem that will skew the race to the top against the United States. China is getting older and America younger. India will be the youngest of the three a couple of decades from now.

Aging is not good for growth, and so China will inevitably slow down, with rapid aging adding pressure to all the other growth brakes embedded in an economy that remains resolutely statist. One cause of aging is the steady gain in life expectancy—from forty years to seventy in half a century—that comes with medical progress and rising prosperity. The other is a fertility rate that has dropped in many places since World War II, but nowhere more brutally than in China, where the rate now stands at 1.5, or even 1.3 as the most dismal estimate has it—down from almost 6 in 1950. At the 1.3 estimate, China lags way behind in the fertility race, limping along in the company of Russia, Eastern Europe, and East Asia (Western Europe isn't doing much better). The economic consequences are bound to be enormous. Figures 14 and 15 tell the gist of the story.

While China ages, the United States is getting younger, thanks to high fertility and immigration, which has always brought the youngish to America's shores.[1] What follows? Basically, an aging population will yield fewer workers who add to the gross national product. This is the "Japan syndrome," the enduring part of the country's stagnation. With its untapped rural masses, China, of course, still has a way to go on the road to industrialization. But it cannot evade the "curse of 2020," as limned by the two curves labeled "China Workers" and "China Dependents" in figure 15. The curse—a shrinking workforce—poses a stark choice between yesterday's boundless growth and tomorrow's rising welfare burden. Second, it presages cultural change that does not bode well for the Declinist assumption that China's growth is eternal.

14.   Graying China, Youthful America, Young India

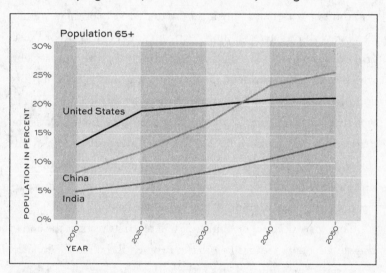

SOURCE: United Nations Department of Economic and Social Affairs, Population Division, *World Population Prospects: The 2010 Revision*, vol. 1, *Comprehensive Tables*. Post-2010 data are projections.

An aging society without immigration not only implies a smaller workforce. It also foreshadows a changing cultural balance between those who seek safety and stability and those who want to risk and acquire—personal traits that are the invisibles of economic growth. If China grows old before it gets rich, it will resemble Western Europe more than the United States, but without the EU's per-person income that now dwarfs China's by a factor of ten. Yet prosperity and social safety have a price. Europe has stopped conquering, having opted for social protection and egalitarianism over "Enrich yourselves!" This unwritten social contract is one reason for the EU's declining performance since the 1970s, when the average growth rate started to decline from more than 3 percent by about half a percentage point decade on decade.

Another reason for slowing growth is the enormous welfare burden, with transfer spending eating up about one-third of Western Europe's GDP, leaving correspondingly less for investment, which is a down payment on tomorrow's growth. Low fertility and high aging rates will increase the welfare burden, in China as well as Europe. Figure 15 shows what the future holds. Or as the demographer Nicholas Eberstadt puts it, "The specter of a swelling population of elderly pensioners dependent for support on a . . . diminishing population of low-income workers suggests some particularly unattractive trade-offs between welfare and growth."[2]

China's working-age population will reach its peak at the end of this decade, and decades before the People's Republic is supposed to overtake the United States.[3] Thereafter, the number of China's toiling masses will continue to decline, all the way to the magic date of 2050, when China, according to *Dreaming with BRICs*, will be $9 trillion ahead of the United States. This is indeed "dreaming with China." By the mid-2010s, the dream will begin to yield to tossing and turning, and China will have lost up to one-third of its working age population by 2050. But trouble looms even sooner for the largest population the world has ever seen.

15. Workers vs. Welfare in China and in
the United States

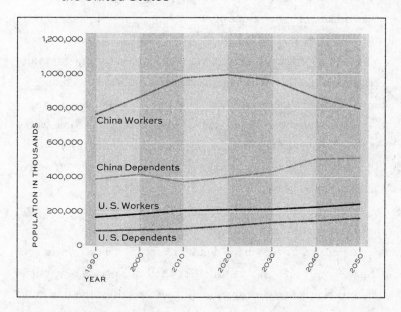

SOURCE: United Nations Department of Economic and Social Affairs, Population Division, *World Population Prospects: The 2010 Revision*, vol. 1, *Comprehensive Tables*. Post-2010 data are projections.

"By 2025, under current UN and Census Bureau projections," writes Eberstadt, "China would account for less than a fifth of the world's population but *almost a fourth of the world's senior citizens*."[4] This glimpse of the near future puts into proper perspective the mesmerizing number of 1.3 billion that is said to provide China's global factory with a bottomless reservoir of able-bodied workers.

By themselves, such numbers do not add up to a nightmare, especially if China compensates for aging by pushing up the labor-participation rate and by investing in education, thus in human capital that makes a country more productive. The torment begins when we tally up the cost of social support for the aged.

A decade ago, three out of four Chinese workers had no pension (and nine out of ten in the countryside).[5] Aware of steady aging, the government recently brought forward its target for universal social security coverage from 2020 to 2013.[6] According to the Chinese Academy of Social Sciences, this is easier promised than done. The report noted that China currently has three workers for every pensioner, but that figure will fall to two for one by 2015 and one for two in thirty years.[7] These ratios are far worse than any in the West.

The nightmare reaches out from the past, when social security was virtually absent, but when large families provided "private" social security, as they have done for centuries. Forty years ago, China's family size was a shade less than five persons; now it is down to bit more than three, mainly as a result of the one-child policy. The consequences are momentous. "Parents of first generation one-only children are in their later years now. One couple caring for four elders and one child is becoming common, meaning the family burden has become very heavy for each young person."[8] Demographers call this the "4-2-1" problem, where one child has to take care of two parents and four grandparents.

The upshot is that the state must step in, now and for the next several decades. Does it really have to? After all, China's savings rate is among the very highest in the world, creating a gigantic nest egg from which the elderly could draw. In theory, yes. The nation's savings have been climbing, topping one-half of GDP, which is the counterpart of the gargantuan investment rate. But now look again: Who is saving, the people or the Party? The government is good for one-tenth of GDP, enterprises (mainly the state, again) are good for another two-tenths. So the state has the lion's share of the stash of cash. Households are left with the cub's share, their savings amounting to a bit more than 20 percent of GDP.[9] So the state will have to deliver. In the process, it will encounter a double whammy.

The first part bids the country to shift resources from investment to medical care and social benefits, something very rich economies like Western Europe's can still handle, if also at the price of shrinking growth rates. But in a developing economy like China's, tilting from overinvestment and underconsumption to social protection will invariably cut into the kind of growth that stands at the center of all "China as No. 1" projections. Older populations don't save, they dis-save to make up for their loss of disposable income after pensions replace wages and salaries. Consequently, less will be left over for investment. This shift is a matter not of choice but of arithmetic, as Japan and Western Europe already show. A burgeoning army of pensioners and infirm will eat up investment funds as a fire will consume oxygen. True, overinvestment, as the chapter about the little Dragons showed, invariably runs into diminishing returns, but underinvestment is no cure when it comes to sustaining an ever-increasing army of nonworkers.

The second part of the double whammy spells strategic trouble. As we saw in chapter 3, China has to scramble mightily to get anywhere near America's sophisticated fighting and projection forces. As it seeks to catch up, China will encounter the crowding-out effect that aging entails. On the one hand, the People's Liberation Army will have to compete ever more strenuously with the civilian sector for highly qualified personnel, hence pay more than for lowly infantry men equipped with rifles and helmets. On the other, as the costs of military personnel and civilian pensions rise, less will be left over for advanced weaponry.

Even after military outlays stopped growing in 2012—after the drawdown in Iraq and Afghanistan—the United States spent $900 billion in fiscal year 2013, including $200 billion for veterans benefits and foreign military aid.[10] The official number for China is $100 billion, also including veterans benefits. So for realism's sake, let's double it to $200 billion. To close the gap, China will have to disburse ever more year after year—and this under the darkening cloud of a demography that will make the aged clamor for an ever-increasing slice of the economic pie. This double squeeze will not soon enable the Middle Kingdom to unseat the greatest military power the world has ever seen.[11]

POWER TODAY AND TOMORROW: EDUCATION

All "Who shall inherit the world?" sweepstakes revolve around power: Who has it, and how much? Chapter 3 shows an unrivaled United States by both present and past standards. This chapter looks at trends that transcend the simple linearity of those splendiferous projections of recent Chinese growth rates so beloved by Declinists. Demographics are also linear, but of a different order. Birthrates might conceivably go up tomorrow, and aging rates would slow down as a result. But such changes take generations to work themselves out. They defy instant meddling by governments and markets.

Economic growth could soar or falter tomorrow, but populations change slowly, because they are rooted in long-term trends and culture. The steady decline of fertility in Western Europe since World War II, now seventy years in the making, is due to a host of irreversible factors, especially expanding female education and labor force participation, plus delayed marriage and faster divorce. In very simple terms, a girl not born today will not reproduce twenty-five years hence. And unless they are already in their dotage, those who are alive today will be so up to ninety years from now.

So let us look at sources of *future* power and performance above and beyond spectacular growth rates that, as the previous risers have shown, do not endure. An obvious candidate in a knowledge economy is education or human capital. Ever since the "Johnny can't read" campaign arose in the 1950s, sounding the death knell for the country's education system has been as American as apple pie—left, right, and center.[12] It is an age-old American obsession, and no wonder in a society that assigns status not to high birth or landed property but to self-betterment and "making it." "Education" and "crisis" are Siamese twins in the American conversation. Entering "American crisis of education" in Google yields more than 400 million entries. Yet it was the United States that invented the world's first system of universal public education from kindergarten to high school. Higher education for the masses is "one of the great achievements of American democracy," notes Columbia University's Nicholas Lemann, adding, "For a system that . . . is deeply in crisis, American higher education is not doing badly."[13]

The Tale of the 600,000 Chinese Engineers. Crisis is an eternal byword of American education. A recent classic reads, "Last year, more than 600,000 engineers graduated from institutions of higher education in China. In India, the figure was 350,000. In America, it was about 70,000."[14] Thus warned the National Academies, which bills itself as "Advisers to the Nation on Science, Engineering, and Medicine." The United States was losing its technological edge once more. Unsurprisingly, the alarm went hand in glove with a call for a lot more federal aid to engineering education. Such statistics always come with a purpose: "dialing for dollars," as a popular U.S. television show had it. Yet *Fortune* magazine swallowed the story in toto, splashing across its cover a brawny Chinese bullying a scrawny Uncle Sam on the beach.[15] The tale of the 600,000 Chinese engineers soon spread unexamined through the media, until it ran into serious fact checking.

For starters, the National Science Foundation, which tracks degree granting in the United States and abroad, cut the 600,000 to one-third as many. India had last given numbers to the NSF fifteen years earlier. Making an educated guess, U.S. academic experts on India cut the 350,000 figure zooming around the United States in half. Why such brutal chops? The hype had ignored the "truth in packaging" principle. About half of China's engineers would be called "technicians" in the United States.

Then a Duke University study made a simple point: Don't look at absolute numbers when measuring the quality of education in countries of vastly disparate population sizes. So per million citizens, the United States was then "producing roughly 470 technology specialists, compared with 340 in China and 130 in India." To boot, official Chinese data tend to "be artificially inflated." Finally, the McKinsey Global Institute waded in by plumbing the employability of Chinese/Indian engineers, that is, their international competitiveness. The upshot: Only one-quarter of the Indians and one-tenth of the Chinese make the cut. By that measure, their American colleagues beat them by multiples, with three Americans for each Chinese and Indian.[16]

So much for the anecdotes and how they stack up against analysis. The general question is this: How do we gauge the accumulation of human capital? One quick, but effective, way is to look at education expenditures as a share of GDP, where the United

States beats China and India hands down. These two BRICs spend around 3.5 percent; the United States spends 7 percent. And this on a population one-quarter the size of China's and one-third the size of India's, and with a GDP that dwarfs the economies of China and India by factors of 2.5 and 10, respectively.

16.   Investing in Human Capital:
      How the United States Outspends the Rest

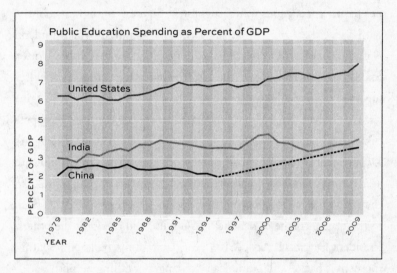

China 1996–2007 estimated. Sources: See explanatory note.[17]

The Leaning Tower of PISA. In the OECD, the United States is at the top in per-student spending on K–12, behind Luxembourg, Switzerland, and Norway. How much output for the input? Since 2000, the OECD has been measuring the scholastic performance of fifteen-year-olds in its PISA rankings.[18] In the most recent one, the United States comes out at the top of midfield in reading and science skills, ahead of their contemporaries in the major West

European countries. This is a lot better than "Johnny can't read" of Sputnik ill fame, but not breathtaking when compared with such highfliers as Finland. On the other hand, in an international test of reading skills of fourth-graders in forty-five countries, the United States comes out in sixth place, behind such usual suspects as Hong Kong and Finland, but ahead of all other Western participants, except Northern Ireland. China as such chose not to be tested.[19]

The United States is doing fine, though not as well as its lavish per-pupil expenditures would suggest. Yet it is an immigrant country, with a vast share of non-native parents and children (which Finland is not). If one corrects for these demographics not just in the United States but also in Europe, the United States rises from midfield to top-field, as one analysis has it—to the No. 7 spot.[20] Still, the winner is . . . Shanghai. "Wow, I'm kind of stunned, I'm thinking Sputnik," exclaimed Chester E. Finn Jr., who served in Ronald Reagan's Department of Education. "I've seen how relentless the Chinese are at accomplishing goals, and if they can do this in Shanghai in 2009, they can do it in 10 cities in 2019, and in 50 cities by 2029." [21] Back to the classic theme of decline; it is up, up, and away for the others. President Obama agreed, "Fifty years later, our generation's Sputnik moment is back," and "America is in danger of falling behind."[22]

That was a good call to arms, but not necessarily good statistics. To begin, PISA's highest honors went to Shanghai—not to China as a whole, which chose to abstain, and for good reasons. Shanghai is a migration hub for the most ambitious and brightest, entry being parceled out by governmental permission. Comparing the richest, best-educated, and privileged city of China with a broad sample of U.S. and European schools is like matching a choice apple against the entire harvest. Pitting Shanghai against Cambridge, Palo Alto, and Bethesda with their "tiger mothers" and "Volvo dads" would have yielded a different tally.

From PISA to Palo Alto. High schoolers, especially in a country with so many first- and second-generation born, are a very diverse bunch of apples. So let's move up on the age scale. A more telling glimpse into a nation's future than the scores of fifteen-year-olds is university performance. The most-often cited ranking comes out of Shanghai's Jiao Tong University, a tally that is skewed toward countables like academic citations and prestigious awards in the natural sciences, hence reasonably objective. Table X of the world's top twenty lists seventeen American universities, which suggests an astounding lead in the race of nations not just today but a generation down the line. Two are British (Cambridge and Oxford), one is Japanese (Tokyo).

Lengthening the list to the top 50 yields 34 American universities. Not a single Chinese university makes this cut. The net has to be cast very wide, to the top 500, to bring in the first Chinese institution. This is Peking University, lodged in the 151–200 bracket. India does not score at all among the world's 500 best. To find an Indian school, we have to leave the overall ranking and scour the subcategory "Engineering/Technology and Computer Sciences." Among the 100 listed there, the Indian Institute of Science makes it into the 76–100 bracket. Yet in this specialized tally, the United States dominates as well, occupying the 15 top slots. Not a single Chinese or Indian school is found in the next subset, the 100 best "Natural Sciences and Mathematics" schools. Here, too, the highest honors go to American schools, with 7 of the 10 best.

Minds and Money. If this lopsided distribution is the future, it belongs to America and a slew of universities in the UK and the rest of the Anglo world. Spectacular economic growth may falter tomorrow. But these institutions groom the cadres of the "commanding heights" in the knowledge economy and produce the research that determines future performance. Now, as in so many realms, China has pledged to climb Mount Olympus in short order. On the way, it will encounter a vexing paradox. On the one hand, knowledge no longer travels the world by horse and slow boat. Today, science and innovation take the digital road, almost at

X. World's Top Twenty Universities

1.	Harvard University
2.	University of California, Berkeley
3.	Stanford University
4.	Massachusetts Institute of Technology
5.	Cambridge University
6.	California Institute of Technology
7.	Princeton University
8.	Columbia University
9.	University of Chicago
10.	Oxford University
11.	Yale University
12.	Cornell University
13.	University of California, Los Angeles
14.	University of California, San Diego
15.	University of Pennsylvania
16.	University of Washington
17.	University of Wisconsin, Madison
18.	Johns Hopkins University
19.	University of California, San Francisco
20.	University of Tokyo

SOURCE: Institute of Higher Education, Shanghai Jiao Tong University, *Academic Ranking of World Universities 2012*, http://www.arwu.org/ARWU2010.jsp.

the speed of light. On the other hand, one critical item has hardly changed in this new cyber world: universities rise slowly. And one Tokyo—the only non-Anglo university among the top twenty— indicates little about the rest of Japan's higher education system.

It took Harvard more than three hundred years to scale the global summit. Life has speeded up since 1636, so one of the recent newcomers, Stanford, got there a bit faster after starting out in 1891. But it took "The Farm," as it is dubbed because of its birth in a vast fruit orchard, half a century before this once regional school reached the mountain top, and then under conditions not easily replicated elsewhere. Stanford has churned out more than fifty Nobel laureates and more Turing Awards than any other university. Did money buy so much recognition? China will undoubtedly throw a mass of cash into the race, just as it has lavished riches on its industrial "national champions" and its Olympic teams. Alas, the career of America's best shows that "money isn't everything," as the old saw goes.

Take the University of Texas at Austin. Some thirty years ago, it set its sight on becoming one of the nation's premier research universities. Money was no object, its home state and its alumni being flush with oil riches thanks to a twelvefold jump in the price of "black gold" in the 1970s. Texas became a magnet for ambition and talent. The university lured away renowned scholars from everywhere. On top of its lavish endowment of $7 billion—the largest of any public university—it is second in federal research grants (after MIT) for universities without a medical school.

And yet. In the 2012 Shanghai ranking, it came in as 38th, a slight decline from seven years earlier.[23] The top floors are still held by the usual suspects. So it takes a while. In the 2011 *U.S. News* listing of the world's 400 best, Austin falls to 76th place.[24] So money, indeed, isn't everything. The causal relationship between riches and renown is a tricky one. Is it wealth that feeds worth, or class that reaps cash? Are Harvard and Stanford, with their huge endowments of $31 billion and $17 billion, great because they are so well-off? The millions may just as well flood into these schools *because* they are at the top of anybody's list. The rich like to give to those who are already outstanding, fame being an irresistible magnet of munificence. A name on the door at Harvard shines more brightly than at a less august place. The relationship between gold and glory remains fuzzy. Columbia has only an $8 billion endowment, and yet it ranks among the top 10. On the other hand, it has been working at it since 1754.

Riches are nice, but not sufficient. The money China wants to plow into its state universities is no guarantee of grandeur, because modernitarianism cannot deliver the right setting—a mix of culture and politics. In the long slog to excellence, "state" and "university" do not a perfect couple make. True, America boasts world-famous public universities such as Berkeley and Michigan. Nonetheless, the top of the crop is private. Some reasons are quite clear. For one, Harvard, Stanford, et al. are not in the business of mass education, whose mission it is to serve the many, hence to broaden access and teach advanced vocational skills like nursing and accounting. Second, these schools are unashamedly elitist in the sense that they select the most gifted (not the richest or best connected) from a limitless pool of applicants. It is *extra vergine*, oil from the first pressing, so to speak. Third, private institutions are not in thrall to fickle legislatures or stifling state bureaucracies. They are free to compete for the best, as well as to experiment and learn from failure.

Such freedom surely explains why America's leading private

universities keep besting Continental Europe's state universities, though some of these go back a thousand years. America's highest-ranked public universities like Berkeley, UCLA, Michigan, and Illinois do better, too, because they are a different breed from their European sisters. America's public universities are practically private by European and certainly by Chinese standards. They depend on their states' taxpayers for a dwindling share of operating expenditure.[25] The rest comes from a hodgepodge of tuition, federal grants, endowments, alumni giving, and business-funded research. Such financial promiscuity has virtuous consequences: the more numerous the sources, the longer the reins of government. Continental Europe's public-funded universities run on a very short leash, and their paymasters—governments—have more fish to fry than only competition and excellence.

Catering to a minuscule, class-based fraction of the age cohort until the 1960s, Europe's public universities now focus on mass education in the name of access and equality. But they do so without the boundless differentiation of the U.S. system with its 4,500 institutions, ranging from the lowly two-year community college to the most selective research university. Even on the public level, American higher education distinguishes between the best and the rest by sorting them in more or less competitive parts of a state's university system. The problem of Europe's universities, notes the former Stanford president Gerhard Casper, is that they "don't want to differentiate too much between the very gifted students and the others."[26]

Given their mission, the one-size-fits-all institutions of Europe and much of the world cannot help stressing equality over excellence, and uniformity over differentiation by task and talent. Tuition is free or symbolic, selectivity spotty. Faculty salaries are mandated nationwide; hence generous financial incentives cannot separate the cream from the crop. Theoretically, these institutions are autonomous; in truth, the education minister has the last word. And those who pay the piper, as they say, call the tune. Governments would rather mediate between vested interests, and thus manage the status quo, than encourage the inequality that is the Siamese twin of academic excellence.

Such features do not breed competition, except for public funds. One size fits all is the opposite of diversity by design, the lively rivalry that typifies American higher education. So it is no accident that in the Shanghai ranking, the best full-fledged European universities (as distinct from narrower technology or medical schools) come in far behind the top U.S. and UK schools. Copenhagen, the highest-ranked, occupies slot forty on the list. German universities, once the world's best when peopled by perhaps 1 percent of the age cohort, start showing up past the fifty mark.

Why are British schools like Oxbridge in the world's top twenty? Because Britain's best are only partially state-funded and thus far more autonomous. Unlike their Continental relatives, they compete across the board. They charge tuition and build endowments. The more they shine, the more they charge—up to £9,000 per student as of 2012 ($14,000), a sum seen as obscenely inequitable in Berlin, Paris, or Rome. Nor would the Continentals ever countenance the harsh selection procedures of the UK's top twenty, known as the Russell Group. By a rough estimate, they accept one out of eight applicants. Across the Channel, such rigor would be "cherry-picking," a blow to equality.

The Clout of Culture. Money can be counted; administrative structures are open to objective analysis. Also, no matter how egalitarian their ideology, governments do impose rigorous selection, as they did in the Soviet bloc and do in China. But then there is the mighty, though unquantifiable, factor of "culture," where the U.S. and the Anglo universities are a world apart from China's as well as Asia's from Ankara to Vladivostok.

Western political culture puts freedom of debate, information, and inquiry at the center of its constitutional order. China is not exactly at the forefront of such liberties. In fact, throughout much of the non-Western world, students still are not taught to ask, "How do you know, professor?" Or to argue among themselves. Or to score by questioning authority rather than by reproducing received wisdom. The more centralized the political system, the less diverse the realm of ideas; this is also the difference between ENA[27] and All Souls.

This author, who entered a highly selective American liberal arts college, Swarthmore, as an eighteen-year-old, would not expect the following dialogue to unfold between a Chinese (or Asian or even European) student and his teacher in an introductory philosophy course. "Could you please suggest some authoritative literature on Descartes?" this acolyte asked.—"What for?"—"For my paper. I need to know what the sages before me have written about the mind-body problem."—"No, you don't. Read the original. You are just as good as they are." This freshman wasn't—and earned a C–. Despite the depressing grade, the point about independent thinking, no matter how untutored, sank in, just like this classic seminar question: "Is A the most interesting thing we can say about this issue X?"

Mark Kitto, who spent sixteen years in China, explains why he was finally leaving: "I want to give my children a decent education." The system, he reports, "does not educate. It is a test centre.

The curriculum is designed to teach children how to pass them. . . . Schools do not produce well-rounded, sociable, self-reliant young people with inquiring minds. They produce winners and losers. Winners go on to college or university to take 'business studies.' Losers go back to the farm or the local factory their parents were hoping they could escape."[28]

In the one-party state that is China, the government is the ultimate guardian over what students and scholars may read, say, and write, even in schools for the elite. The state holds the power of the purse. It makes the senior appointments. It controls the Internet, routinely blocking troublesome sites. The state selects those who depend on public funds for study abroad, but ideological fealties and fertile minds are not necessarily twinned. The Communist Party, though it has loosened its grip over society, remains in control of teaching and research. Such a regime, no matter how eager to catapult its universities into the international Hall of Fame, rules from the top down, and in the crunch, it will subordinate free inquiry to state interest. Unconventional ideas and intellectual risk taking grow not out of the Politburo but from below. The government can shower money on the chosen, funding particle accelerators and space exploration. Yet the hardware will grind and grate without the right "software," call it "culture of freedom" or "intellectual anarchy."

Top-down, modernitarian states are not good at fabricating the intellectual explosives that crack old molds and break new paths. How is America's liberal democracy different? At first glance, not that much. The federal government was hardly a waif when it came to bankrolling education in the twentieth century. Driven by World War II and the Cold War, Washington poured hundreds of billions into America's universities and labs, into basic and applied research. And it continues to do so, disbursing $36 billion annually to universities just for science and engineering R&D.[29] The input may be similar, but the output is not.

The Story of Stanford. Take Stanford again, a middling regional university into the 1940s. Given its rapid rise to global eminence, it looks like a fitting model for the academic shooting stars China intends to launch. Could Beijing, the state's cornucopia at the ready, replicate the trick today—from "Farm" to fame? The answer: An illiberal state like China could not re-create those "only in America" conditions that fueled Stanford's meteoric rise in the space of just two generations.

The ingredients—who, how?—are not easily separated decades later. But one figure, unimaginable in Chinese academia, stands out in every account. Present at the creation was an academic entrepreneur—nay, a buccaneer—by the name of Frederick Terman. The engineering professor, who would later become provost, was obsessed with building "steeples of excellence" at The Farm. As a by-product, he launched Silicon Valley, which would grow in symbiosis with Stanford, each nourishing the other. The unwitting founding act occurred in 1939 when Terman prodded two of his students, David Packard and William Hewlett, to start a little electronics company, now a very big one, in a Palo Alto garage. Fittingly, the garage is a museum today, commemorating the birth of Hewlett-Packard and Silicon Valley. In 2001, the Hewlett Foundation returned the 1939 favor with interest, a gift of $400 million for the humanities and sciences.

Terman also had a hand in Varian Associates, which began with $22,000 and a few Stanford affiliates and went on to build the Stanford Industrial Park (renamed Stanford Research Park) on the edge of the campus. Touted as "spawning ground of Silicon Valley," the park would grow into the world's premier research outfit, with Stanfordians migrating back and forth. The empire builder Terman then lured back William Shockley.[30] The inventor of the transistor set up Shockley Semiconductors, a prototypical start-up. The plot thickened a few years later when the Nobel laureate got into a fight with his minions. As disgruntled Harvard clergymen emigrated to establish Yale College, so the Shockley renegades went off to found Fairchild Semiconductors with a $1.5 million investment from New York's Fairchild Camera, the first of the venture capitalists or "angels" who populate Sandhill Road on Stanford's northern border today. How could a state-controlled economy duplicate the diversity and depth of the American capital market?

The revolt triggered the chain reaction that made Silicon Valley what it is today. The nuclei kept fissioning. Gordon Moore and Robert Noyce, two of Shockley's "Traitorous Eight," absconded once more, leaving Fairchild to form a start-up by the name of Intel. The rest is history. Within twenty years, those eight Shockley defectors "gave forth 65 new enterprises, which then went on to do the same."[31] Among the most famous progeny of Stanford are two students by the name of Sergey Brin (an immigrants' son) and Larry Page, the founders of Google. Google licenses its Internet search technology from Stanford, where the "father of the Internet," Vinton Cerf, had developed the TCP/IP protocol, the standard language between computers.

As payment for the license, Stanford received initial Google shares it has since sold for $336 million.[32] The former Stanford student and Yahoo cofounder Jerry Yang led a successful $1 billion fund-raising drive and gave $75 million of his own hoard. As early as 1999, the Netscape founder Jim Clark, a former engineering professor, contributed $90 million to Stanford's coffers. Jawed

Karim, a Bengali born in East Germany and cofounder of You-Tube, cashed out when Google bought the company for $1.65 billion, retiring to Stanford at the age of twenty-seven to earn an advanced degree in computer science. So Stanford is Silicon Valley, and Silicon Valley is Stanford—a serendipitous, but very American, synergism a state-run economy cannot engineer. Nor can these fabulously rich patrons tell Stanford what to do and whom to hire with the money—another critical difference between the Chinese state and America's private benefactors.

There is, of course, plenty of federal money in this tale of "The University and the Valley," from the U.S. Atomic Energy Commission to the Defense Advanced Research Projects Agency (DARPA), which funded an early version of the Internet developed at Stanford. Munificence is easy to replicate for a government hankering for first-class universities. It is also easy to build prestige projects like the Shanghai maglev train or the Three Gorges monster dams, which displaced 1.3 million people and would not pass muster in the democratic and environmentally correct West. The moral of the Stanford tale transcends federal largesse. It is also about private capital, which is a bit harder to raise in China. Even harder to imagine are academic conquistadores like Terman and ambitious, footloose youngsters who would trade the safety of a state university for the exhilarating unknown, including abject failure. Finally, the most critical difference of them all: a surfeit of freedom, clad in law.

Recall the "Traitorous Eight" who defected to form competing companies, taking their skills and experience with them. It is hard to imagine Chinese engineers running from the state and living more happily ever after in their own country. In California they could. Here is why. "It was in California . . . that a particular law emerged in 1872 [which] defended the employee's freedom of movement, the right to leave his or her employer at any moment, even to immediately go to work in direct competition with their former employer. . . ."[33]

QED. It is freedom, mobility, and "entrepreneurial anarchy" that makes the most decisive difference. It is the freedom to listen to inspiration, follow ambition, and transform dreams into companies like Intel. The one-party state, which insists on occupying the "commanding heights," can deliver such freedom only at the price of its self-demotion. A Bengali born in East Germany could not scale these heights in China, not in a country whose ancient culture ties citizenship so tightly to ethnicity. Nor would a Chinese elite university, coddled as it may be, give such a wide berth to academic freebooters like Frederick Terman.

THE POWER OF INVENTION

China et al. grow faster, hence they will outstrip the United States—that is Declinism's central article of faith. Naturally, the same kind of alarm has always been sounded in the intellectual engine room of the U.S. economy, in STEM (science, technology, engineering, and mathematics). As we noted in chapter 2 on "The Uses of Declinism," doom is closely tied to dollars. Piles of public monies must be thrown into the race against those nimble, harderworking foreigners who are about to leave the United States in the dust. A generation ago, *A Nation at Risk*, a much ballyhooed "Report to the Nation," warned the federal government, "Our once unchallenged preeminence in commerce, industry, science, and technological innovation is being overtaken by competitors throughout the world." To stem the tide, the federal government had to take "primary responsibility" and "fund" what the "national interest" demanded.[34] Doom determines the national interest and then opens the national purse.

Growth, as the career of the East Asians shows, can crest tomorrow. By contrast, funds are the future—the seed that produces the harvest. What a nation puts into research and development (R&D) is a driver of future performance. What is the future in the twenty-first century? Standardized mass production, built on high fixed investment and plentiful labor drawn from the countryside, was the engine of the two preceding centuries. Tomorrow, it will be basic research, computing power, software design, artificial intelligence and robotics, nano- and biotechnology, imaging and recognition, consumer conveniences like e-commerce, Apple's Siri, and a million apps. In addition, such American traits as restlessness, inventiveness, and hustling. Plus deep and diverse capital markets. And a culture like Silicon Valley's that helps to transform dreams into "stuff," digital or real.

In the old world, China's bottomless labor pool and low wages made it a global factory, as Britain had been in the nineteenth century. These advantages are bound to dwindle. Industrial labor was the queen of the nineteenth and twentieth centuries. But in the twenty-first, notes Tyler Cowen of George Mason University, "the factory has been reinvented as a quiet place."[35] A joke sharpens the point: "A modern textile mill employs only a man and a dog—the man to feed the dog, and the dog to keep the man away from the machines."[36] This is the next industrial revolution, and the future is now. It does not depend on cheap labor.

Is America's future running out of money, as Declinism has had it since "Johnny can't read"?

A good glimpse of tomorrow is investment in R&D. Figure 17 shows that no other nation spends more on R&D than the

United States. It lays out three times more than China, even in PPP dollars, which give China a hefty extra boost. Nor is U.S. spending slowing, as the straight-up trend line in figure 18 shows. That growth rate, about 5 percent annually in real terms, has been in place for sixty years, silencing the alarm rung by each new generation of Cassandras.

17.   Spending on R&D: The United States vs. Others

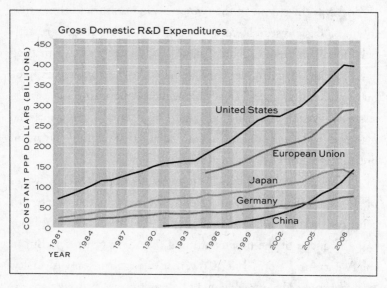

SOURCE: National Science Foundation, *Science and Engineering Indicators 2012*.

Such are the basic numbers, with R&D outlays as a rough-and-ready measure of America's investment in the future. They bespeak neither flagging effort nor backsliding in the race against rivals, as the Cassandras have been warning decade after decade. Only the EU is a worthy competitor, but the gap between those 500 million Europeans and the 300 million Americans has been wid-

18.   U.S. R&D Outlays: Sixty Years of Expansion

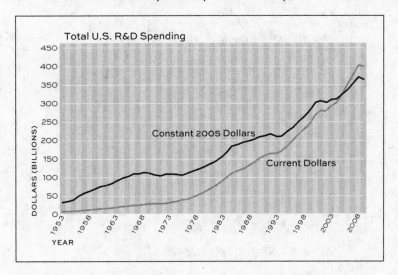

SOURCE: National Science Foundation, *Science and Engineering Indicators 2012.*

ening. China has been speeding up, but the United States holds a comfortable spending advantage of three to one.

Generating Intellectual Capital. Money, the input, isn't everything, as we observed in the university race; output matters. So what does the money buy? The United States produces more science and engineering journal articles than Asia's top ten together, and three times more than China.[37] "World citations to U.S. research articles," reports the National Science Foundation, "show that [these] continue to have the highest citation rates across all broad fields of S&E."[38] China has been coming up, but so has the sum total of the world's academic output since the mid-1990s. Let's therefore look not at mass but at impact. In the world's top 1 percent bracket of most-cited articles, the United States bests China

19.   Shares of Global Scientific Output

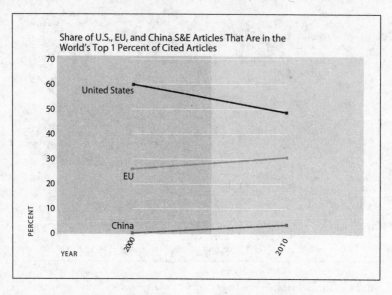

Share of U.S., EU, and China S&E Articles That Are in the World's Top 1 Percent of Cited Articles

SOURCE: National Science Foundation, *Science and Engineering Indicators 2012*, Table 5-24.

49 percent to 4 percent in all fields. It is dramatically more lopsided in subfields like astronomy and biology.[39]

Patents and Performance. Universities, where the United States rules the global roost, are the "production lines" of human capital. Citations reflect the early returns, measuring the quantity and quality of intellectual output. Patents are the next stage. They "are one of the most commonly used indicators [of] innovative activity," notes the RAND Corporation in an exhaustive study of U.S. competiveness in science and technology.[40]

In the most recent OECD ranking of global performance, the United States leads the pack on "triadic patents," those registered in the United States, the EU, and Japan. The West beats the rest by

85 percent to 15 percent. The BRICs come in at 2 percent. China is listed at the bottom with 1 percent, between Belgium and Austria with their minuscule populations of 11 million and 8 million.[41] (Triadic patents, awarded in the United States, EU, and Japan, are the most significant measure because they are validated in the world's hubs of invention.)

In the triadic patents arena, China vs. the United States isn't even a race, as figure 20 shows. If the future is ICT and Biotech, then America's, though less shiny than at the height of the dot-com bubble, is bright. It filed thirteen times more biotech patents than China (figure 21). In ICT, China has been doing better, but the United States still holds a three-to-one edge. Here as elsewhere on the scale of national strength, the United States remains comfortably ensconced on the top floor, and China will have to scramble mightily to dislodge No. 1.

20.   United States vs. China: Number of Triadic Patents

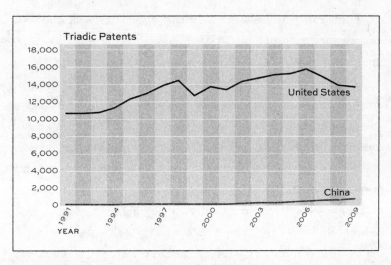

SOURCE: OECD, Main Science and Technology Indicators database, January 2012.

21.   United States vs. China: Biotech Patents

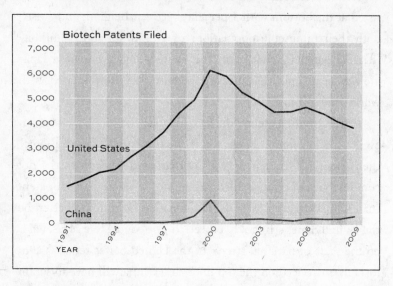

SOURCE: OECD, Main Science and Technology Indicators database, January 2012.

From Paper to Production. Patents reflect scientific prowess, but technological progress is another story. The world has been mesmerized by China's export steamroller, though that behemoth has been moving more slowly since the Crash of 2008, its fabulous GDP growth dropping below double-digit. So let us take a closer look at exports, especially at its sources. In a seminal piece of research, debunking at its best, the Tufts scholar Michael Beckley has shown how long China must scramble before it can generate innovation on its own.[42]

What looks from afar like an emerging technology superpower, Beckley writes, is in fact a piggyback economy. "China's high-technology exports are 'not very Chinese, and not very high-tech'—more than 90 percent are produced by foreign firms and consist of imported components that are merely assembled in China, a practice known as 'export processing.'"[43] Indeed, the foreign share of high-tech exports has risen during the naughts, which is a sign of slowdown rather than indigenous tech mastery. The foreign share of exports at the end of the naughts was where it had been in the mid-1990s.[44] Apparently, "a powerful work ethic and huge pent-up aspirations for prosperity," as two sober authors put it with regard to China, are not enough to vault as a nation to the top of the class.[45]

What would propel China to technological preeminence? Another RAND study has looked at the most powerful drivers across twenty-nine countries. It lists a lot more than diligence and acquisitiveness, richly present in China and India. The catalog ranges from plentiful capital via good governance and political stability to education and R&D—ten factors in all.[46] Declinists take note: "Scientifically advanced nations" such as the United States, the EU, and Japan will be "*highly* capable" of fielding "new technology."[47] China and India have only "*partial* capability." In other words, it will take a while. The doomsday that *Newsweek* predicted in 2011 has already passed. Citing the Conference Board, a U.S. business network whose Leading Economic Index tries to plumb the future, the magazine announced that China would be the world's largest economy (by PPP) "as early as next year."[48] The year 2012 came and went, and the United States was still No. 1 by a very comfortable margin.

THE POWER OF IMMIGRATION

The United States is unique in the company of Europeans and Asians. For it has been and will be a nation of immigrants—more so even than the other countries of English settlement, be they Canada, Australia, or New Zealand. Founded by settlers, as well, these nations have always rationed the influx of immigrants. So did the United States after World War I. But it still takes in one million legal and roughly 400,000 illegal immigrants per year.[49] Immigrants are seen as a problem in most of the world; in U.S. history, they have periodically also been targeted as a threat ever since non-WASPs flooded into the country. Yet for all the nativist revolts right into the twenty-first century, they continue to fuel the American engine that will keep decay at bay.

In the nineteenth century, the population grew fifteenfold, mainly as result of immigration. The inflow has had a profound impact on the history of the United States, and it will continue to do so. In the process, the country became the world's first "universal nation," peopled by a myriad of nationalities. The consequences were enormous and are replicated nowhere else. This universal nation, especially with its vast open spaces, would be much better equipped to accept and "nationalize" newcomers than the rest of the world.

It is instructive to compare the United States with Europe. In the modern European nation-state, energized by the rising force of nationalism in the late eighteenth century, citizenship, rights, and status were chained to ethnicity, custom, and faith. In the United States that link would soon be cut, a historical first. It wasn't so in the beginning, the "melting pot" coming a lot later. As Samuel Huntington has shown,[50] the country started out as a transplanted Britain, as a North American offshoot of the island empire, which replicated its culture and institutions on the other side of the Atlantic. It was peopled by white Anglo-Saxon Protestants, setting aside 600,000 African slaves and millions of descendants, who were systematically denied full citizenship rights until the middle of the twentieth century.

America started out as a WASP nation-state that endured into the early nineteenth century. Then its national identity began to change as millions of Catholics and Jews, Germans, Irish and Scandinavians, East Europeans and Russians arrived on America's shores, to be followed by Asians and Latinos. Those who came voluntarily were not born as Americans but *became* Americans. That was the critical difference between this new nation and the Old World, and it still is when the United States is compared with Asia. It was the historical difference between a society founded practically ex nihilo and the entrenched nation-states whose ethnic roots went back to the Roman Empire—to places named Hispania, Gallia, and Germania.

Not that it was so easy for non-Protestant and non-Anglo newcomers; the influx triggered discrimination and successive waves of hostility from day one. As one early critic of the Constitution thundered, religious equality might bring about "a papist, a Mohomatan, a deist, yeah, an atheist at the helm of government."[51] The idea of an inclusive citizenship, where faith and origin pale, actually did not triumph until the middle of the twentieth century when the Civil Rights and the Voting Rights Acts, enfranchising African Americans, began to conclude the most shameful chapter in the peopling of America. In the end, the "American Creed"—a civil religion stripped of bloodline, belief, and heritage—did win out. Group after group could join the Creed. Its catechism was secular and universal: individualism, equality before the law, democracy, limited government, property rights, and freedom of speech, worship, and movement. The Creed was enshrined in documents like the Declaration of Independence, the Constitution, the Bill of

Rights, and the Gettysburg Address, as well as countless inaugural addresses.

Add less lofty, but perhaps even mightier, engines of attraction: "making it" and the "land of opportunity" where the "streets are paved with gold." Tocqueville found in the "equality of social conditions"[52] one of the most remarkable differences between the Old World and the New. Commoners did not have to defer to hereditary elites, be they ennobled by property or "divine right." Nor did they have to bow to a priestly caste; there was no such caste in a land of myriad, mostly dissident churches. The dominant ethos was acquisition and hard work, labor being accorded a dignity it did not have in the Old World. "Making it" was also the fruit of vast open spaces, loose hierarchies, and weak governments. Those who didn't make it in one place could pick up and go to another. "Go west, young man," a slogan ascribed to the nineteenth-century author Horace Greeley, remains deeply embedded in American folk culture. It was spoofed by the Marx Brothers in their movie *Go West*—to the "land, sonny," where "you will have a lot of money."

Until this day, Americans are the most mobile population in the West, moving to and fro in search of careers and betterment. To sign on to the Creed was a lot easier than shedding inherited status and breaking into closed guilds in the Old World. Hence the allure of this *novus ordo seclorum* of which Tom Paine, the Revolution's most famous pamphleteer, wrote, "We have it in our power to begin the world over again."[53] Becoming an American, who was free to do and go, was better than the life of a serf or tenant in Europe, who could not own land, nor marry without his lord's permission.

In this "New Country," a newcomer could remake himself, breaking the chains of his past. America's civil religion found its counterpart in the real thing. The country's ur-religion, Puritanism, was an English version of Calvinism. Once it had sunk roots on the other side of the ocean, it shed its dour and unforgiving doctrine in favor of optimistic self-helpism. Instead of predestined damnation or salvation, Evangelical Protestantism invented the heartening notion of "born again."[54]

This was the spiritual side of the "second chance"—or Barack Obama's "yes, we can!" No more "unconditional election" or the "complete corruption of humanity" through original sin, as Calvin had it. Baptism could be chosen at any time in life, and born-again man could find salvation by his own effort. The God of Calvin had decreed man's fate in the Hereafter—no way out. But now God would help those who helped themselves. Nowhere else does religion feed a secular ideology centered on self-reliance and transcendence in the here and now. "Bornagainism" both reflects and reinforces the individualism and optimism of the American secular experience.

Add to this "supply-side religion." Having built a "wall of separation between Church & State," as Thomas Jefferson put it in 1802, "God's Own Country" could be owned by many Gods. In this "free market," so to speak, anybody could be an entrepreneur of the cloth. Hence countless denominations, hence the religious hucksterism scathingly portrayed in the novels of Sinclair Lewis. Yet for all the sordid profiteering, do-it-yourself religion had a nice political upside. "Who is your God?"—a deadly question in the Middle East and not so long ago in Europe—does not pit insiders against outsides. Nor does "Where are you from?" betray suspicion or disdain. It is a conversation starter that reflects polite curiosity. Once the WASP Republic had lost its grip, the questions that matter became "Where did you go to school?" and "What do you do?"

Such queries probe acquired, not handed-down, traits. Yesterday's passport matters less than today's advanced degree.

China and India haven't even begun to think about immigration, Japan has done so only barely. A "real" Chinese is still a Han, and a "real" Russian is still a Russian-born. Mark Kitto, the Briton who tried to become Chinese for sixteen years and gave up, puts it *tout court*: "A China that leads the world will not offer the chance to be Chinese, because it is impossible to become Chinese."[55] The Indian constitution proscribes discrimination by caste, and over the decades affirmative action has tried to pierce the iron walls of descent. De facto, though, the caste system remains a powerful reality that constrains competition and upward mobility.

Only very recently have the Continental Europeans begun to accept "real" immigrants, that is, those who *want* to come, stay, and naturalize, as opposed to "guest workers" and refugees who are supposedly temporary residents. Unlike the United States, which got there by the middle of the last century, the European and for sure the Asian countries, have a long way to go in "nationalizing" outsiders of different color, bloodline, and faith, let alone viewing them as a precious national resource.

Like the rest of the world, Americans, too, have always seen immigration as a threat to their core identity, starting with the Irish in the 1820s. Yet wave after wave was eventually "Americanized." Recall *The Godfather*, *Gangs of New York*, and *Hester Street*—movies that chronicle the travails and tragedies of Italian, Irish, and Jewish immigrants. In the end, an Italian by the name of Enrico Fermi entered American history as the "father of the atom bomb." John F. Kennedy, a Catholic of Irish stock, became president. These narratives have become an integral part of American folklore. In fact, one-half of America's presidents proudly claim Irish ancestry, Barack Obama being the most recent one. The son of a German-Jewish schoolteacher, Henry Kissinger, rose to be secretary of state. So did Madeleine Albright, born as Marie Jana Korbelová in Prague. America resented whoever came after, but closure just as regularly ran afoul of the brute dynamism the newcomers embodied. In the simplest terms: In a country where ambition meets opportunity, immigrants do get to crack the mold. Russian Jews, who could not break into WASP-held industries and banks, founded Hollywood, the world's behemoth of entertainment. Silicon Valley started out as a WASP enterprise; today it is more like a microcosm of Chinese, Indians, Israelis, Germans, and Frenchmen.

In his *Rise and Decline of Nations*, Mancur Olson argues that closed societies freeze up—victims of rent-seeking elites who capture political power to cement economic privilege and stifle the competition that fuels rejuvenation. Once on top, they pull up the ladder. That is not the fate of a "universal nation" created as "something new under the sun" and which worships self-reinvention as a reigning ideology. In such a culture, newcomers manage to pull the ladder down again and to climb it. Where status is fluid and fleeting, the top is not an easy chair for the *beati possidentes* but a free-for-all. Desire and hustling, skill and ingenuity are the rungs on this ladder. Hungry and driven, they climbed it all: Germans, Irish, Jews, Italians, now Asians and Latinos, pushing, jostling, and dislodging. They could because in a country born in rejection of the Old World—of nobles, priests, and guilds—the "New New Thing"[56] is part of the civil religion.

The fruits of such a dispensation won't soon be harvested elsewhere. Those who crave them—Chinese, Indians, even Europeans—go to America instead. "Take immigrants out of Silicon Valley and you have no Silicon Valley," gushed the Welsh-born Michael Moritz of Sequoia Capital.[57] One-half of the valley's engineers were born abroad.[58] Here are some numbers to fill out the picture. One-quarter of all the high-tech companies founded in the United States between 1995 to 2005 had at least one foreign-born founder. The figure rises to 40 percent in California. Nationwide, these immigrant-founded companies produced $52 billion in sales and employed 450,000 workers in 2005.[59] By another count, more than two-fifths of Silicon Valley start-ups were founded by immigrants in 2012.[60]

Such data help put into perspective the perennial claim that the United States is running out of scientists and engineers and thus out of steam. Hence it is said to go the way of previous empires— first rot, then decline. Claims that "certain other countries produce a greater proportion of scientist and engineering students . . . have been made for almost 50 years," notes Roger Pielke of the University of Colorado, adding drily that the U.S. economy has "done quite well" in that period.[61] Its real GDP grew fourfold. Today, the top three software companies in the world are American, so are eight of the top ten. Of the ten fastest-growing, six are American. There are no Chinese or Indian outfits in this lineup.[62] Overall, the ten most valuable brands were American in 2011, all but one of them having added value since 2010. There is no Chinese company among the top one hundred.

Whether the United States is lagging in the production of scientists and engineers depends on how much is enough, and on the level of educational achievement. Only about 15 percent of all B.A. degrees are awarded in "hard" science and engineering (that is, minus the social sciences). Master's degrees add up to a similarly low fraction. So not enough. Yet the share rises sharply at the summit of educational attainment. Almost one-half of Ph.D.'s in the United States are awarded in the hard sciences and in engineering. How much is enough? One answer: No other country in the world produces more Ph.D.'s in S&E than the United States, about 17 percent of the global total for a population one-twentieth the size.[63]

Critics of U.S. higher education argue that such numbers still conceal underperformance in S&E by pointing to the growing share of foreign-born students in the system. After a falloff in the aftermath of 9/11, that share has been growing again. The United States remains the destination for the largest number of foreign students worldwide, followed by the UK, Germany, and France. The United States is, so to speak, the world's largest S&E university, having awarded 223,245 Ph.D.'s to foreigners in a twenty-year stretch (1989–2009). Of these, 150,000 have gone to students of the top four: China, India, South Korea, and Taiwan.[64]

Doesn't such a surfeit of foreigners prove the Declinists' point? Not quite, for an overwhelming number of these recipients stay: almost seven out of ten. The retention list was headed by Chinese (92 percent) and Indians (81 percent).[65] So instead of illustrating an ominous American deficit, these imports become a "national" resource. They fill whatever gap is being created by the latter-day Marys of Sputnik ill fame who have "barely mastered the fourth-grade arithmetic fundamentals" or the Johnnys who prefer an M.B.A. to the rigors of hard science. These foreigners are an import of the special kind. The intake is not consumed like Japanese cars and Chinese-made (though American-designed) running shoes. Hence the "talent deficit" in S&E should not be confused with America's perennial trade deficit, which indeed betrays a wide gap between consumption and production. The U.S.-trained brain gain represents an investment in the future that bears fruit by the

22. Foreign Percentage of S&E Degrees, 1997–2006

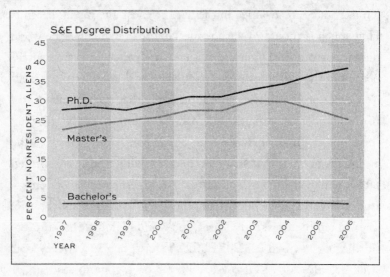

SOURCE: National Science Foundation, Division of Science Resources Statistics, 2010, "Science and Engineering Degrees, by Race/Ethnicity of Recipients: 1997–2006," http://nsf.gov/statistics/nsf10300/content.cfm?pub_id=3786&id=2.

multiple—as gifted immigrants have done since Benjamin Franklin, the son of an English candlemaker, who invented the lightning rod and a dozen other useful things.

The import of foreign talent is proof not of decline but of the opposite: the power to pull in the world's skilled and ambitious. Offering them a professional haven or heaven is the story of America, and it has no end. It continues even if there is no longer a Hitler, who drove the greatest of twentieth-century science to America's shores, among them Albert Einstein, Hans Bethe, Niels Bohr, Leo Szilard, and John von Neumann.[66] More than three out of every four patents at the top ten patent-producing U.S. universities had at least one foreign-born inventor. More than half of all patents were awarded to foreign inventors at the beginning of their careers: students, postdoctoral fellows, or staff researchers. Foreign-born inventors played especially large roles in cutting-edge fields that shape the future.[67] The United States leads the list of Nobel Laureates with 331, more than three times the number of the two next-best, Britain and Germany. But the number is less interesting than the provenance. One-quarter of the luminaries were born abroad.

Russia's greatest wealth—oil, gas, minerals—comes out of the ground. America has those, too, but its most precious riches— talent and aspiration—come from the world. This supply is virtually inexhaustible as long as the country stays open and welcoming. The import bespeaks enduring attraction, not imperial exhaustion. The world might fault the United States for cherry-picking, pointing to the fact that the saplings were planted elsewhere. On the other hand, the twenty-first century is about the most mobile capital of all: men and women of ability and ambition. That capital does not wander off to the BRICs.

The societies that are best equipped to draw and nourish these talents will be best prepared for the global long-distance race. Among those—count in the British offshoots and Israel—the first "universal nation" will stay in the lead unless it closes its gates or others fling open theirs. If the United States does shut itself in, as it seemed to do during the 9/11 moment, the Declinist prophecy might yet come true. To replicate America's unique advantage, that is, to "universalize" their national identities, yesterday's and today's risers have a long way to go. Europe has just started to open up, but it is weighed down by historical handicaps and egalitarian habits that are not easily overcome.

Modernitarianism vs. the Liberal Model

The last three chapters belong together. Chapter 4 surveyed the past, looking at the Asian model as first practiced by Taiwan, Japan, and South Korea—how growth exploded and why it flattened in due time. Chapter 5 portrayed the model's descendant, China's State Capitalism 2.0. The refurbished version displays all the ailments that had weakened the earlier Dragons, plus those that stem from enduring semitotalitarian rule. The present chapter has compared China and the United States in terms of five critical drivers: demography, education, R&D, invention, and immigration. These reflect long-term trends and hence have a claim on the future. In demography, above all, the "is" determines the "will be." Harbingers of future performance, these drivers take us beyond yesterday and open the curtain on a drama yet to be enacted, but with a standard caveat: Keep in mind the follies of past predictions.

Together, chapters 4, 5, and 6 lay out the case against Declinism—the evergreen of America as has been, laid low by its own failings or left behind by the rising rest. The context is set by chapter 1, which relates how the tide of doom has always receded. The contenders slowed while the United States bounced back from real or make-believe disaster. Will Decline 5.0, the rise of the rest, be different?

Chapters 4 to 6 argue "no" or "not so soon." All the wunderkinder of decades past have lost their earlier vigor. The miracles of modernitarianism do not last. China, following a similar blueprint, doesn't quite duplicate that model. First, its industrial "reserve army" will not be exhausted as quickly. Second, China is bigger by orders of magnitude, in both size and population; it will make its weight felt in the international system no matter what. China's international strategy—globalization from day one—marks a third difference. Yet thirty years later, even globalizing state capitalism is running up against its own limits. Chapter 5 has tried to explain why.

First, spectacular growth is soon overtaken by rising wages not fully compensated for by productivity gains. Second, the demographics are not as permissive as the country's 1.3 billion people suggest. Aging is the most cruel drag on growth. The projections point to the middle of this decade as tipping point. This is when the ratio between workers and dependents will begin to shrink (see figure 15). There will be too few workers for too many dependents. Add, third, the built-in fault lines of unrepentant statism. By its very nature, the system protects the status quo from competition and "creative destruction" while consistently misallocating resources. Farther down the line lurks the *existential* problem of modernitarianism *Made in China*. Its core is the unspoken motto "Enrich yourselves, but leave the driving to us." Unless China is Deng Xiao-ping Country from here to eternity, it will not be able to banish the specter of regime change forever, which creates a new set of problems, indeed, a double bind.

Dilemmas and Double Binds. Dengism, capitalism plus statism minus freedom, has dazzled the world with a long-running spectacle of superlative economic success. But China's modernitarianism, like the earlier Dragons', is bumping up against its built-in ceilings, setting up a cruel dilemma between changing and staying the course. One horn of the dilemma—liberalization—warns the Party: If you loosen up, you lose supremacy. So stay the course. But if you do, you run into the other side of the predicament and risk the very stability that has allowed you to unleash the economy without freeing the polity. The most cruel feature of the dilemma is that the wondrous growth, which has lifted China from miserable poverty, will go in either case, whether it is despotism or democracy. Liberalization and repression set up a perfect double bind.

Liberalization. The pressure is on because the miracle comes with a curse that hit the older Dragons as they moved from indigence into middle income. As noted in chapter 5, middle income implies a middle class that in due time claims a larger voice and larger share. This has been the historical pattern in the West, which eventually spilled over into East Asia, only faster: first rich, then rowdy. As income rises, so does the clamor for stakeholder rights. The formula reads: Prosperity plus education plus urbanization equal pushback. First it is property rights, then voting rights, then social security, then such familiar Western acquaintances as environmentalism and NIMBY ("not in my back yard"). Both militate against the careless exploitation of nature that underlay East Asia's and China's skyrocketing growth.

Everywhere, middle income has led to the redistribution of resources both material and symbolic—from investment to consumption, from enforced saving to social protection, from the state to the individual. Everywhere, the migration of power from state to society has slowed the blinding speed of the takeoff phase. In the process, modernitarianism runs out of cheap funds and steam; hence economic miracles tend to undo themselves. Democratization does not harmonize with frantic industrialization, as the careers of the little Dragons suggest. The historical correlation has been solid, and it harbors plenty of causation. Riches fuel dissent, which wrings concessions from the almighty state. These whet the appetite for more, further eroding regime authority while shifting wealth from state to society.

That path, of course, is strewn with bloody setbacks; Taiwan and South Korea did not become democracies overnight; nor did France after the Revolution of 1789. Still, once the cork pops, the genie won't be pushed back into the bottle. The Chinese regime has labored mightily (and deftly) to imprison this demon, democracy being the Beelzebub of the *nomenklatura*. The Party has tried to exorcize it by drawing legitimacy and consent from stellar economic accomplishment that, alas, falters in mature modernitarianism for all the reasons outlined in this chapter. Unless China dwells on another planet, the pressures from below—tens of thousands of civil disturbances per year[68]—will not abate, for docile consumers eventually turn into raucous citizens. So on to the other horn of the dilemma.

Repression. The regime's nightmare is Tiananmen, when output collapsed in the bloody crackdown that followed. Terror, as the mayhem of 1989 illustrates, breaks not only people but also seemingly unstoppable economic expansion. So did the final convulsion of Maoism known as the Cultural Revolution. The trauma of 1989 is as old as China itself. Call it the "Ming-to-Quing cycle": centuries of uprisings and murderous revenge escalating into civil war. In the course of that half millennium, a towering empire lost both its wealth and its greatness.

Repression may keep the *nomenklatura* alive, but not an economy that has thrived on obedience at home and massive investments from abroad. A succession of Tiananmens would put paid to regime legitimacy as well as to the inflow of capital. A mass uprising might follow nonetheless, if Chinese history is a guide. So despotism renewed is just as unpalatable as are democracy and a true market economy. Since revolts are the hardest part of the soothsaying business, let us assume that the regime stays in the saddle, especially since the Party has proven so adept at containing the "revolution of rising expectations" that historically has come with rapid growth. Hence the most likely regime choice is the status quo—dilemma management, so to speak. The continuity scenario might be labeled "Supreme Party, Slowing Economy," a future that, according to our argument, lurks in the very nature of modernitarianism.

The system forged ahead nicely during takeoff, when plentiful resources do not exact efficient allocation. Yet state capitalism, whatever its coloration, is *inherently* inefficient, as illustrated most dramatically by its virtually nonviolent collapse in the Soviet Union. In China, the typical warning signs are housing bubbles, tottering banks, and lavish subsidies to low- or no-profit state-owned enterprises. Such a syndrome reflects the system's built-in misallocation of resources. All of these deadweights began to drag on the Chinese economy before the Crash of 2008—and for similar reasons as in the West, where overspending, easy money, and rampant speculation culminated in the longest crisis since the Great Depression. Yet the analogies should not be overdrawn.

East and West—Where the Twain Don't Meet. The bigger the state, the harsher the handicaps, and there is conspicuously more state in China than in the Western economies. In fact, the state *is* the economy, as chapter 5 has shown. And where the state rules, collusion beats competition, innovation, and elite rejuvenation. Alas, creation and destruction is the lifeblood of any economy, and nowhere more so than in a knowledge economy. Not too many American dot-coms and high-tech companies of the 1990s are still alive today.

Take a telling Western example of state-driven technology: France's Minitel, a telephone-based videotext service. A rudimentary search engine, it was launched by France's PTT in 1982. It survived, courtesy of the centralized state, until 2012, twenty years into the Internet age. The moral of this drawn-out tale is an old one. Governments, which need not obsess about bottom lines, do well when a new investment is "bulky" and capital costs are high. Precisely because of the high start-up costs, they raise walls of protection around their "national champions."

When technological cycles were long—as in days of the nineteenth-century railroad and the twentieth-century mechanical phone system—the government's brake on "creative destruction" didn't bite for decades. The harm done by market barriers was outweighed by the blessings of the new infrastructure. In the digital age, the bottom line soon turns bright red. When it is Minitel vs. Google, the government's showpiece soon outlives its usefulness, eating up resources and freezing invention. Apropos of Google, it might not exist today if the U.S. government had sheltered Hotbot, AltaVista, and Lycos, search engines that have been long forgotten.

State intervention that remains limited explains why the United States with its entrepreneurial anarchy and rich capital markets outperforms State Capitalism 2.0 in the innovation race. This happy verdict holds true even if the United States suffers from ample pathologies to inspire Declinist melancholy: dysfunctional government, polarized parties, inequality of incomes and wealth, ballooning entitlements, pork and patronage, strained infrastructures. . . . Nonetheless, a one-party regime faces problems of a different magnitude. State-sponsored rent seeking—the fusion of political and economic power—weighs ever harder as a backward economy moves up on the ladder of sophistication. It is easier to churn out tens of thousands of primitive T-34 tanks, as Stalinist Russia did in World War II, than to shift from mass to class in the civilian sector. Nor do statist economies, sidelining the "crazy" and creative, excel at inventing the "New New Thing."

Western capitalism, of course, isn't so laissez-faire any more, the state consuming an ever larger chunk of GDP—around one-half, as in Europe. This share is ten times higher than it was in peacetime 150 years ago. Yet for all this expansion, production is effectively private in the West, as it is not in China; indeed, in the last quarter century, the democratic state has pulled back, selling publicly held enterprises and deregulating entire industries. While public spending has surged since World War II, the wealth-producing part of the system has had to brave the rising winds of competition from within and without. Antitrust enforcement has expanded for a century while trade and capital barriers have fallen.

More state *and* more market is the most delicious paradox of the modern Western welfare state. Indeed, without a vigorous market economy, it couldn't carry the mounting load of redistribution. Another difference—in kind, not degree—between China and the West is the rule of law. This system, which long preceded democracy, holds in check corruption, cronyism, and rent seeking, all of which are the enemies of economic dynamism. So history whispers that the fabulous success of China and its illiberal comrades in growth cannot endure, because the institutions don't fit.[69]

Hence the perfect predicament confronting China's elite: lose-lose. If it loosens the reins, the horse will eventually throw off the Party, with democracy inevitably slowing the breakneck speed of the economy. If, on the other hand, the regime sticks to modernitarianism (markets minus freedom), it risks a Tiananmen and its twin, a crashing economy. The mildest scenario is dilemma management, as practiced by the current regime. Tweaking the status quo has a third set of considerable risks of its own: ossification and a drawn-out descent. In other words, no matter how the red emperors try to extricate themselves, they will pay the price of waning growth or worse. And there evaporates that mesmerizing economic miracle that has inspired worldwide adulation while promising global primacy in short order.

Nor is this the end of the story, for there is more to global primacy than the economic "substructure"—the modes and relations of production (the "how to" and the "who owns" of an economy). Karl Marx put technology, labor, and capital at the center of his universe, while pooh-poohing the "superstructure," such as religion, philosophy, and *Bewusstsein* (awkwardly translated as "consciousness"). He overdid it; the *Überbau*, culture in the widest sense, *does* matter. GDP is but a necessary condition of preeminence. The other critical strengths flow from the invisibles of power: ideology and outlook, global interest and responsibility. Again, let history be our guide. Liberal empires—Britain and the United States—have assembled a much better record in running the world than their illiberal forebears from Habsburg to Russia, whether Moscow belonged to the tsars or the communists. What it takes, and who has it, is the theme of the concluding chapter.

CHAPTER SEVEN

America, the West, and the Rest: Who Will Own the Twenty-First Century?

THE WORLD'S NEW POWER MAP

A five-power world dominated the eighteenth and nineteenth centuries. It came to an end in 1945, when only two—the United States and the Soviet Union—were left standing. In turn, this two-power world vanished when the USSR left the ring in 1991, the empire collapsing without a shot being fired. Yet America's "unipolar moment"[1]—its old enemy gone, its own might unshackled—was to be brief.

A heady moment it was. No longer checked by a mortal rival, the United States launched three wars in places where it would never have dared tread while Soviet power was still whole—in Afghanistan and twice in Iraq. In the old days, those battlefields were off-limits; such were the rules of bipolarity, where trespassing into the other's sphere was strictly verboten. Kabul was too close to the Soviet *imperium*, Baghdad a long-standing ally in all but name. Suddenly, a stellar moment spelled opportunity without risk, so why not? "We've got the ships, we've got the men, and got the money too!" they sang in nineteenth-century London at the height of the British Empire. America had it all. Without putting the nation on a war footing, the United States was able to dispatch 700,000 men halfway around the world to crush Saddam Hussein's Iraq in 1991. The country was back with a large land army in 2003, while prosecuting another war in Afghanistan. No other power in history could have replicated that feat—not on this scale, not at this speed.

Some twenty years later, the United States had left Iraq while pulling out of Afghanistan—undefeated, but frustrated. Unable to impose an American order on these far-away countries, the nation had become wary of foreign entanglement, and for sound reasons. It was facing the longest stretch of high unemployment since the Great Depression and tasting the bitter fruits of super-Keynesian deficit spending. The federal shortfall had topped 10 percent of GDP, declining only slightly at the time of Barack Obama's reelection in 2012. Debt was climbing toward the historic peak of World War II, when it stood at 120 percent of GDP.

Long and inconclusive wars have a sobering effect on nations— recall Vietnam a generation earlier. As then, though, the climb down from imperial adventure came with a nice upside. America remained unchallenged, a remarkable outcome that betrayed a larger truth. Truly great powers can blunder coming and going. They can go too far or pull back and still remain unscathed. It is their large margin of error that marks them off from lesser players. The wrong choices of weaker nations can prove fatal.

Real giants, on the other hand, do not risk deadly retribution when they throw their weight around, as the United States did after the fall of the Soviet Union. With No. 2 out, nobody was left to take on No. 1. A "hyperpower," as the French foreign minister Hubert Védrine had it, can suffer military misfortune without losing its perch. Such a power can also afford to scale back without risking its standing. This happy state is called "existential deterrence"—safety by dint of size, weight, and retaliatory strength. Retraction was Barack Obama's choice in the aftermath of George W. Bush. Now the Obama administration would "lead from behind"[2] rather than strike out; it was drones rather than boots on the ground. Still, who would test the giant's strength?

Yesterday's mortal rival, the Soviet Union, had committed suicide. Its Russian heir was a world-class power no more. America's new rival, China, was not ready to take on the reigning superpower—not regionally, as Imperial Japan had tried to do in the 1940s, and certainly not globally, as had the Soviet Union in the Cold War. Democratic Japan, touted as new master of the economic universe during Decline 4.0, was trapped in long-term stagnation, remaining an American security client, to boot. Europe, another former candidate for the top spot, had plenty of muscle to give the United States a good run. It had size, population, and riches, but neither the will nor the wherewithal, as the steady drop in defense spending indicated after the end of the Cold War. None of the contenders posed a serious threat to American primacy, even while Gulliver was stumbling once again, as he had from Decline 1.0 to 4.0. During Decline 5.0, the schadenfreude of the rest was muted by economic calamity all around, from Berlin to Beijing.

The Decathlon Power. What is the world like today? It is no longer unipolar, if it ever was, with one nation on top and all the others defining their position in relation to the "unipole," let alone deferring to it. In fact, the United States never could lord it over the rest in the sense that it got its way everywhere, not even at the height of its soi-disant unipolar moment, and certainly not before, when its power was checked directly by China in Korea and indirectly by the USSR in Vietnam. That said, the world is far from multipolar: a system of several coequal powers balancing one another while jostling or fighting for advantage. Some can equal or even best the United States in some currencies of power, be they economic or demographic, but they can't match it overall. A fitting metaphor (not to be confused with the real ranking of nations) was the Olympic decathlon of 2012. Other nations excelled in individual sports, but the United States scored gold and silver in the ten-discipline contest, as it had in most Olympics since World War II.

So what is the world like today? Above all, it is like no other international system since the rise of the modern nation-state, when "power" usually came with "balance." Nobody could have put it more vividly than Paul Kennedy, the most learned and influential of modern Declinists:

Nothing has ever existed like this disparity of power; nothing. I have returned to all of the comparative defense spending and military personnel statistics over the past 500 years that I compiled in *The Rise and Fall of the Great Powers*, and no other nation comes close. The Pax Britannica was run on the cheap, Britain's army was much smaller than European armies, and even the Royal Navy was equal only to the next two navies—right now all the other navies in the world combined could not dent American maritime supremacy.

Charlemagne's empire was merely Western European in its reach. The Roman empire stretched farther afield, but there was another great empire in Persia, and a larger one in China. There is, therefore, no comparison.[3]

This was penned in 2002, at the high point of the "unipolar moment"—and then in the wake of the Yale historian's thrilling moment on the flight deck of the USS *Enterprise*, which packed more punch than the entire Royal Navy at the peak of British power.[4] But subtract awe and admiration, and the assessment still holds a decade later. Previous empires always rubbed up against others, courting war or extinction. If they didn't fall under their own weight, because they couldn't control an ever larger expanse, they spent their careers grabbing more or defending what they had. Neither fixation added to the coffers of the state and the wealth of its subjects.

A Virtual Empire. In contrast to previous empires, America's is not the sum total of core, conquests, and colonies. It is like the twenty-first-century economy, a blend of the digital and the real. It is a globe-encircling network of influence, girded by unmatched air and sea power, space-based surveillance, and brick-and-mortar bases. Command and control are in real time; power projection is measured in hours. This "empire" needs no corrupt viziers and rapacious tax collectors who drive the natives to rebellion. A state without a state religion, the American empire does not impose its faith on other peoples. Rome did so in Judea, Habsburg-Spain in Latin America, and Moscow, the "Fourth Rome," in Eastern Europe, where it installed the Communist Church. All reaped costly revolt.

The American empire usually comes in brogues, not in hobnail boots. When it moves on tank treads, it doesn't fight for possession, as traditional imperial powers have done. A goodly number of America's wars have been willful or aggressive. Its empire was not one of boundless virtue, given its conquests of Indian and Mexican lands, its domination of Latin America, or its second war against Iraq. But America stands out by grace of sheer luck. Its physical empire was at home, a vast continent without mighty rivals. It expanded from the thirteen colonies to the fifty states without running into formidable foes. The British had extruded the French from the Northeast before the United States was born. They handed over the Northwest in 1846. "To conquer without war" was the "first fact" of the young republic's grand strategy, observed the French diplomat Louis-Marie Turreau.[5]

Gobbling up the real estate was a steal. One-third of the country was bought from the French in the Louisiana Purchase. So was Florida from Spain, and Alaska from Russia—and all for a pittance, ranging from $15 million to $7 million in then dollars.[6] Rome fought, America bought. The rest—the Southwest and Texas—was wrested from an outgunned Mexico. There is in American history no Thermopylae, where the Greek general Themistocles faced a Persian force fifty times larger. Unlike any other empire, the United States never had to fight for its very existence, not even in World War II.

So add the economy of power to the surfeit of power, as celebrated by Paul Kennedy on the flight deck of the *Enterprise*. No other empire has ever enjoyed such a pretty balance sheet. Virtual empires based on allies, investments, trade, finance, and cultural draw are cheaper and less strenuous than the traditional version. This is a new thing under the imperial sun, and a soothing one, to boot. America's network empire irks affiliates and riles rivals, but its longevity reflects an acceptance that physical empires enjoyed only fitfully in the past. Evidently, this global mesh serves more non-American interests than it harms. This neo-*imperium* also bears a reassuring message for its own people: It will not be ruined by overextension or war.

Only the United States can bring down the United States. If the burden becomes unbearable, the calamity will be homegrown. The country could lose its economic vigor, social cohesion, or competitive spirit. It might go on consuming more than it produces; this is the ugly warning uttered by intractable trade and federal deficits, the latter shooting skyward during Decline 5.0. The United States might close the door to immigration, this inexhaustible wellspring of rejuvenation, and freeze up. It might lose its national ethos and its warrior culture. It might become more like the rest of the West, preferring equality to acquisition, and social safety to personal riches. Or it might lose both equality and "making it" in a system that cements privilege and blocks mobility. Whatever the poison, it will be brewed inside the United States.

On Top, Not in Control. Like any decathlon gold medalist, the United States is not the first in every discipline. Nor is it the master of the universe who gets his way at will. It never could, even when the rest, including the West, was flat on its face after World War II. The United States fought to a draw in Korea, and it failed in Vietnam. It lost its economic supremacy long ago, as Europe and Japan recovered from history's bloodiest war. Also some forty years ago, the "almighty dollar" was taken down a few pegs, when the Nixon administration closed the "gold window," ending the greenback's cast-in-concrete convertibility into bullion. Decades ago, the United States also lost its grip on the global institutions it founded, such as the UN, the International Monetary Fund, the World Bank, and the GATT, rechristened World Trade Organization. Wherever it is one nation, one vote, the United States is only first among equals.

The power of oil devolved to OPEC in the 1970s. The U.S. balance of trade went negative in 1971, staying there ever since. *Never* has the United States proven able to fully impose its will on smaller allies like France, West Germany, or Israel. It could not deter Moscow from forcibly "recentralizing" its East European empire in the 1950s and 1960s when it quashed revolts in East Berlin, Budapest, and Prague. The last time Washington pulled off a nonmilitary regime change in a major country was in 1953, when the CIA and Britain's MI–6 toppled Mohammad Mossadeq in Tehran and reinstalled the Shah. In short, the United States has always faced a distinct gap between what it had in the bank and what it could buy with the hoard.

If this twenty-first-century world is not uni-, bi-, or multipolar, if it is run neither by one power, nor by a twosome, nor by a committee of states, what is it? Is it none of the above? Is it, to stay with the academic nomenclature, "apolar" or "nonpolar"? At first blush, it may seem so, given that this planet is now populated by five times as many states as it was at the end of World War II. Capturing the mood at the beginning of Decline 5.0, the president of the U.S. Council on Foreign Relations argued in "The Age of Nonpolarity" that the new world would be dominated not "by one or two or even several states but rather by dozens [with] various kinds of power." This new dispensation represented "a tectonic shift from the past," and "power is now found in many hands and in many places."

Where Kissinger and Nixon had sketched a five-power world during Decline 2.0 half a century ago, there were now six. These were America and the four usual suspects, China, Europe, Japan, and Russia, plus India as newcomer. Behind them trailed the regional greats. Brazil was leading the Latin American league, followed by Argentina. Africa's regional heavyweights were Nigeria and South Africa; in the Middle East, Egypt, Iran, Israel, and Saudi Arabia were vying for dominance. In South Asia, Pakistan stood out; in East Asia, Indonesia and South Korea occupied the second tier; in Oceania, Australia was head of the class.

Nor was the new power map defined only by states. Add several new species: supranational leaders like the EU and subnational spoilers like al-Qaeda, Hezbollah, and the drug cartels. Count in a slew of multinational institutions like the International Monetary Fund, the UN, OPEC, the Arab League. . . . And global media like Al-Jazeera as well as a thousand NGOs like Greenpeace and Human Rights Watch.

In short, the stage was populated by many actors with many assets and ambitions both benign and noxious. Hence the "emergence of alternative power centers" had "weakened [America's] position relative to them."[7] So less for the United States and more for the rest. This dictum had a familiar ring, being the sostenuto of six decades of Declinism. Yet it was followed by an incontrovertible truth: "In this world, the United States is and will long remain the largest single aggregation of power." Indeed, especially since there is no meaningful way to describe Argentina or Nigeria as great powers.

Chips and Gaming Tables. Clearly, one feature of world politics is both novel and enduring. Power has diffused and diversified while trickling down to many players. Yet this is not the whole story. The very inflation of power has also devalued it—the way a dollar today buys only one-eighth of what it fetched fifty years ago. To map this world, we might recruit the gaming table as a metaphor. Let us not only count all the new players who have thronged the table but also look at the nature and number of their chips. Then another truth emerges. In a world of many, it takes more to score—not just this or that *jeton* but large piles of different color and shape.

Those who don't bring enough to the table may not last out the evening. To belabor the metaphor: In a casino, anybody can play—even with white one-dollar chips, be it at the roulette or blackjack table. To play for larger stakes, he'll need the purple ($500) or gray rectangular ($5,000) plastic.[8] To score in the global power game, a would-be winner needs more than a handful of chips. He must come armed for the long haul, and then with many different chips that fit many games and tables.

Out in the real world, the games are military, commercial, financial, diplomatic, and cultural; the tables are local, regional, and global. Riches are not enough. A nation must *want* to play, that is, bring a keen sense of global interest or, even better, responsibility to the contest. Sustainable power, that is, authority or legitimacy, must be married to a larger purpose than just "more for myself." A would-be winner must also be *able* to compete. To prevail, a nation needs a knack for multitasking, skills honed by experience, real-time information on a global scale, and a gift for making friends, aka allies. In this world, even the mighty can rarely win by themselves. They require networks of influence that can be tapped when the stakes are too high for a single player.

To put it in yet other terms: In this globalized arena of many players, regional or single-asset advantage is not enough to go planetary in the way of the Europeans from the Age of Discovery to the rise of the United States. The strategic reach of Britain, Habsburg, and France, and even the tiny Netherlands spanned much of the globe in their days, enabling them to amass empires from Asia to the Americas. No more, not in a world where the locals have traded their flintlocks for handheld missiles, and their scimitars for improvised explosive devices.

China, Russia, and India have mass, but their global influence is not commensurate. Europe musters fabulous riches, but not the ambition of a global strategic player. Among the second-tier nations, Saudi Arabia has oil and the money to spread its dour Wahhabite doctrine around the world, but despite its bulging armory, it has offshored its security to the United States. Iran attracts with a messianic Shia creed, but it repels both the Sunni and the Western world, ruining its economy in the process. The Soviet Union had a Marxist ideology that won loyalties around the world. Post-Soviet Russia has no such universalist appeal, nor does China.

The IMF can try to dictate the fiscal policy of failing economies; it cannot save the euro. The Gates Foundation can disburse millions to Africa, but it cannot teach peace to potentates who war against their own peoples and their neighbors. If lucky, the UN can legitimize, but not launch interventions against the malfeasants of the day. For all its demographic clout and nuclear weapons, India will not soon commit to the management of global order. It cannot even resolve the local issue of Kashmir against the will of its much smaller Pakistani neighbor, with whom it has fought three wars since the departure of the British.

Al-Qaeda and offshoots wield the weapons of terror with vicious skill, defying drones above and U.S. forces below. But look again. Al-Qaeda's anticolonialist forebears, say, the FLN in Algeria, also exploited terror. The difference is that the Algerian insurgents did achieve their strategic objective, driving out the French from *l'Algérie française* in less than a decade. So did the FLN's brethren who expelled their colonial overlords throughout Africa and Asia. But al-Qaeda cannot do more than maim and murder; it cannot dislodge armies or regimes. Nor will Fatah, Hamas, and Hezbollah oust the Jews from the Levant. Contemporary terror, spectacular as it is, scores tactical gains, but not strategic ones.

It takes lots of chips, and of many denominations, to make a mark; that is the moral of this twenty-first-century's tale. Others, states and nonstates, have acquired more of them, but only the United States has them all, and the biggest stacks, to boot— except for population, where it is outclassed by China and India, and GDP, where the EU weighs in with a slightly larger one. But the EU and Japan, first and third in the GDP ranking, are allies of sixty years' standing.

The Uni- and the Multipolar. To assess the distribution of power, let us resort to the contradiction in terms coined by Samuel Huntington in 1999, at the very height of America's "unipolar moment." This world, he argued, is "uni-multipolar," a "strange hybrid." What is the "uni" part? The United States is first in "every domain of power." It is also in a league of its own with the "reach and capabilities to promote its interests in virtually every part of the world." The "multi" part consists of "major regional powers" without the same global sweep. These are our old acquaintances Europe, Russia, and China, plus "potentially" Japan and India. Add Brazil, Iran, South Africa, and Nigeria in their various regional arenas.

How does the "uni" relate to the "multi"? Huntington responds judiciously. On the one hand, "the settlement of key international issues requires action by the single superpower." On the other, the United States must always recruit a "combination of other major states." Nonetheless, Washington can "veto action on key issues by combinations of other states."[9] Finally, no coalition, let alone a single state, can defeat the United States in the way previous greats were overpowered by their enemies. This is as true today as it was one or five decades ago.

It is also true that, until this day, the United States could never play Rome to the rest, unless its targets were small Central American states. In all other cases, from Korea to Afghanistan, action required coalitions, as in the case of Britain. Conversely, no "combination of other states" could inflict its will on this überpower,[10] forcing it to adhere to climate conventions or to submit to the International Court of Justice. In that respect, the United States remains a "veto-proof" country.

The overall balance of power remains tilted in favor of the United States, but with one critical caveat. The proliferation of players has blunted America's influence over the world's institutions of collective action. Since its imperial heyday from the 1940s to the 1960s, Washington has had to cajole, co-opt, and bribe more frequently, and sometimes with little to show for the effort. When North Korea attacked the South, the United States could simply circumvent the UN Security Council and go to the General Assembly for a mandate, aka the "Uniting for Peace Resolution." Those days are gone for good. But they went decades ago. Ever since, it has been the Rolling Stones for the United States: "You can't always get what you want." There is, and has always been, a distinct gap between the assets and the achievements of power. This basic truth does not yet dispose of another critical question amid a plethora of tables and contestants: What does it take to play well? Let us look at nonphysical assets—at history, culture, ideology, and identity.

THE LURE OF LIBERAL EMPIRE

The bulk of this book has analyzed the "visibles" of power, the chips that nations bring to the table. How are they acquired, how do they stack up? Let us now turn to the game itself. Who has the appropriate traditions and skills, and how so? The long and the short of it is that *liberal* empires do better for reasons rooted in their domestic order. Or make that liberal empires that start out on an island like Britain. Or better yet, on a very large, continent-sized island like the United States. Insularity spelled safety, and safety bred liberty. From that grew a network of global rule less vulnerable and more economical than the methods of dynastic or totalitarian empires.

Alexis de Tocqueville dwelled at length on the link between geography and safety: "Separated from the rest of the world by the ocean," the United States "has no enemies."[11] Why isn't "the American Union . . . dissolved by a great war? It is because it has no great wars to fear. The Union is almost as much insulated from the world as if all its frontiers were girt by the ocean." It is America's "geographical position which renders . . . wars extremely improbable."[12]

The master was wrong on one count. The Union *was* almost done in by a "great war." But that calamity was a *civil* war, the bloodiest in American history, not a foreign one. The same goes for England/Britain, the "parent," which imprinted its culture, institutions, and outlook on the United States. Mortal enemies like Spain, France, and Germany have not set foot on the island since 1066. The Civil War and the Glorious Revolution of the seventeenth century could have broken the country. Yet England, too, was lucky or, more precisely, sheltered by a maritime moat that thwarted foreign intervention. By contrast, the French Revolution attracted the major powers of Europe almost from the start, and in the existential struggle against the invaders, liberty lost out to terror and dictatorship.

By a stroke of good fortune, England's internal wars did not reaffirm tyranny, but improved substantially on the Magna Carta of 1215, the ur-document of the liberal state. With a little help from

William of Orange, who had been *invited* to intervene, Parliament put paid to absolutist royal power. Henceforth, the monarch could no longer suspend laws, levy taxes, appoint royal officials, or keep a standing army in peacetime without Parliament's say-so. These gains strengthened the separation of powers and the rule of law—historically the *conditio sine qua non* of liberal democracy. The liberal state had behavioral consequences for Britain and then for its American offspring, as we shall see.

Safety (or a fortunate geography) marks the critical difference between the island powers and history's other greats. Absent those existential perils that would torment Continental Europe (and China) all the way into the middle of the twentieth century, liberty found a much warmer climate in the Anglo-American world. Mortal threats from the outside usually favor despots on the inside who instinctively follow Henry IV's advice to his son and successor in the eponymous Shakespearean drama: "Be it thy course, dear Harry, to busy giddy minds with foreign quarrels." That was the best way to secure his personal rule, the dying king counseled. When core security—physical immunity—is given, bourgeois revolutions do not turn into Bonapartist dictatorships, nor republics (like Weimar Germany) into totalitarian systems. In such a benign setting, it is hard to wield the "primacy of foreign policy" to impose one-man rule. Without a sense of looming victimization, strongmen and the "garrison state"[13] cannot easily overwhelm democratic experiments. In short, no Hobbesian threat, no behemoth state.[14]

This happy career set Britain and the United States, the two first liberal states, apart from Europe's great powers. The civil religion of liberty, steeped in dissident Protestantism, did not keep them from amassing global empires. Britain's was real, stretching literally around the world to become history's largest. America's, give or take the Philippines, was essentially virtual. Both Anglo powers played diplomatic and military hardball with the worst of them, and they never stopped fighting. Both fought wars of aggression and aggrandizement. They owned and traded slaves. They conquered continents and in the process killed legions of natives. Yet theirs was still a liberal imperialism—certainly in terms of self-perception, and of deeds, as well. As liberal polities, they pursued selfish interests in ways that happened to serve others, too. Was it good sense or just serendipity? In any case, this coincidence defines the critical difference between liberal and traditional empires.

To illustrate the point, take a long line of European and Asian conquerors and compare their ways with the Anglo ways. Charles V and Philip II of Spain did not intend to bring the blessings of liberty to South America, not even to their own kind; the purpose was gold and silver, sugar and enslavement, plus personal aggrandizement. When these emperors went after France and Britain in the struggle for mastery, the aim was hegemony pure and simple. On the French side of this fateful struggle, Francis I simply wanted to control Italy and break Habsburg-Spain's stranglehold on the Continent.[15] Louis XIV, the Sun King, fought five wars in his lifetime not to extend *haute culture* to the Low Countries and Central Europe but to grab land and establish French supremacy. Napoleon started at the head of France's democratic revolution, then crowned himself emperor and proceeded to implant puppet regimes all over Europe.

When Frederick the Great launched Prussia's expansion by attacking Maria Theresa of Austria in 1740, he wasted no words on embellishing aggression. Instead, he listed "always ready troops," "well-filled coffers," and the "liveliness of my temperament" as reasons. Plus "ambition, interest and the desire to have people talk about me."[16] Wilhelm II, the next to reach for German hegemony, wanted a "place in the sun" for his Reich, as his chancellor put it. Hitler wanted to enslave and colonize Europe in the name of the "master race." Stalin promised earthly salvation, but delivered only oppression to his half of Europe. Their imperialism did not earn them loyalty, let alone friendship, and subjugation did not build a durable order. From Bonaparte to the red tsars of Russia, empire proved short-lived. Napoleon's and Hitler's lasted but a dozen years, Stalin's in Eastern Europe only fifty.

The British conquered, and with plenty of cant to mask selfish interest laced with racism and xenophobia, but in the process, as the historian Niall Ferguson puts it, they also disseminated "certain distinctive features of their own society."[17] Among them were the rule of law, the limited state, representative government, property, and the anti-hierarchical faith of Protestantism. All of these were liberal institutions in the sense that they limited power both temporal and ecclesiastical.

Domestic Order and International Conduct. Liberty and empire did not a harmonious couple make. This is how Winston Churchill put the clash between the two. For sure, the British Empire was progress incarnate. "What enterprise . . . of an enlightened community," he asked, "is more noble and more profitable than the reclamation from barbarism of fertile regions and large populations? To give peace to warring tribes, to administer justice . . . ?" Then he shifted to the dark side—the "ugly scaffolding" of goodness, another name for "ideology." Thus, "industrious races are displayed stinted and starved for the sake of an expensive Imperialism. . . . Wild peoples, . . . tenacious of liberty, are seen to resist with fury the philanthropic invaders." Among them were the "greedy trader, the inopportune missionary, the ambitious soldier, and the lying speculator." Given these "sinister features," how could one "believe that any fair prospect is approached by so foul a path"?[18]

By condemning "so foul a path," Churchill demonstrated a central characteristic of liberal empire: the faculty to cut through its own pretensions. France's and Spain's grandees never did, and those who raised their voices against Stalin and Hitler ended up in prison camp or dead. In China, critics are silenced, as well, and "reeducation camps" still dot the land. In Britain, a tyrannical governor-general of the East India Company, Warren Hastings, ended up in the court of the House of Commons in 1788, where Edmund Burke famously thundered, "I impeach him in the name of the English nation, whose ancient honor he had sullied. [And] in the name of the people of India, whose rights he has trodden under foot." Hastings was the "common enemy and oppressor of all."[19]

Scarcely fifty years later, Thomas Macaulay delivered a rousing speech in the Commons in which he recalled the company's "shameful abuses." In the next breath, he celebrated the achievements: "I see that we have established order where we found confusion." Britain had reconstructed "a decomposed society" done in by "all the evils of despotism and . . . anarchy."[20] This rosy Whig narrative of Britain as a progressive force wasn't just empty oratory. There were limits to what Britain could and would do; this is the central part of a story that distinguishes a liberal polity from standard empire.

A contemporary student of the empire, John Darwin, elucidates the many-faced nature of the beast:

Those who disliked one face of British imperialism could usually find an alternative, more liberal, human or respectful. *This was no accident.* It reflected the fact that by the eighteenth century at latest, Britain had become a remarkably pluralistic society, tolerating different religions, sustaining different subcultures (regional, religious, intellectual and class-based) and with a political system open to new wealth and new ideological influences [like evangelicalism and anti-slavery]. . . . Since the prime motive was profit, and not the glory of Church or king, this was an empire of commercial experiments, not an empire of rule by design.[21]

There are at least four differences between liberal empire and traditional empire.

Culture. An open culture, at least by the standards of the time, makes for an open empire. That is the rough-and-ready link between society and international system in the British and American case. It was conquest *and* co-optation, exploitation *and* inclusion—all the way to self-government in the lands of English settlement. The difference is the one between French Canada and British Canada: administration by royal officials vs. governance devolving to locals in the Anglophone parts, though under the Union Jack. Closed, hierarchical cultures like Imperial China, Ottoman Turkey, and Soviet Russia knew only satrapies, cherishing autonomy neither at home nor abroad. The liberal polity that took hold in Britain did not end at the water's edge but imprinted itself in varying degrees across its possessions.

Economy. Capitalism, arising first in the British realm, marks a second difference. The system allowed the economy to decouple from throne and altar. Capitalists worship money, not emperors, popes, or secular godheads like Lenin. Greed breeds acquisition, risk taking, and initiative, lengthening the distance to the powers that be at home as well as in Britain's possessions. Even better: Where soulless machines replace workers, power over men and land—the hallmark of preindustrial empires—matters less than mastery over the impersonal forces of capital and technology.

This shift in the "modes of production" turned freedom into a more compelling proposition than in feudal-agrarian societies. In those, the rulers, with the priesthood at their side, invented instruments and ideologies that tied their subjects to the land and kept them in thrall. Serfdom and subsistence agriculture were the norm. In the Spanish empire, the extraction of precious metals was based on forced labor. In the Russian and Habsburg empires, serfdom ended only in the middle of the nineteenth century. None of them exported freedom even to their own colonial overclass.

Not that the capitalist-industrialist system was so saintly. Yet it offered alternatives willy-nilly. People could free themselves from their overlords by migrating to the cities. Those who could not find a livelihood in the factories departed to the colonies, in particular to North America, where land was free and cheap. Britons went first, followed by Germans, Irish, and East Europeans escaping from want or oppression. Freedom exported itself, so to speak, turning tenants and serfs into freeholders and shopkeepers.[22] In this world, liberty was not just a lofty Lockean ideal but also a physical reality.

Religion. Faith helped as well. Max Weber, the great German sociologist, thought that Calvinist predestination spawned capitalism because earthly success presaged a man's future place in heaven. Hard work and riches foretold salvation. The theory has not withstood the test of comparative history. There is a better conceptual path from Protestantism to capitalism. The dissident version, which has been a pillar of Anglo-American culture, broke ecclesiastical monopolies—be they Catholic or Anglican—and so evened the playing field for the competitors of the cloth. As early as 1644, John Milton's *Aeropagitica* delivered a flaming plea for "the liberty to know, to utter, and to argue freely according to conscience." Once such "market barriers" are flattened, what is good for religion—the freedom to compete and succeed—is also good for the economic realm, breaking down privilege and protection. Capitalism, argues Walter Russell Mead in *God and Gold*, is both a "product" and a "motor" of an open society,[23] which in turn makes for an open empire.

For those who question such a shiny neo-Whig portrayal of Anglo culture, there is more hardheaded stuff to mark the difference. Britain outlawed slavery at home as early as 1772, and sixty years later throughout the empire; subsequently, the Royal Navy went after the slave trade on the Atlantic. The moral pressure came from a liberal society below; the state followed. Interest, of course, was also in play; the navy made sure rival nations wouldn't profit from a trade Britain had proscribed for itself. But whatever the intentions, the empire had produced a public moral good by prohibiting the trafficking in human lives.

Trade. Free trade was also a selfish interest that produced an international public good for the rest. The essence of a public good like an open trading system is that everybody can partake of it once it exists, and without having to pay for it. The principle came into full bloom with the abolition of the Navigation Acts in the mid-nineteenth century. For two hundred years, these had restricted foreign shipping between England and its colonies. Why the turn away from "managed trade," as it is called today? First, the Napoleonic Wars had undone Britain's mercantilist rivals, and the seas were now cleared of worthy opponents. Second, as "first industrializer," the island state enjoyed a profitable cost advantage in manufacturing; so free trade was a no-brainer, a boon to British industry. The third factor derives from a darker chapter of "early capitalism," which drew legions of uprooted peasants into the hellholes of Manchester and Leeds.

Low wages required low food prices, and so a rising manufacturing class went into combat against the landed gentry and won. Ideology helped as well. The industrialists were aided by disinterested liberals like David Ricardo, the economist, and parliamentary luminaries like John Bright and Richard Cobden who were motivated by the plight of Britain's urban poor. The import-restricting Corn Laws fell in 1846, opening up the country to cheap grain from the North American prairies. Thus, crass class interest added to the public good of free trade. It took the Continentals until the twentieth century to break the power of the landed classes, and some argue that it was the fateful alliance between "Iron" (German industry in the west) and "Rye" (the landed aristocracy in the east) that ended the free-trading career of Bismarckian Germany while stifling the country's democratic evolution.[24]

Balance of Power. A final example of the confluence between egotism and serendipity is the balance of power. "'Tis Britain's care to watch o'er Europe's fate," sang the poet Joseph Addison, "and hold in balance each contending state / To threaten bold presumptuous kings with war / And answer her afflicted neigbours' pray'r."[25] Two hundred years earlier, an admiring chronicler had celebrated

Elizabeth I as the "Umpire between the Spaniards, the French and the Estates," and "England was the Holder of the Balance."[26]

Unsurprisingly, the island nation developed an obsessive interest in chastening, as Winston Churchill put it, "the strongest or the potentially dominant tyrant"[27] across the Channel. For the most selfish of reasons, the British delivered a valuable service to the rest—all the way to the twentieth century when they took on Wilhelm, Hitler, and Stalin (though by then with a little help from their American cousins). Balance-of-power systems that preserve the independence of its members—another public good—don't manage themselves. Like all public goods, they need a leader who organizes the coalitions and keeps them going. Even better is a mastermind who does not go for mastery himself, but acts according to the maxim. Do for yourself, do for others as a by-product, and then leave well enough alone.

So after Napoleon's defeat, the Foreign Office laid down the principle that staying in Europe "will necessarily involve us deeply in all the politics of the Continent, whereas our true policy has always been not to interfere except in great emergencies." Worse, there were domestic costs to consider. So the instruction stressed that the people of Britain might fear for their liberties, seeing the court consorting with "great despotic monarchs" who were scheming to quell the "revolutionary spirit."[28] In other words, staying aloof and keeping a watchful eye on the balance of power was good for Britain's freedom as well as for Europe's.

Call it serendipity or selfishness—the fact is that the Anglo nations, which rode to primacy on the back of a liberal-capitalist order, pursued careers quite distinct from other imperial powers. What Britain began, the United States continued. It started with the Barbary Wars just a couple of decades after independence.

With Britain gone, American shipping was no longer protected by the Royal Navy. North African pirate states were capturing and enslaving American as well as European seamen, trading them for ransom or demanding tribute. In 1801, Thomas Jefferson dispatched a naval squadron; the war—actually two—was won in 1815, and piracy ended in those waters. The United States did it for itself; other Western nations plying the Mediterranean profited— that is the essence of international public goods.

Liberal Empire Made in U.S.A.

Young America, born as a WASP republic, was the child of Britain and the Scottish-English Enlightenment. Both played a power game quite distinct from the ways of their rivals whose ideas about man and the state were rooted in feudalism and absolutism—from Spain and France to Russia and China. The difference between the Anglo and the Continental Enlightenment is the one between Locke and Hume, on one side of the Channel, and Rousseau and Voltaire, on the other. The islanders put the individual and his conscience at the center of their universe, whence tolerance, republicanism, and democracy followed. Rousseau's central concept was the "general will," philosophically a liberal idea, given that it was to promulgate only what *everybody* could accept and so enslave none. In historical practice, the *volonté générale* paved the way to the totalitarianism of the French Revolution, which dealt with the individual by breaking him, and with tolerance by abolishing Christianity and imposing a fanatical secular creed. "Ecrasez l'infâme"—crush the infamous church—Voltaire famously thundered.

Naturally, young America thought it had invented something completely new under the sun—the *novus ordo seclorum*: no more

coldhearted reason of state and power mongering. Such evil machinations were the corrupt games of princes and potentates. "I have,"
wrote Jefferson "but one system of ethics for men & for nations—to
be grateful, to be faithful to all engagements and, under all circumstances, to be open & generous." The new morality would promote
"in the long run even the interests of both."[29] This was an early
definition of a public good. And yet, goodness had its limits; balance-of-power politics made an early debut in American thinking.

Before long, Alexander Hamilton postulated in the *Federalist
No. 11*: "We may hope to become the arbiter of Europe in America,
and to be able to incline the balance of European competitions in
this part of the world. . . ." If you can't boot them out, read this
maxim, then balance among them. Still in infancy, the Republic
engaged in power politics as if tutored by Richelieu, pitting France
against Britain after independence and playing all the great powers
against one another in order to grab half a continent. Never has
peaceful expansion or, more accurately, "peaceable coercion" been
so profitable.[30]

There were liberal ideals, and there were hardheaded interests.
Yet the new ideology did color the interests throughout American
history. "Open covenants, openly arrived at," the first of Woodrow Wilson's "Fourteen Points," echoes Jefferson's injunction "to be
open & generous." Jefferson's "one system of ethics for men & for
nations" foreshadowed the human rights rhetoric of Franklin D.
Roosevelt, Jimmy Carter, and Ronald ("Mr. Gorbachev, tear down
this Wall") Reagan. Tainted as it was by realpolitik, the idealism
of America's latter-day presidents still cannot be separated from
Jefferson's exalted conceptions of what America *should* be and do.

Take free trade, an early American idea that defied the mercantilist spirit of the times. Was it driven by ideals or interests?

Freedom of navigation and trade were informed by *both*, which is the key point—the ideals nicely reinforced the interests. As early as 1776, the Model Treaty laid down the most-favored nation rule for America's intercourse with the rest—not quite free trade, but a liberal design nonetheless because it transcended the reigning system of exclusive access to ports, routes, and partners.

Vast open spaces and agricultural surpluses demanded markets for American exports; that was the interest, a mercantilist classic. Yet idealists like Jefferson's Republicans favored imports, as well—the very opposite of the old zero-sum game, where winning meant selling more and buying less. The motive was part and parcel of the *novus ordo seclorum* ideology. How so? Stuff bought abroad would keep manufacturing from America's shores, a good thing. For the Republic must not become like Europe. To preserve its liberty and undercut class strife, to maintain a "healthy society," the nation had to live the simple life of freeholding farmers instead of separating into rich and poor, owners and workers. For that reason, counseled Jefferson, "let our workshops remain in Europe."[31] The Europeans must have clapped their hands in delight over such naïveté.

Ideals and interests meshed in yet another way. A nation with a tiny army and a measly navy could not fight the established powers for trade routes and privileges. Nor should the young polity *want* a large standing army, which was a threat to republican liberty. As Jefferson put it, "our constitution is a peace establishment—it is not calculated for war," which "would endanger its existence."[32] Trade, according to the liberal faith, was inherently peaceable, hence a perfect substitute for war. It would advance the mutual interest and prevent ruinous fighting. "War is not the best engine for us to resort to; nature has given us one *in our commerce*, which, if properly managed, will be a better instrument for obliging . . . Europe to treat us with justice."[33]

Another early and consequential precedent is America's second war against Britain. The War of 1812 was the "strangest in American history."[34] Why take on the mightiest navy on earth? This second round was fought for some of the traditional reasons—honor, power, and aggrandizement. The British were impressing American sailors into their navy. They were supporting Indian tribes standing in the way of westward expansion. Northward enlargement beckoned as well; so why not grab a piece of Canada, a dream that had failed in the Revolutionary War? The major interest, though, was the freedom of navigation and trade across the Atlantic, which Britain was trying to control in its mortal struggle against Napoleon. Thus, the freedom of the seas, a public good, was imprinted early on in the American DNA, though the ideal of free trade was hardly an iron law. As the nineteenth century progressed, the United States, like all developing nations, became a high-tariff country. The average peaked at 45 percent in 1870; today it is 1.3 percent.

Still, Jeffersonian idealism, though conveniently framed by self-interest, made for a commercial policy quite different from France's in the eighteenth or China's in the twenty-first century.[35] Rather than "more for me, less for you," it was the Open Door, a liberal trading order that would deliver free access and trade to all. Such lofty principles were, of course, particularly useful for a young nation up against established powers that had carved up the world's commerce among themselves. Yet the rest, too, stood to benefit from the self-serving rhetoric. According to the liberal faith promulgated by Smith, Ricardo, and colleagues, *everybody* would profit. Even better, unfettered economic intercourse would lift the curse of war from the world. Why conquer if you can trade peacefully and get rich without shedding a drop of blood? Mutual gain beats mutual mayhem.[36] As economic warfare leads to war, economic cooperation leads to peace—this conviction runs through American history from the founding fathers until this day.

In modern American parlance, the magic word is "interdependence," a robust web of international relations that would guarantee peace and cooperation. Samuel Berger, Bill Clinton's national security adviser, sounded like Jefferson redivivus:

> We have consciously tried to define and pursue our interests in a way that is consistent with the common good. . . . Consider our economic policies. In the last few years, we have . . . fought for open markets, here and abroad [and] the impact on the world . . . has been remarkable. . . . [T]he President quite deliberately undertook to keep our markets open, knowing our trade deficit would increase substantially. As a result, we made a bigger contribution than any other country toward easing the [Asian financial] crisis. . . . [37]

The tone was self-congratulatory, a classic of great-power oratory. Yet the underlying message was that of a liberal empire whose interests are rooted in a liberal domestic order. Russian or Chinese officials rarely articulate the national interest in such a universalist language.

AMERICA AS XXL BRITAIN

Informing interest and action, ideology is not just window dressing. It reflects historical experience and, in the British and American case, a happy, insular existence that vindicated the Liberal creed. That is the continuity between Jefferson and Obama. It took until the twentieth century for America to become Britain writ large. In that tortured century, the United States fought three very large wars (one cold) à la Britain—not to overturn but to restore the balance. The purpose was not conquest but order, a public good prized by leaders as well as followers. The United States fought like Britain, which according to Churchill, had always taken up arms against whoever sought to unify Europe under his knout. The United States saved Europe from Wilhelm II, Adolf Hitler, and Joseph Stalin. In East Asia, it did the same by defeating Imperial Japan; in the Cold War, the United States held the line against Stalin's successors around the world until the Soviet Union collapsed.

Much has been made of American isolationism, the opposite of public-goods production, in the interwar period. There was indeed withdrawal after World War I and the refusal to join the League of Nations, the forerunner of the UN. The consequences were catastrophic, as the rise of fascism and World War II would show. Still, the United States quickly reengaged on the economic front. It was obviously in the American interest to restore Europe's economies so as to regain healthy customers for its exports. The problem was Germany, which was being bled dry by astronomical reparations charges. How could Weimar Germany buy if it could not pay? American self-interest was clearly the engine, but it was deployed in such a way as to pull Europe's cars along as well.

Acting for the government, the Chicago banker Charles G. Dawes proposed to lighten the burden until Germany could carry it. A $200 million ($2.7 billion current) loan was floated in the United States and quickly oversubscribed. So much goodness was also good for American capitalism. The United States lent money to Germany, which it used for reparations to France and Britain. In turn, these could repay their war loans from the United States. The recycling was nonetheless a boon for the entire Western economy, as the Roaring Twenties showed. In 1928, Owen D. Young promised a new loan of $300 million. The Crash of 1929 put an end to such calculated generosity, but Young's brainchild—the Bank of International Settlements— exists to this day. Thus did self-interest segue into an institution that presaged the towering institutional architecture the United States erected after World War II.

Was it empire building? Yes, but light-years away from what Persia, Rome, or Soviet Russia did. Some, like the UN founded in San Francisco in 1944, were universally inclusive. Others, like the trade-promoting GATT or the liquidity-generating IMF,[38] were empire by invitation: you can join if you meet the membership criteria. Again others—NATO and regional compacts like SEATO (Southeast Asia) and CENTO (Middle East)—were traditional alliances, but with a new twist. In the classic ways of public-goods production, the United States assumed the largest burden; indeed, these institutions were more like unilateral security guarantees than coalitions of equals.

Evidently, all these organizations served American interests in a big way. NATO was America's forward defense against the Muscovite empire, but it also sheltered Europe from the Atlantic to the Elbe River. The IMF, a global lender of last resort, gushed forth dollars that funded Europe's recovery and eventually found their way back into the American economy. Still, what was good for the United States was also good for the rest, which was hungering for scarce capital in the days of the "dollar gap."

The Marshall Plan, worth $30 billion in today's money, jump-started Europe's shattered economies and so turned them into profitable outlets for America's agri-industrial machine. It was a two-way blessing—and more. The condition of American largesse was European unity: Western Europe as a whole, the German pariah included, would have to apply as one. This was the birth of European integration and the beginning of the end of the "arch enmity" between Gaul and German. For suddenly there was a bigger player in the game who would protect each against the other, and both against the Soviet Union. Previous empires have also leashed warring tribes, but they never tried to unify them.

By the light of traditional power politics, European unification, both political and economic, was a woolly-headed project for an imperial power. Yet this American interest made perfect sense in terms of an ideology that saw the near suicide of Europe rooted in the bad old ways the *novus ordo* had transcended. The logic, laid out in copious official oratory, went as follows: National sovereignty had bred rivalry and war, which, in turn, had favored tyranny. Political unity would eliminate the prime cause of bloodshed, while economic well-being would nourish democracy. And democracy, according to the Liberal faith, would finally spell peace in Western Europe—just the kind of sturdy order America wanted for itself, especially in its global struggle against the Soviet Union. Thus, realpolitik and idealpolitik came together in a mutually beneficial marriage.

Here is a typical example of the creed: "Peace and stability are the very cornerstones of prosperity. When our diplomats and military forces combine to help create stability and security in a . . . region, that same stability and security attracts investment. Investment generates prosperity. And prosperity strengthens democracy, which creates more stability and more security." The world has never seen a more virtuous circle, this portrayal of American grand strategy suggested. But there is even more. For "there is only one nation with the power and reach to fill this role," namely the United States.[39] So virtue came with its own reward, which was the validation of American leadership.

To deflate such rhetoric as mere posturing misses the larger point. Those who justly admire the grand experiment of European integration might recall that it was Big Brother from across the sea who set the stage and built the shelter. By becoming a power in Europe for its own reasons, America delivered ample benefits to the rest. The United States was protector, pacifier, and start-up "angel" rolled into one.[40] Add Japan, Taiwan, and South Korea to the list. Assuming a role Britain had played only fitfully, the United States was pursuing its own advantage by systematically producing international public goods. Traditional empires, built on possession, control, and servitude, had other fish to fry. It did not enter into the minds of Romans or Ottomans to turn their Middle Eastern conquests into an "Arab Union," let alone into a future economic competitor. Nor does such thinking inspire today's might-be global powers, whether China, India, or Russia, where zero-sum thinking prevails. It takes a liberal polity to build a liberal empire that benefits more than just itself.

THE DEFAULT POWER

Institution building was yesterday, financed by a surfeit of American power and money, and driven by the imperatives of the Cold War. This cosmic conflict over, America faces a different world in the twenty-first century. Power has indeed diffused. Other nations, like China, are rising. Post-Soviet Russia is eager for a comeback.

Europe is rich and populous. Japan, even after twenty years of stagnation, is still the world's third-largest economy. India will be the youngest large nation in midcentury. Power has also diversified, as Terror International demonstrated even before 9/11. Though it lacks strategic punch, Islamist terror keeps imposing gargantuan "transaction taxes" on the world, ranging from millions of work hours lost waiting in airport checkpoint lines to the billions spent on huge internal security apparatuses like the new U.S. Homeland Security Department. It eats up $70 billion per annum and employs a quarter of a million people.[41]

Power is a most elusive concept, and yet it stands at the center of the Declinist debate. The three eternal issues are: What is it, who has it, who is losing it? The answer that springs to mind first focuses on physical assets, the "cash" a nation has in the bank: riches, armies, population. The next answer fastens on "cash flows," the dynamics of power—up or down? In the last sixty years, the spectacular growth of up-and-coming economies has been routinely invoked to illustrate America's decline. Yet a closer look at the fortunes of nations bids us to be wary.

Europe and Japan, the champions of the 1960s and 1970s, have drifted into slow or no growth. Worse, Europe's weight is shrinking. At fault isn't just the deadly crisis of its common currency that erupted in the second decade of the twenty-first century. Behind the battle for the euro lurked long-term economic decline. Growth has fallen decade by decade since the heady seventies; ever since, the EU's share of the global product has shrunk by ten percentage points in real terms (see table III). Japan has been imprisoned in secular stagnation and the developed world's worst debt-to-GDP ratio. Soviet Russia has simply disappeared, and its heir's riches remain tied to the price of natural resources. China, as we peer into the second decade of this century, may be slowing, following the natural trajectory of start-up economies and bumping against the built-in limits of modernitarianism—authoritarian modernization.

Clearly, power has spread across this new world, but primacy is more than physical assets. As the EU shows, GDP and population are not enough to tilt the global scales. If they were, Europe would have intervened in Serbia and Libya without American help. India and Brazil, the two BRIC stars, bring size and weight to the table, but not much beyond modest regional ambitions balanced by large neighbors. What Argentina is to Brazil, nuclear-armed China, Russia, and Pakistan are to India, only more so. Not for India and Brazil the toils and troubles of the world, not even a strategic blueprint for a great-power future to come.

If assets are but a necessary condition of primacy, what other chips must a nation invest? With its one billion people and economic growth, India best exemplifies the difference between "necessary" and "sufficient." To make the cut, it takes a broad array of material and immaterial assets. The material resources are economic, financial, and military. But just as critical are the immaterial advantages: global interests and responsibilities.

Measured against these benchmarks, India is a very large country, indeed, a subcontinent, but not a global player. Harking back to an old tradition of nonalignment, India prefers abstention to commitment in forums like the UN Security Council. Indifference or diffidence tends to dwarf involvement. The giant does not project power beyond the Indian Ocean. Its size and population are not matched by the country's cultural draw. Unlike the United States, India exports rather than imports brains, giving away the twenty-first century's most precious "natural resource." India churns out ten times more movies per year than Hollywood.

Yet, the Oscar-winning *Slumdog Millionaire* (2009), celebrated as Bollywood's global breakthrough, was actually made by a British director and three British companies.

Lasting primacy or leadership requires a certain culture or mindset—what the French call *prise de conscience*, a global outlook and vocation. It also requires a global toolbox, ranging from projection forces via alliances and commercial-financial networks to the intangible conditions of influence. Among those are the English language as the "operating system" of the world's economy. International transactions are not usually conducted in Russian or Chinese, and once a standard exists, it tends to perpetuate itself—just like the dollar, which for all its ups and downs will not soon yield to the euro or the renminbi. Nor will Chinese, Russian, or Indian culture soon shoulder aside the American version—high or low—whose draw is embodied by Harvard and Hollywood. History supports the point. As "operating systems," Latin and French outlived the strategic preeminence of Rome and France. By such measures, no other rival, not even China, the star of Decline 5.0, comes close to America, whatever the country's many familiar failings and the riches of the rising rest.

How the United States Is Different. The United States, to recapitulate, is no Rome, which used to be conterminous with the international system of the time. It enjoys neither supremacy nor an unlimited writ across the planet. It is not first in all disciplines, but it surpasses all other contestants in the decathlon. Call it "primacy" or "being No. 1." A more useful term is "default power."[42] In technology, "default" is the state to which a system returns when new settings prove deficient or deleterious. In international politics, a "default power" is a nation to which others look when nobody else steps forward. The United States is the Default Power that occupies center stage because it does what other actors cannot or will not do. America's default role implies that it defines the issue, sets the agenda, and convenes the rest. If it comes to collective action, this Default Power usually assumes the largest burden and acquires most of the shares. In a truly competitive multipolar system, other actors would press forward. Yet Europe, China, Russia, Japan, or India rarely, if ever, do. Hence the default phenomenon.

The examples abound. When tribal slaughter devastated Rwanda, the United States did not intervene, but neither did anybody else. A decade later, the same fate befell the Darfur region of Sudan; when the United States held back, nobody else stepped up to stop the mayhem. Following on the Kyoto Protocol, the UN climate conferences in Copenhagen (2009), Durban (2011), and Doha (2012), where the United States did not put its shoulder to the wheel, spawned no new commitment on CO_2 reduction, but ample mutual recrimination. Crowds ranging from 10,000 to 17,000 participants do not produce public goods unless there is a leader who recruits a coalition of the willing that sets the agenda and pressures the fence-sitters. When civil war broke out in Syria in 2011, the United States refrained from the use of force,[43] but so did everybody else, above all, the rising rest: China, Russia, India, and Brazil.

In the First Iraq War, it was the United States that harnessed a coalition of thirty members to expel Saddam Hussein from Kuwait. At the end of the 1990s, it was neither the UN nor the EU that led the charge against Serbian expansionism and "ethnic cleansing," but the U.S. Air Force. After 9/11, the United States marshaled virtually a global alliance of belligerents and supporters to defeat the Taliban in Afghanistan. Even during the Second

Iraq War (2003), when a noisy wave of anti-Americanism coursed through the world, George W. Bush managed to corral more than thirty nations. In recent memory, only one country—France—has ridden out in front. The French charged ahead in 2011 against Libya's Muammar Khadafy, and in 2013 against Islamists in Mali. But when its European followers ran out of ordnance in the Libyan campaign, they had to borrow it from the United States, which also supplied the space-based and battlefield surveillance.

This side of military action, the Default Power bundles the many strands of global diplomacy. It was Jimmy Carter who convened Egypt and Israel in Camp David in 1978, extracting a historic peace agreement from both. It was Bill Clinton who forced Yitzhak Rabin and the PLO's Yasser Arafat to shake hands in the Rose Garden of the White House in 1993. These two examples are particularly instructive. Why the United States rather than Europe, Russia, or China, actors that all take a major interest in the Middle East? Because a successful "honest broker" must have lots of chips, both symbolic and material—authority, clout, and (literally) cash to spare.

No other player in the Middle East has them all. Authority or legitimacy implies a broker who can count on receptive partners in Jerusalem as well as in Arab capitals. They may hate each other, but they will listen to a credible go-between who is willing to put his prestige on the line. Power delivers two additional advantages. First, clients want to remain on the good side of a mediator who has the capacity to reward and to punish. Second, a convener stronger than either can ensure both against the consequences of misplaced credulity. The United States was, and remains, the security lender of the last resort for Israel while also acting as implicit protector of whatever Arab player chooses to treat with Jerusalem, be it Egypt or the Palestinian Authority.

The Default Power can give and withhold vital benefits. China et al. will not or cannot put up the necessary resources. These are authority and the ability to bribe and to blackmail. Where pressure does not work, side payments will. Thus, Egypt and Israel have enjoyed double-digit billions in military aid since Camp David. More recently, the annual $1.3 billion arms subsidy to Egypt gave the United States leverage over post-Mubarak Egypt. Even an Islamist Egypt will not lightly risk this lifeline by abrogating the peace treaty with Israel. If peace ever comes to Israelis and Palestinians, it will be brokered by Washington, the world's only player willing and able to underwrite the security of either—and bribe them with subsidies, to boot.

Bill Clinton proclaimed the United States an "indispensable nation" in 1997; Barack Obama used exactly the same term three administrations later, adding, "Even [in] countries where the United States is criticized, they still want our leadership, and they still look to us to make sure that we're providing opportunity and peace."44 Such rhetoric may smack of triumphalism, but it rolls "default power" and "public goods" into one—the two assets that constitute the unique advantage of American diplomacy.

When it comes to preventing the spread of nuclear weapons, a top item on the global agenda, the United States does the orchestrating. The Six-Party Talks with North Korea were organized by the America of George W. Bush, who was more "criticized," as Obama politely put it, than any other recent president. When Iran came forward with a proposal on its nuclear program, it addressed Bush's America first—in May 2003, the month following on the frightful display of American military power in Iraq. Subsequently, the EU and Russia waded in. These forays went nowhere. By 2005, the Bush administration had started turning the sanctions screw in earnest, pulling the UN and the EU along. By 2012, the EU had joined the United States in an oil embargo, while Iran was cut off from the international banking system. How to explain the consent? A nonnuclear Iran is an international public good cherished from Lisbon to Riyadh, yet none of its would-be consumers can produce it without the United States' taking the lead and backing it up with the threat of coercion.[45]

Regional and Global Balances. The Default Power does what others cannot or will not do. The United States is the only player in the game that, like Britain in the past, preserves regional balances and ties them together globally.[46] The United States underwrites Europe's security against a resurgent Russia; hence American troops remain welcome even twenty years after Moscow's surrender in the Cold War. The United States helps the Europeans to take care of local malfeasants like Serbia's Slobodan Milosevic or Libya's Muammar Khadafy. It counters whoever reaches for mastery over the Middle East, recalling Churchill's famous line about always opposing "the strongest, most aggressive, most dominating Power on the Continent." This had "nothing to do with rulers or nations; it is concerned solely with whoever is the strongest or dominant tyrant."[47] Balancing trumped kinship and previous loyalties.

The United States has followed the same icy logic. It has armed Israel against Soviet clients like Egypt and Syria. Yet when Cairo bolted from the Soviet embrace, it became America's first choice among the Arabs. Iraq was coddled, then coerced. The United States helped Saddam Hussein, the worst tyrant in the region, against Khomeini's Iran in the Gulf War of 1980–88, though Baghdad had started it. When Saddam occupied Kuwait, threat-ening the oil fields of Saudi Arabia, the United States turned on its onetime protégé, defanging Iraq in the wars of 1991 and 2003. Ever since, the target of containment (and possibly war) has been Iran, though under the Shah it had been a pillar of U.S. strategy in the Middle East. Such flexibility was the hallmark of "perfidious Albion" in centuries past.

After Reza Pahlavi's fall in 1979, Khomeinist Iran, the new pretender to regional hegemony, became a natural target of American attention. It fielded a revolutionary Shia ideology that recalled the expansionist doctrines of Nazi Germany and Communist Russia. It threatened Sunni neighbors with terror and subversion, and Israel by proxy—Hamas in the south and Hezbollah in the north. Finally, Iran was obsessively working on nuclear weapons and long-range missilery. The United States has therefore been leading the sanctions alliance against Tehran, with war an ever-present option. The Fifth Fleet—there is no other—remains close to Gulf waters.

While supporting the cause of the Palestinians, the United States guarantees the survival of Israel, Jordan, the Gulf States, and ultimately Egypt. Hence, Israelis and Arabs have all carried their complaints to Washington, even in the days of George W. Bush. When he convened the Middle East conference in Annapolis in 2007, all forty invitees came—Arabs, Europeans, and Asians. It strains the imagination to see Europe, Russia, India, or China in that role, important though the Middle East is to all of them. This foursome lacks clout, credibility, and commitment. In the Syrian civil war, it was the United States that would lead military action against the regime's chemical weapons.

Farther afield, in the Great Game of Central Asia, the United States offers itself as silent protector against Russian attempts to craft a sphere of domination where it once ruled over captive peoples. Having led the renewed battle against the Taliban, the United States will not again wash its hands of Afghanistan, as it did after quick victory in 2002. Washington signals ever so softly that it will sequester Pakistan's nuclear weapons if chaos widens into collapse. At the same time, the United States is the only player who can rein in both Pakistan and India, and protect each against the other. India has been drawn into the American orbit and so adds to the informal balance against China that the United States is orchestrating in East Asia. Dreams of Asia rising may founder on a strategic reality that has been—and remains—centered on the United States as guarantor of regional security. Whether Vietnam or Japan, South Korea or Australia—they all count on the United States to keep China on its best behavior, and Japan from going nuclear.

Pivoting to the Pacific. Though intermittently overshadowed by America's wars in Korea and Vietnam, Europe remained the central arena of the Forty Years' War, aka Cold War. In Germany, the regional and global balance came together as one—with one million men stationed on either side of the Iron Curtain. In the worst moments, 300,000 American troops and thousands of tactical nuclear weapons were deployed in the European theater. By the beginning of the 2010s, the nuclear stockpile had dwindled to about 200, and the force to 30,000. The Europeans were not wringing their hands in despair. Gone was the Soviet Union, whose shock troops used to be dug in at the gates of Hamburg. Europe, the greatest prize of the Cold War, currently faces no strategic threat as far as the eye (and space-based sensors) can see. Neither does the United States fear a remake of those conflicts that sucked it into Europe three times in the twentieth century—from hot to cold war.

A strategic era had come to an end, hence the "rebalancing" or "pivot" to the Pacific, the central arena of the twenty-first century, where the United States faces China as the new challenger. The game is far more subtle than in the days of Nazi Germany and Soviet Russia. One critical difference is the one between a revolutionary and a revisionist power. Revisionists like Wilhelmine Germany want a "place in the sun" that certifies their new status as a great power. They want a seat at the table and a privileged say in world affairs. They want access, respect, spheres of influence, in short, a larger slice of the global pie.

Revolutionary powers like Hitler's Germany and Bolshevik Russia don't just want more for themselves. Driven by a consuming ideology that has allegedly put them on the right side of history, they want to change the game itself—to overturn the table, so to speak. Recall Leon Trotsky, the first foreign affairs commissar, who preached the "permanent revolution" that would prevail "not only in one country but in all the leading countries of the world."[48] Hitler didn't just want to break the chains of the Versailles settlement or gain a bit more lebensraum. He wanted to crush, kill, and enslave—to build a new Germanic order on the ruins of the old state system. Promising young Nazis, groomed in special Adolf Hitler Schools, dreamed of becoming "governor in Chicago," as one of them confided to this author decades later.

Revolutionary nations like Iran today cannot be appeased; they must either be defeated or quarantined until the "breakup" or "mellowing" of their power, as George F. Kennan famously put it when he designed the containment of the Soviet Union. For all its Communist coloration, China is merely a revisionist power that wants more, but not all. Such powers are amenable to a deal that confirms their new status and position. Yet whatever the accommodation, their might must be balanced in the traditional ways—by armaments and alliances, by deterrence and diplomacy. This is precisely the thrust of American grand strategy in the twenty-first century.

It is "not a Cold War situation," as Secretary of Defense Leon Panetta put it in a programmatic speech in 2012; "this is a different world." Nor is the United States in Asia what it used to be in Europe. Then it was American divisions on the ground; now it is American fleets across the Pacific. Then the United States assembled a tightly integrated alliance with a huge standing army under the control of an American supreme commander. Now it is orchestration, not integration. Then the United States put itself directly in harm's way with men and nuclear weapons. Variously known as "trip wire" and "forward defense," the posture signaled to the Soviet Union: If you attack our allies, you will have to attack America itself. In Asia, Japan and South Korea were similarly sheltered. Tying America's hands would reassure allies and disillusion adversaries. It was bonding rather than balancing à l'anglaise. Now it is a new mix—free or only loosely tied hands—that will outlive Barack Obama's eight years in office.

The purpose, shades of Britain again, is to minimize costs and to maximize options. It isn't just "pivoting" from one theater to another. The revised strategy is tilted toward balancing, though not as systematically or exclusively as in the British case. Britain never committed to permanent alliances, opportunistically recruiting coalitions as the need arose. Outside its colonies, Britain usually dispatched expeditionary forces only during war. To project power, Her Majesty's Government relied on fleets, the rule being offshore balancing. Britain's American heir is keeping a larger bundle of arrows in the quiver, ranging from long-standing alliances via à la carte commitments to over-the-horizon balancing with mobile forces.

As in the Cold War, it remains bonding by way of formal treaties with Japan, South Korea, and Australia, and with troops on the ground in all three places. Farther away, bases strung out across the Pacific form a second tier of ready and reinforcable forces. Guam and Hawaii are two key staging areas. World War II bases like Tinian in the Marianas have been refurbished in a move fraught with symbolism. For this is where the B–29s took off that rained nuclear devastation on Hiroshima and Nagasaki in 1945. Minor bases with growth potential are located in Thailand, Singapore, and the Philippines. Cam Ranh Bay in Vietnam is an offstage candidate likely to move toward the center if China increases pressure on the country, once a colony for a thousand years.

"Rebalancing" toward Asia comes in the guise of a much-touted "60–40" shift. The U.S. Navy will homeport 60 percent of its vessels in bases along the Pacific by 2020. Only 40 percent will remain in Atlantic waters, down from one-half in decades past. Such is the lineup for the "different world" of the twenty-first century, as Leon Panetta put it during the first Obama administration. In this world, the United States will no longer "simply charge in" and "build permanent bases." Instead, it will assert its power in a precautionary manner by fielding its own forces and outsourcing security to others. It will be "rotational deployments and exercises" so as to help "other nations" to "develop their own security." Anybody can join this Pacific orchestra, "including Myanmar," with the United States as conductor.[49]

It is both burden shifting and burden shedding. It is synergism à la Albion plus regional security against China—balance-of-power politics plus public-goods production in the classic way of twentieth-century America. Is this lower profile a response to Decline 5.0? The old-new strategy is certainly more economical, flexible, and subtle than yesterday's. Rather than a concession to weakness, the policy is tailored to a muted, not yet mature rivalry that doesn't replicate the "children of darkness vs. children of light" struggle against the Soviet Union. Mercifully absent is the revolutionary impetus that animated the Soviet general secretary Nikita Khrushchev to fling his apocalyptical "We shall bury you!" against the West in 1956. China's ambition is not ideological but geopolitical, and victory neither urgent nor foregone. Mercifully present is a manifold mutual dependency. China's astronomical dollar surpluses hinge on an open American market. Mutual deterrence functions on many levels, and it is encased by caution and cooperation.

And yet it is "advantage U.S.A.," as they call out on the tennis court, and for reasons both structural and cultural. The Default Power's position in Asia resembles Britain's in Europe as guardian of the status quo (though by no means in the rest of the world, where it was expansion and conquest). The balancer is never the "balancee," the player against which others unite. It is the anchor of the system, hence a boon for the rest. It is not selfless *noblesse* that confers the conductor's baton on the United States, but the revisionist dragon overshadowing the Pacific. With its growing muscle and weight, China poses a threat to its neighbors willy-nilly, no matter what its ambitions might be (though plentiful they are). Naturally, all the others—from tiny Singapore to 250 million Indonesians—look to the status quo power that is America. It has the interest in holding off China, and it has the means. The United States roams the Pacific with the world's most awesome projection forces.

Some Pacific nations might tacitly or formally bandwagon with

Beijing, an ever-present choice for those who are up against an overweening power next door. But history does not record many instances where weaker states have ganged up on the balancer, which is the United States. So they all look to the United States: Tokyo, Canberra, Jakarta, Hanoi, Singapore, Bangkok, Seoul. . . . The reason, it bears stressing, is structural, and neither accidental nor ideological. It is safer to seek shelter under the wings of a distant patron than to slip into the embrace of a nearby giant with a long history of expansion and domination.

A default power is the player to which others turn when they cannot score on their own. In this role, the United States profits not only from hard structural realities but also from its peculiar culture and tradition. Revisionists—add Russia—are in the game for themselves, viewing it as a zero-sum contest where their own gain is another's loss. Self-interest unalloyed by attention to the common interest makes for submission, not for loyalty. "More for myself and less for you" breeds fear rather than consent. Such a posture also threatens the existing order, hence each and all.

The challenge is perennially manifested in Beijing's claim to various pieces of the South China Sea where China rubs up against so many players: Japan, Indonesia, the Philippines, Taiwan, Vietnam, and Malaysia. China is not in the public-goods business that envelops self-seeking into shared benefits such as order and stability; such a vocation is not a conspicuous feature of Chinese imperial history. History in general does not abound with authoritarian or totalitarian regimes that have respected the independence of the rest while assuming responsibility for the greater good.

The United States hails from a different tradition. Practically from day one, and certainly after World War II, the American Republic has harkened to a liberal ideology that, by intent or good fortune, has softened the *sacro egoismo* of states with the balm of the wider interest. The creed of a liberal empire does not guarantee benevolence, as America's many imperial ventures show, starting with the power politics practiced by the founding fathers that netted them victory over Britain and half a continent. Yet a liberal polity comes with the mindset and the habits that turn zero-sum into non-zero-sum games. When "liberal" trumps "empire," the United States has been able to transform raw power into consent, and selfish ambitions into authority. Among the world's heavyweights, liberal-democratic Europe could play the same role, but it lacks the global outlook and means.

THE PROSPECTS OF AMERICAN POWER

In 2011, a Chinese scholar representing a think tank of the State Security Ministry delivered a remarkable assessment of American power at Washington's Woodrow Wilson Center.[50] Reporting on a study of his institute, he listed fifteen components. Ten, he argued, were American advantages in the global contest:

1. Population, geographic position, and natural resources.
2. Military muscle.
3. High technology and education.
4. Cultural/soft power.
5. Cyber power.
6. Allies, the United States having more than any other state.
7. Geopolitical strength, as embodied in global projection forces.
8. Intelligence capabilities, as demonstrated by the killing of Osama bin Laden.

9. Intellectual power, fed by a plethora of U.S. think tanks and the "revolving door" between research institutions and government.
10. Strategic power, the United States being the world's only country with a truly global strategy.

On the other hand, the United States has lost ground in terms of:

1. Political power, as manifested by the breakdown of bipartisanship.
2. Economic power, as illustrated by the post-2007 slowdown.
3. Financial power, given intractable deficits and rising debt.
4. Social power, as weakened by societal polarization.
5. Institutional power, since the United States can no longer dominate global institutions.

What follows? First, a rhetorical point. China, at least this official analyst, may be less impressed by American failings than are Declinists inside and elsewhere outside the United States. Second, this assessment—the good and the bad—is largely on target, with a sober sense of what matters in world politics. Third, the analysis confirms the metaphor of the Decathlon Power as ahead in most, but not all, disciplines, be they hard or soft. Finally, as four of the five loss leaders show, America's future will be determined at home.

The Reticent Power. In the end, the three D's of Deficits, Debt, and Dysfunctionality will claim their due. Such dire warnings have been uttered from Decline 1.0 to 5.0, though without materializing. They are easy to make because they come without a date.

Yet beware. Just because Declinists have always been wrong does not guarantee that they will never be right. Empires *do* fall and disappear. On the other hand, America's defects do not spell out the *Mene, Tekel* of biblical prophecy; the fate of the *novus ordo* is not foreordained, as Babylon's was.

Secular, not cyclical, trends spell doom. Unfortunately, it is not vouchsafed to the human mind to distinguish between the two; hence, the many false prophecies of the last sixty years. Chapter 6 argued that unique American advantages such as demography, immigration, and innovation will not soon dissolve in the mist of history. They transcend economic cycles, even long slowdowns like America's and the world's in the early twenty-first century. Indeed, these types of strength promise to reinvigorate economic health.

Add two new trends likely to endure and to feed the reindustrialization of the United States. One reflects historical experience. As start-up economies like China's accumulate wealth, costs rise faster than productivity, and so their competitiveness as "factories of the world" wanes. As a result, jobs return to the most advanced economies. The second trend goes by the name of "fracking," the exploitation of new technologies to extract previously inaccessible gas and oil reserves. The data suggest a colossal windfall for the American economy by the end of this century's second decade. Cheap gas will fuel the industrial machine while holding out energy independence to the United States—a boon that will reduce, perhaps even reverse the endemic trade deficits of half a century.

No natural bounty, however, will by itself reverse the budget deficit that has been climbing toward levels last seen during World War II. One cause is cyclical, the trillion-dollar toll levied on the economy after the Crash of 2008, the birth of Decline 5.0. The deeper cause is structural, rooted in the nature of democratic politics throughout the West. With few exceptions, democratic polities spend more than they take in, with entitlements and group benefits rising faster than income. Indeed, the present value of future disbursements is such that every Western government would be bankrupt if it kept its books in good order. These books are so hard to balance because the imperatives of electoral power dictate paying off ever-shifting domestic coalitions. Peter gets without taking from what Paul got yesterday, and so the burden rises.

For the great democracies of Europe and Japan, the load is not as weighty as it is for the United States. The former are not in the business of world order; in fact, they have been steadily shifting from warfare to welfare. Twenty-first century America is straggling, but moving in the same direction. This is something new under the sun. For almost a century, since the first election of Franklin D. Roosevelt, the United States had managed to combine both welfare and world-order politics, whether the White House was occupied by Democrats or Republicans. Athwart the center-left, Democrats used to live comfortably with both welfarism and nationalism. In the twenty-first century they have bolted to the left while the GOP, once ensconced on the center-right, has swung to farther reaches. Bipartisanship in favor of an activist America is but a distant memory, while both outer left and outer right play with the even older idea of isolationism.

This new America is not polarized; its parties are.[51] But it is victorious parties that set the agenda. By fits and starts, the Obama administration and the Democratic Senate have opened a new chapter in the "social-democratization" or "domestication" of America. The oft repeated motto runs, "After a decade of war that's cost us thousands of lives and over a trillion dollars, the nation we need to build is right here, right here at home."[52] Say good-bye to Bill Clinton's nation building abroad, and hello to George McGovern in his 1972 campaign: "Come home, America!"

The shift was driven by hard times and by soft purpose. Financial calamity and ideological preference, affirmed twice by more than half of the electorate, have converged to lower America's strategic profile. Leading the charge in Libya, Syria, and Mali was not to be; at best, it was riding along or passing the ammunition. Three instances may be enough to spell out a pattern.

International activism, soft or hard, has waned. Preoccupied with itself, the United States has become a reticent power. In global politics, the country has narrowed its interests, no longer pursuing the sweeping designs that characterized earlier eras. In the American tradition, Roosevelt, Truman, and Eisenhower stand for muscular containment and international institution building. Kennedy and Johnson, Democrats both, hark back to Andrew Jackson and Theodore Roosevelt, representing assertive nationalism. From Wilson via Jimmy Carter to George W. Bush, a global democratic agenda held sway, "regime change" included.

Barack Obama's two terms do not fit smoothly into any of these traditions. It is neither isolationism nor interventionism, exceptionalism or universalism, nationalism or institutionalism. It is the politics of reticence abroad coupled with the expansion of the "social state," as the Europeans call it, at home. In matters military, defense budgets are declining in ways not seen since demobilization after V-J Day. The use of force has shifted from massive deployment to over-the-horizon balancing and to pinpoint attacks exploiting the economy and safety of high-precision standoff weapons. This is not "Europeanization," but a distinct turn from "exceptionalism" and reflexive entanglement in the travails of the world.

Does such a posture betray decline, and decline for good? No great power has ever *chosen* decline. Great powers are *pulled* off center stage by their debilities at home, and then *pushed* into the wings by hungry risers. But trends do not yet spell doom, as the history of Declinism suggests. In terms of assets—"cash" in the bank—the United States remains the Decathlon Power. In terms of its enduring strengths, it is not fated to sink steadily like Babylon and ancient China, Habsburg, and Soviet Russia. The direction is sideways—toward retraction and disentanglement, a road chosen after World War I and for a brief spell, circa 1945–47, after World War II. The question of the twenty-first century is whether the Decathlon Power will still act as the Default Power.

Whatever the country wishes to be, it cannot easily unshoulder this role, for there is no other. France can fly into nearby Libya and Mali, but not take on distant, let alone stronger, opponents. Nor might the rest, so often the victim of American *hauteur*, want to look forward to the abdication of the United States. International order is not self-generating; even a balance of power requires an orchestrator. Yet liberal giants who have learned to insert self-interest into the wider weal are more reassuring conductors than indifferent or domineering rivals. It is easier to live with a bumbling bull, even if it occasionally throws its weight around, than with charging dragons or bears. Content in their pastures, democracies like India and Europe do not hanker for global responsibility. Pushing against the fences, revisionists like China and Russia threaten to break into the global commons. They need to be contained and socialized. Others like revolutionary Iran or Terror International, which respect neither fences nor rules, must be defanged, a task that demands collective action and hence a leader who harnesses and maintains the coalition.

A rules-based world requires a caretaker. Yet "a world in which America turned inward," cautions the *Economist*, "would be far less predicable and a less safe one."[53] The resistible rise of previous contenders—like Japan, Russia, and Europe—might give pause to those who either cheer or fear America's abdication. But even if the next chapter in the story, Decline 6.0, were the real thing, there is still a point to ponder. How would the world fare if the global commons were run by China or Russia, illiberal giants both? Or even by democratic India, Japan, or Europe, which cannot take care of their own back yards? Not even those who have been trading in glee or gloom since Decline 1.0 might live happily ever after with any or all of them as housekeepers of the world.

Acknowledgments

No book arises ex nihilo. An ideal setting was provided by the Freeman-Spogli Institute for International Studies and the Hoover Institution, both at Stanford, where the author was privileged to work as Senior Fellow, respectively, as Marc and Anita Abramowitz Fellow of International Relations. The intellectual stimuli came from many directions. My students in PoliSci 213, an advanced undergraduate seminar on American foreign policy, contributed challenge and curiosity. Colleagues at the university provided the vital conversations. Among them are David Brady, an original mind and astute observer of American politics and society; Stephen Krasner, an old friend from Harvard days; Francis Fukuyama, with whom I sit on the executive committee of the *American Interest*, a journal we cofounded with Zbigniew Brzezinski and Eliot Cohen; Gerhard Casper, the former, German-born president, who added his comparative perspective to the mix.

These are the "invisibles" of creativity. Tangible inspiration was provided by three more scholars outside of Stanford. One is the late Samuel Huntington, a teacher who became a friend. He coined the term "Declinism," and he was also the first to stress the cyclical nature of the phenomenon. He also taught me how to think more subtly about the nature of America's national identity. More recently, Nicholas Eberstadt, one of the country's foremost demographers, and Mark L. Haas pointed me to the central role of demography in the assessment of future power, especially in the latter's "A Geriatric Peace? The Future of U.S. Power in a World of Aging Populations," in *International Security*. Michael Beckley, in his "China's Century? Why America's Edge Will Endure," also published in *International Security,* wrote a pathbreaking analysis that cut through mountains of Declinist lore. As noted in the text, some of my graphs (e.g., on the enduring gap between China's and America's GDP) are inspired by his. Such intellectual debt requires more than a footnote; hence this additional acknowledgment.

Yet my greatest thanks go to my two research assistants, Moritz Zander and Paul Ockelmann, both at Stanford at the time. Moritz put together important historical tables and unearthed many illustrative quotations sprinkled through the first chapter. Paul, a former student, traveled the longest distance with me. A drawer of graphs and hewer of data, he has been an indispensable collaborator of highest intelligence and even greater patience—all the way to the final proofreading. Without him, as they say, this book would not have seen the light of day, or at least not so soon. A writer could not have received more valuable support.

Last, but absolutely not least: Robert Weil of W. W. Norton. This is my second book under his guidance. Perhaps, they don't make editors like him any more, but writers should consider themselves lucky to have such a Cicerone. Unfailingly, he speared grammatical, stylistic, and intellectual soft spots—commenting, querying, and improving. Otto Sonntag went over the text with a fine-tooth comb, catching wobbly grammar, incomplete quotations, and missing references. As long as there are Bob Weils and his lieutenants in the book business, the English language and clearheaded thinking shall not perish from this earth.

Josef Joffe,
Stanford, Summer 2013

Notes

Introduction

1 For the citations, see Philippe Roger, *The American Enemy: The History of French Anti-Americanism*, trans. Sharon Bowman (Chicago: University of Chicago Press, 2005), pp. 16–25, passim.

Chapter One

1 As quoted in Paul Dickson, "The Sputnik Shock, Then and Now," *Globalist* online magazine, 3 October 2007, http://www.theglobalist.com/Story Id.aspx?StoryId=2218.

2 This term was first coined by Samuel Huntington in his "The U.S.—Decline or Renewal," *Foreign Affairs*, Winter 1988–89, pp. 76–96, which describes the first four waves. Actually, there were four and a half. The dress rehearsal of "Declinism" took place in 1950, right after the Soviet Union had exploded its first nuclear device, breaking the U.S. nuclear monopoly. In response, the Committee on the Present Danger was formed, predicting impending doom. It would reemerge again and again, all the way into the twenty-first century. Warning that the Soviet Union was reaching for strategic superiority, it called for massive rearmament. See also below, n. 27.

3 The literal translation from the Aramaic is meaningless, referring to coins and measures: "two minas, a shekel and two parts." Only Daniel could decode the phrase.

4   *Life*, March 24, 1958, pp. 25–37.

5   "The Saturday Essay," *Wall Street Journal*, 8 January 2011.

6   http://www.whitehouse.gov/the-press-office/2011/01/25/remarks
     -president-barack-obama-state-union-address-prepared-delivery. Obama
     had used the same term in "Our Generation's Sputnik Moment Is Now,"
     address in Winston, N.C., 8 December 2010.

7   "Man of the Year," *Time*, 6 January 1958.

8   Dated 7 November 1957, the declassified report can be found on a website
     of George Washington University: http://www.gwu.edu/~nsarchiv/NSA
     EBB/NSAEBB139/nitze02.pdf. The quotations to follow are from pp.
     1 and 4.

9   In the U.S. Senate on 14 August 1958, citation from John F. Kennedy,
     Strategy of Peace (New York: Harper & Brothers, 1960), p. 60.

10   As quoted by the *Baltimore Sun*, 25 September 1958, p. 5, citation taken
     from Christopher A. Preble, "Who Ever Believed in the 'Missile Gap'?:
     John F. Kennedy and the Politics of National Security," *Presidential
     Studies Quarterly* 33 (December 2003): 807.

11   At the Municipal Auditorium, Canton, Ohio, 27 September 1960. See John
     F. Kennedy Presidential Library and Resources, http://www.jfklibrary
     .org/Historical+Resources/Archives/Reference+Desk/Speeches/JFK
     /JFK+Pre-Pres/1953/002PREPRES12SPEECHES_60SEP27e.htm.

12   *The Necessity for Choice: Prospects of American Policy* (New York: Harper,
     1961), p. 3.

13   "The Legacy of the Late Sixties," in Stephen Macedo, ed., *Reassessing
     the Sixties: Debating the Political and Cultural Legacy* (New York: W. W.
     Norton, 1997), p. 21.

14   Doris Kearns, *Lyndon Johnson and the American Dream* (New York:
     Harper and Row, 1976), pp. 282–83.

15   *Do It! Scenarios of the Revolution* (New York: Simon and Schuster, 1970),
     p. 23.

16   Allen J. Matusow, *The Unraveling of America: A History of Liberalism in
     the 1960s* (New York: Harper and Row, 1984). The "suicide" theme was
     struck by the British historian Paul Johnson in *Modern Times: The World
     from the Twenties to the Eighties* (New York: Harper and Row, 1983), in
     the heading of chap. 18.

17   As quoted in Jules Witover, *85 Days: The Last Campaign of Robert Ken-
     nedy* (New York: Putnam, 1969), pp. 109, 116.

18 "Address by Richard M. Nixon to the Bohemian Club," 29 July 1967, in U.S. Department of State, *Foreign Relations, 1969–1976*, vol. 1, doc. 2, http://www.history.state.gov/historicaldocuments/frus1969-76v01/d2.

19 Arnold J. Toynbee, a British "metahistorian," wrote *A Study of History* (1934–61), a twelve-volume oeuvre chronicling the rise and inevitable fall of civilizations. Oswald Spengler, a German historian, wrote *The Decline of the West* after World War I, a dark tale of inexorable decay.

20 Nixon, "Remarks to Midwestern News Media Executives Attending a Briefing on Domestic Policy in Kansas City," 6 July 1971, in *The American Presidency Project*, http://www.presidency.ucsb.edu/ws/index.php?pid =3069&st=Media+Executives&st1=Kansas+City.

21 "Central Issues for American Foreign Policy," written in 1968 and reproduced in *American Foreign Policy: Three Essays by Henry Kissinger* (New York: W. W. Norton, 1969), p. 58.

22 This conversation is related by Walter Isaacson in *Kissinger: A Biography* (New York: Simon and Schuster, 1992), pp. 696–97.

23 Robert S. Litwak, *Détente and the Nixon Doctrine: American Foreign Policy and the Pursuit of Stability, 1969–1976* (Cambridge: Cambridge University Press, 1984), p. 50.

24 What came to be known as the Nixon Doctrine was laid out as early as 1967 in Nixon's "Asia after Viet Nam," *Foreign Affairs*, October 1967, pp. 111–25.

25 James Reston, "Excerpts from Interview with Kissinger: Eight Years in Washington Evaluated," *New York Times*, 20 January 1977, p. 77. Full text: *Department of State Bulletin*, no. 1963, 7 February 1977, p. 102.

26 Historical note: "Socialism in one country" was Stalin's famous phrase, following the defeat of communism in Europe after World War I. Henceforth, the Soviet Union would maintain the revolution even while capitalism endured elsewhere.

27 "Address to the Nation on Energy and National Goals: The 'Malaise Speech,'" 15 July 1979, http://www.presidency.ucsb.edu/ws/index.php?pid =32596&st=&st1=.

28 As cited by Russell Watson et al., "Has the U.S. Lost Its Clout?," *Newsweek*, 26 November 1979, p. 46.

29 "America in Decline: The Foreign Policy of 'Maturity.'" *Foreign Affairs— America and the World 1979*, 1979, pp. 456, 481.

30 All quoted in "Has the U.S. Lost Its Clout?," p. 46.

31 "Straight Talk from Kissinger," *Newsweek*, 11 December 1978, p. 56.

32 The CPD was originally established in 1950 as a "citizen's lobby" to alert the country to the "present danger" posed by the Soviet Union and to push for the implementation of the National Security Council's top-secret NSC-68 Report. The report proposed a massive buildup to maintain military superiority over an enemy "unlike previous aspirants to hegemony . . . animated by a new fanatic faith, antithetical to our own." Like Declinism, the CPD keeps reappearing. It reemerged in the 1970s and in 2004.

33 "The Russian Bear Redux?," *Newsweek*, 10 January 1977, p. 23.

34 "Can the U.S. Defend Itself?," *Time*, 3 February 1978, p. 20.

35 "Ayatullah Khomeini," *Time*, 7 January 1980, p. 8.

36 "Losing the Balance of Power," *Newsweek*, 13 November 1978, p. 35.

37 Commission on Presidential Debates, "The Carter-Reagan Presidential Debate," 28 October 1980, http://www.debates.org/index.php?page=october-28-1980-debate-transcript.

38 "Ronald Reagan Acceptance Speech," Republican National Convention, Detroit, 17 July 1980, http://www.4president.org/speeches/reagan1980convention.htm.

39 "The U.S.—Decline or Renewal?," p. 95.

40 http://www.youtube.com/watch?v=EU-IBF8nwSY.

41 David P. Calleo and Benjamin M. Rowland, *America and the World Political Economy* (Bloomington: Indiana University Press, 1973), p. 197.

42 Explanatory note on historical usage of GNP and GDP: Current standard practice measures economic size in terms of gross domestic product (GDP). That is the total value of the *country's* production and services, according to the following formula: consumption + investment + government spending + the difference between exports and imports. Until the 1970s, the standard measure was gross national product (GNP), which is GDP plus capital gains from overseas investment minus income earned by foreign nationals in the United States.

43 Arthur J. Hughes, in *Public Productivity Review* 7 (June 1983): 203.

44 "Capitalism in Japan," *Time*, 21 April 1980, http://www.time.com/time/magazine/article/0,9171,924020,00.html.

45 As quoted in "From Superrich to Superpower," *Time*, 4 July 1988, p. 28.

46 Clyde V. Prestowitz, *Trading Places: How We Are Giving Our Future to Japan and How to Reclaim It* (New York: Basic Books, 1988), p. 493.

47 The figures in this and the preceding two paragraphs are taken from http://www.ers.usda.gov/Data/macroeconomics/Data/HistoricalRealGDPValues.xls.

48 For instance, the Australian academic Gavan McCormack, "From Number One to Number Nothing: Japan's Fin de Siècle Blues," no date, http://rspas.anu.edu.au/papers/findesiecle.html (preceding two quotes). In 1990, Jon Woronoff published a book with the apt title *Japan as Anything But Number One* (Tokyo: Yohan, 1990).

49 National Bureau of Economic Research, "US Business Cycle Expansions and Contractions," http://www.nber.org/cycles.html.

50 *Beyond American Hegemony: The Future of the Western Alliance* (New York: Basic Books, 1987), p. 220.

51 *The Bankrupting of America: How the Federal Budget Is Impoverishing the Nation* (New York: William Morrow, 1992), p. 167.

52 For a quick take on comparative productivity, see Robert J. Samuelson, "We're Not a National Laundromat," *Newsweek*, 9 July 1984, p. 61. See also his book skewering a plethora of instant wisdom in economics, *Untruth: Why the Conventional Wisdom Is (Almost Always) Wrong* (New York: Random House, 2001).

53 Note: Data for Germany before 1991 pertain to the former West Germany.

54 *Beyond American Hegemony*, p. 220.

55 *The Bankrupting of America*, pp. 164, 190.

56 *The End of Work: The Decline of the Global Labor Force and the Dawn of the Post-Market Era* (New York: Putnam, 1995). By the mid-1990s, "marketism" was sweeping postcommunist Europe, India, and China—about one-third of humanity.

57 Paul Kennedy, *The Rise and Fall of the Great Powers* (New York: Vintage Books, 1987), p. 515 (the quotation is from the paperback edition of 1989).

58 "The End of Empire: Can We Decline as Gracefully as Great Britain?," *Washington Post*, 24 January 1988, p. C1.

59 *The Rise and Fall*, p. 534.

60 "The U.S.—Decline or Renewal?"

61 Huntington writes, "A situation in which one country accounted for

up to 50 percent of the global economic action was clearly a temporary product of the war." Ibid., p. 82.

62 U.S. Department of Agriculture, Economic Research Service, "GDP Shares by Country and Region—Historical," http://www.ers.usda.gov/Data/Macro economics/Data/HistoricalGDPSharesValues.xls. The ten-year averages are for 1970–79 and 2000–09.

63 *The Rise and Fall*, p. 500.

64 A prescient exception was Andrei Amalrik's *Will the Soviet Union Survive until 1984?* (New York: Harper and Row, 1970).

65 See "Historical Crude Oil Prices," http://www.inflationdata.com/inflation /Inflation_Rate/Historical_Oil_Prices_Table.asp.

66 Walden Bello, "American Resurgence, Japanese Malaise," http://focus web.org/publications/1997/American%20Resurgence,%20Japanese%20 Malaise.htm. Bello was codirector of "Focus on the Global South" at Chullalongkorn University in Bangkok.

67 "Albright's Interview on NBC-TV, February 19, 1998," *USIS Washington File*, 19 February 1998.

68 "Bless Our Pax Americana," *Washington Post*, 22 March 1991, p. A25.

69 "Dear Dr. Greenspan," *New York Times*, 9 February 1997.

70 "Is America on the Way Down?," *Commentary*, March 1992, pp. 16, 21.

71 "American Power Is on the Wane," *Wall Street Journal Europe*, 15 January 2009, p. 24.

72 "Is This the End of the American Era?," *Sunday Times* (London), 12 October 2008, p. 14.

73 Roger C. Altman, "The Great Crash, 2008: A Geopolitical Setback for the West," *Foreign Affairs*, January–February 2009, p. 14.

74 Before the German Bundestag, 25 September 2008, http://www.bundes regierung.de/Content/DE/Bulletin/2008/09/97-1-bmf-bt-regerkl.html.

75 "Aftershocks," *Washington Post*, 21 September 2008, p. B1.

76 "Complexity and Collapse: Empires on the Edge of Chaos," *Foreign Affairs*, March–April 2010, p. 32.

77 "A Shattering Moment in America's Fall from Power," *Guardian*, 28 September 2008.

78 Historical note: In 2007 and early 2008, the U.S. military was indeed in trouble, having to fight a second war inside Iraq to battle the insurgency, which naturally gave rise to melancholy speculations. During

the "surge," 20,000 new troops were committed to secure Baghdad and Anbar Province. By the summer of 2008, the insurgency was quashed.

79 "Waving Goodbye to Hegemony," *New York Times Magazine*, 27 January 2008, passim.

80 David Calleo, *The Bankrupting of America: How the Federal Budget Is Impoverishing the Nation* (New York: William Morrow, 1992), p. 177.

81 Thus the title of *Time*'s cover story on 8 March 2010 (international ed.). Another cover version of the same issue asked, "Where Did Europe Go?"

82 David S. Mason, *The End of the American Century* (Lanham, Md.: Rowman & Littlefield, 2009), p. xii, xiii (emphasis added).

83 Cotton Mather, famous for his fire-and-brimstone sermons, deserves the title of "First American Declinist." Forever castigating his flock in the Massachusetts Bay Colony for cheating, lying, and defiling God's plan for America as "God's City," he predicted divine retribution for 1697, 1716, and 1736, when the world would come to an end.

84 (New York: Public Affairs, 2008), pp. 123, 130, 216.

85 Ibid., pp. 236, 237, 239.

86 Dmitry Orlov, *Reinventing Collapse: The Soviet Example and American Prospects* (Gabriola Island, B.C.: New Society, 2008), pp. 15, 104. For a shorter take, see the profile of Orlov by Ben McGrath, "The Dystopians: American Chronicles," *New Yorker*, 26 January 2009, pp. 40–49.

87 (New York: Perseus, 2005).

88 Bill Emmott, *Rivals: How the Power Struggle between China, India and Japan Will Shape Our Next Decade* (Orlando, Fla.: Harcourt, 2008).

89 Thus the title of his book published by W. W. Norton in 2008. As this author wrote in a review of *The Post-American World* ("The New New World," *New York Times Book Review*, 11 May 2008), his book is not "another exercise in declinism," because it "eschews simple-minded projections from crisis to collapse."

90 "In China's Orbit," *Wall Street Journal*, 20/21 November 2010, p. C2.

91 *Economist*, 14 July 2012, p. 8.

92 *American Interest*, May–June 2012 issue.

93 Ruchir Sharma, "Broken BRICs: Why the Rest Stopped Rising," *Foreign Affairs*, November–December 2012, p. 2. Caveat: at this point, the entire world economy was suffering from declining or zero growth rates.

So, as always in the soothsaying business, it was difficult to distinguish between the cyclical and the secular.

94 See "The Great Crash, 2008."

95 "The U.S. Economy May Surprise Us All," *Financial Times*, 3 September 2012, http://www.ft.com/intl/cms/s/0/f7ec3e66-f5ac-11e1-bf76-00144 feabdc0.html#axzz25rcvCaGp.

96 Bill Emmott, "The American Century Is Not Over," *Prospect* (London), December 2012, pp. 28, 31 (emphasis added).

97 Clyde Prestowitz, "The Miracle Trap," *Foreign Policy* (blog), 4 January 2013, http://prestowitz.foreignpolicy.com/posts/2013/01/04/the_miracle_trap.

98 In response to a journalist's question, he said at the NATO meeting in Strasbourg in April, "I believe in American exceptionalism, just as I suspect that the Brits believe in British exceptionalism and the Greeks believe in Greek exceptionalism." Strasbourg, 4 April 2009, http://www .whitehouse.gov/the-press-office/news-conference-president-obama -4042009.

99 "Address to the Convention of the Veterans of Foreign Wars," Reno, Nev., 24 July 2012, typescript, http://www.vfw.org/VFWNationalConvention.

100 http://www.whitehouse.gov/the-press-office/2012/01/24/remarks -president-state-union-address.

Chapter Two

1 Pollyanna is a character from the 1913 children's classic *Pollyanna: The First Glad Book*. The character of the Henny Penny fable can also be found in the story "Daddabha Jataka" in Buddhist scripture. The role of the chicken is played by a hare who believes that a falling fruit portends the end of the world and starts a stampede among the animals. A wise lion stops the panic by counseling careful observation and sober reasoning. The phrase "The sky is falling" has entered English as a common idiom indicating a mistaken or hysterical belief in the imminence of disaster.

2 Actually, it was in the American Civil War of 1861–65 that the use of modern weaponry like the machine gun foreshadowed the mass slaughter of World War I. Yet this "dress rehearsal" was either ignored or misunderstood in Europe.

3 Thus the title of a chapter in Judith Shklar, *Political Thought and Political Thinkers*, ed. Stanley Hoffmann (Chicago: University of Chicago Press,

1998), pp. 175–92, published posthumously. *After Utopia* (1957), her most famous book, had given the answer forty years earlier. The evils perpetrated in the first half of the twentieth century had put an end to the Enlightenment's faith in the ineluctable march of moral progress.

4   Introd. and chap. 1 of *The Decline of the West*, vol. 1, *Form and Actuality* (London: Allen & Unwin, n.d.), p. 18. Originally published as *Untergang des Abendlandes: Gestalt und Wirklichkeit* (Munich: C. H. Beck, 1918 and 1922).

5   Matt Ridley, *The Rational Optimist: How Prosperity Evolves* (New York: HarperCollins, 2010), p. 294.

6   Bernard J. James, *The Death of Progress* (New York: Alfred A. Knopf, 1973), p. 10.

7   (New York: Alfred A. Knopf, 1982), p. 63.

8   Their best-known attack on the Enlightenment and its faith in reason and progress is *Dialektik der Aufklärung* (The Dialectics of the Enlightenment), written in the United States between 1939 and 1944.

9   Christopher Lasch, *The Culture of Narcissism: American Life in an Age of Diminishing Expectations* (New York: W. W. Norton, 1978), p. xiii.

10 Ibid., p. 235.

11 "The U.S.—Decline or Renewal," *Foreign Affairs*, Winter 1988–89, p. 96.

12 Merton continues, "This specious validity of the self-fulfilling prophecy perpetuates a reign of error. For the prophet will cite the actual course of events as proof that he was right from the very beginning." Robert K. Merton, *Social Theory and Social Structure*, enl. ed. (New York: Free Press, 1968), p. 477.

13 "The Unanticipated Consequences of Purposive Social Action," *American Sociological Review* 1 (December 1936): 903–4.

14 Kennedy, *Strategy of Peace* (New York: Harper & Brothers, 1960), p. 45.

15 Inaugural Address, 20 January 1961, http://www.jfklibrary.org/Asset -Viewer/BqXIEM9F4024ntF17SVAjA.aspx.

16 http://www.youtube.com/watch?v=EU-IBF8nwSY.

17 In the U.S. Senate on 14 August 1958, citation from Kennedy, *Strategy of Peace*, p. 60.

18 At the Municipal Auditorium, Canton, Ohio, 27 September 1960. See John F. Kennedy Presidential Library and Museum, http://www .jfklibrary.org/Research/Research-Aides/Ready-Reference/JFK-Speeches

/Remarks-of-Senator-John-F-Kennedy-at-Municipal-Auditorium
-Canton-Ohio-September-27-1960.aspx.

19 By September 1961, a National Intelligence Estimate had concluded
that the USSR possessed no more than twenty-five ICBMs and would
not possess more in the near future. There *was* a "missile gap," but
greatly in favor of the United States.

20 "Ronald Reagan Nomination Acceptance Speech," Republican National
Convention, Detroit, 17 July 1980, http://www.4president.org/speeches
/reagan1980convention.htm.

21 "Address to the Nation on Energy and National Goals: 'The Malaise
Speech,'" 15 July 1979, http://www.presidency.ucsb.edu/ws/index.php
?pid=32596&st=&st1=.

22 *NSC 68: A Report to the President Pursuant to the President's Directive
of January 31, 1950*, citation from first paragraph, "Background of the
Present Crisis," http://www.fas.org/irp/offdocs/nsc-hst/NSC-68-1.htm.

23 Marc Trachtenberg, "A 'Wasting Asset': American Strategy and the
Shifting Nuclear Balance, 1949–1954," *International Security* 13, no. 3
(Winter 1988–89): 29.

24 *The Unraveling of America* is the title of a book on the period by Allen J.
Matusow (New York: Harper and Row, 1984).

25 It was quite a change from Nixon's previous career. As a young congress-
man, he had reached national prominence as a fire-breathing member of
the House Un-American Activities Committee, a stance he maintained
all the way to his 1968 run for the presidency. In foreign policy, he was
a relentless advocate of nuclear superiority over the Soviet Union. Now
that the Soviet Union is gone, it is easy to forget what a good career
builder anticommunism was during the Cold War.

26 Richard Nixon, "First Annual Report to the Congress on United States
Foreign Policy for the 1970s," 18 February 1970, http://www.presidency
.ucsb.edu/ws/index.php?pid=2835.

27 For the numbers, see http://www.usgovernmentspending.com/down
chart_gs.php?year=1948_1968&view=1&expand=&units=b&fy=fy11
&chart=20-fed&bar=1&stack=1&size=m&title=&state=US&color
=c&local=s.

28 In the "Hearings before a Subcommittee of the Committee . . . Relating
to Educational Programs," pt. 3 (Washington, D.C.: U.S. Government
Printing Office, 1958), p. 1309.

29 For the French output, see the excellent account by Philippe Roger, *The American Enemy: The History of French Anti-Americanism*, trans. Sharon Bowman (Chicago: University of Chicago Press, 2005).

30 *Considerations on France* (Cambridge: Cambridge University Press, 1994), p. 61, as quoted in Roger, *American Enemy*, p. 46.

31 Josef Joffe, "A Canvas, Not a Country: How Europe Sees America," in Peter Schuck and James Q. Wilson, eds., *Understanding America: The Anatomy of an Exceptional Nation* (New York: Public Affairs, 2008), pp. 597–98.

32 *Weltgeschichtliche Betrachtungen* (a series of lectures between 1868 and 1872, published posthumously). Quotations are from a facsimile (German) ed. (New York: Arno Press, 1979), pp. 421, 425, 254.

33 For other indictments of America as dystopia, see Joffe, "A Canvas, Not a Country," pp. 609–15.

34 John Gray, "The Great Atlantic Drift," *Guardian*, 12 December 1994, p. 18; "A Shattering Moment in America's Fall from Power," ibid., 28 September 2008, http://www.guardian.co.uk/commentisfree/2008/sep/28/usforeignpolicy.useconomicgrowth.

35 Hannah Arendt's "Dream and Nightmare" is an essay on America and anti-Americanism written in the 1954 and republished in her *Essays in Understanding, 1930–1945*, ed. Jerome Kohn (New York: Harcourt, Brace, 1993), pp. 409–17. The *Spiegel* piece nicely exemplifies the recycling of motifs and phrases endemic in Declinism.

36 "Good Night, America," *Der Spiegel*, 1 November 2010, pp. 72–82. The English translation used here is taken from "Superpower in Decline: Is the American Dream Over?," http://www.spiegel.de/international/world/0,1518,726447,00.html.

37 This is the most often quoted part of a sermon, "A Model of Christian Charity," that John Winthrop, the governor of the Massachusetts Bay Company, delivered on the *Arbella* (or *Arabella*), which took Puritan emigrants from England to Salem in 1630. "For we must consider that we shall be as a city upon a hill. The eyes of all people are upon us" are the words seen as the original expression of American exceptionalism. In recent times, John F. Kennedy and Ronald Reagan have invoked the City in their oratory. Winthrop employed a prophetic-declinist motif at the end of the sermon: "We shall surely perish out of the good land whither we pass over this vast sea to possess it" if "we deal falsely with our God in this work we have undertaken."

38 *The Federalist Papers No. 11*, http://avalon.law.yale.edu/eighteenth_century /fed11.asp.

39 *TR Inaugural Site*, http://www.trsite.org/content/pages/speaking-loudly.

40 *The Papers of Thomas Jefferson*, vol. 33: 17 February to 30 April 1801 (Princeton: Princeton University Press, 2006), pp. 148–52, http://www .princeton.edu/~tjpapers/inaugural/infinal.html.

41 *An Address Delivered at the Request of the Committee of Arrangements . . . on the Fourth of July 1821* (Cambridge: Hilliard and Metcalf, 1821), p. 32, http://digital.library.umsystem.edu/cgi/t/text/pageviewer-idx?c=jul ;idno=jul000088.

42 "State of the Union Address," 24 January 2012, http://www.white house.gov/the-press-office/2012/01/24/remarks-president-state -union-address.

43 As related by Daron Aceglu and James A. Robinson in their masterly treatise *Why Nations Fail: The Origins of Power, Prosperity and Poverty* (New York: Random House, 2012), p. 128.

44 See chapter 1 for the predictions of repeat Declinists like David Calleo, Clyde Prestowitz, and Paul Kennedy.

45 *New Yorker*, 25 March 2009, p. 24.

46 *The Rational Optimist: How Prosperity Evolves* (New York: HarperCollins, 2010), p. 295.

47 In an interview with the German daily *Frankfurter Allgemeine Zeitung*, http://www.faz.net/aktuell/wirtschaft/dennis-meadows-im-gespraech -wir-haben-die-welt-nicht-gerettet-11671491.html.

48 "An Insatiable Desire to Peer into the Future," *Financial Times*, 28 December 2012, http://www.ft.com/intl/cms/s/e7cb6e88-4a18-11e2-a7b1-00144 feab49a,Authorised=false.html?_i_location=http%3A%2F%2Fwww .ft.com%2Fcms%2Fs%2F0%2Fe7cb6e88-4a18-11e2-a7b1-00144 feab49a.html&_i_referer=http%3A%2F%2Fsearch.ft.com%2F search%3FftsearchType%3Dtype_news%26queryText%3DTim%2520 Harford#axzz2GS3cPKSG.

49 The full title is *Expert Political Judgement: How Good Is It? How Can We Know?* (Princeton: Princeton University Press, 2005). The review is by Louis Menand, "Everybody's an Expert," *New Yorker*, 5 December 2005, pp. 98–101.

50 This one is known as the "inductionist fallacy," the assumption that what

was will be—that regular occurrence bespeaks an unchanging reality that extends from the past into the future. A vivid illustration of the fallacy is the chicken that has seen the sun rise every day and so believes that it will do so again tomorrow. Fatal to the chicken and the theory is the farmer who decides to chop off the fowl's head for dinner.

Chapter Three

1 Kissinger doesn't recall having made it, nor can his associates of the time, as related by his former colleague Peter Rodman in *Drifting Apart?* (Washington, D.C.: Nixon Center, 1999), p. 27.

2 This is the heading of the first chapter in Fareed Zakaria's *The Post-American World* (New York: W. W. Norton, 2008).

3 To dramatize America's decline, the end of World War II is often taken as a starting point, when the U.S. share was commonly assessed as 50 percent. Yet this baseline is misleading. In 1945, all the world's major economies were down or destroyed. Naturally that left the United States in an abnormally elevated position.

4 U.S. Department of Agriculture, Economic Research Service, "Real Historical Shares Values," www.ers.usda.gov/Data/Macroeconomics /Data/HistoricalGDPSharesValues.xls.

5 Calculated from Angus Maddison, *The World Economy: Historical Statistics* (Paris: OECD, 2003), table 1b, pp. 48–49.

6 For Germany, the average annual rate between 1870 and 1913 was 2.81 percent; for China it was 6.71 percent between 1973 and 2001. Ibid., table 8b, p. 260.

7 Angus Maddison, *The World Economy: A Millennial Perspective* (Paris: OECD, 2001), p. 127.

8 U.S. Department of Agriculture, Economic Research Service, "Real Historical GDP Values," www.ers.usda.gov/Data/Macroeconomics/Data /HistoricalGDPSharesValues.xls. The figures for Japan (by the decade) are: 4.5 percent in the 1970s and 0.86 percent in the naughts, with an uptick since.

9 "China's Century? Why America's Edge Will Endure," *International Security* 36, no. 3 (Winter 2011–12): 41–78.

10 "China's Q3 GDP Slows to 7.4 Pct," http://news.xinhuanet.com/english /china/2012-10/18/c_131914081.htm.

11 http://www.usgovernmentspending.com/us_defense_spending_30 .html.

12 This number refers to 203 fighting ships above 2,000 tons displacement and excludes ballistic-missile submarines, mine-warfare ships, and supply and support ships, which bring the total USN number to 280.

13 Numbers are taken from Robert O. Work, *The U.S. Navy: Charting a Course for Tomorrow's Fleet* (Washington, D.C.: Center for Strategic and Budgetary Assessment, 2008), p. 7. See also Robert O. Work, *Winning the Race: A Naval Fleet Platform Architecture for Enduring Maritime Supremacy* (Washington, D.C.: Center for Strategic and Budgetary Assessments, 2005).

14 Formal allies are Australia, Canada, France, Germany, Greece, Italy, Japan, Netherlands, South Korea, Spain, Turkey, and Britain. Friendlies are Peru, Brazil, Indonesia, and Singapore. Balancing against Russia and China, India is an implicit strategic partner of the United States.

15 Work, *The U.S. Navy*, pp. 9, 10.

16 "The Greatest Superpower Ever," *New Perspectives Quarterly*, Spring 2002, http://www.digitalnpq.org/archive/2002_spring/kennedy.html. A largely identical piece, "The Eagle Has Landed," appeared in the *Financial Times*, 2 February 2002.

17 "Remarks at Eisenhower Library," Abilene, Kan., 8 May 2010, http://www.defense.gov/speeches/speech.aspx?speechid=1467.

18 The United States contributed more to the action in Libya than is generally recognized. After Britain, it made the largest financial contribution. It deployed eleven navy ships. In addition to tankers, U.S. ground-attack aircraft, stealth bombers, electronic-warfare planes, and fighter bombers were involved in Libya.

19 "Empire of Bases" is the term employed by Chalmers Johnson, *The Sorrows of Empire: Militarism, Secrecy and the End of the Republic* (New York: Henry Holt, 2004), heading of chap. 6.

20 Secretary of Defense Robert Gates and Secretary of State Condoleezza Rice in an op-ed for the *Washington Post*, "What We Need in Iraq," 13 February 2008, http://www.washingtonpost.com/wp-dyn/content /article/2008/02/12/AR2008021202001.html. For a general analysis, see R. Chuck Mason, *Status of Forces Agreement (SOFA):What Is It, and How Has It Been Utilized?* (Washington, D.C.: Congressional

Research Service, June 18, 2009), http://www.fas.org/sgp/crs/natsec/RL34531.pdf.

21 If one believes the *Times of India*, which reported on 28 January 2010, "China Mulls Setting Up Military Base in Pakistan."

22 Department of Defense, "Active Duty Military Personnel Strengths by Regional Area and by Country, December 31, 2010," http://siadapp.dmdc.osd.mil/personnel/MILITARY/history/hst1012.pdf.

23 For the figures, see "US Government Spending Chart," http://www.usgovernmentspending.com/spending_chart_1902_2015USp_30f.

24 "The Military-Extraction Gap and the Wary Titan: The Fiscal-Sociology of British Defence Policy, 1870–1913," *Journal of European Economic History* 22 (Winter 1993): 498. Another instructive example is Israel, currently spending 6.5 percent of GDP, the highest ratio in the West (six times larger than that in many EU countries); it was growing very nicely in the 3–5 percent range during the 2010s.

Chapter Four

1 U.S. Department of Agriculture, Economic Research Service, "Real Historical GDP Values," www.ers.usda.gov/Data/Macroeconomics/Data/HistoricalGDPSharesValues.xls. The naughts of the twenty-first century are being left out because the cyclical factors clearly dwarfed structural ones.

2 Susan Shirk, *China: Fragile Superpower* (New York: Oxford University Press, 2008), p. 7.

3 "Enrichissez-vous!"—enrich yourselves—is a phrase ascribed to François Guizot, Fench interior minister in the mid-nineteenth century, meaning that there were now enough social and political rights. Deng Xiao-ping was reputed to have said the same at the beginning of his reforms.

4 Clyde V. Prestowitz, as quoted in "From Superrich to Superpower," *Time*, 4 July 1988, p. 28.

5 Clyde V. Prestowitz, *Trading Places: How We Are Giving Our Future to Japan and How to Reclaim It* (New York: Basic Books, 1988), p. 493.

6 http://www.usgovernmentspending.com/spending_chart_1860_1900USk_13s1li011mcn__US_Gross_Domestic_Product_GDP_History.

7 From 1929 to the deepest trough of 1933. Source: U.S. Department of

Commerce, Bureau of Economic Analysis, "National Income and Product Accounts."

8   *Time*, 4 July 1988, p. 28.

9   This nice correlation between an appreciating currency and declining growth should not be confused with causation. Evidently, many other factors are also in play, above all the tendency of all catch-up economies to slow down once they are back in business.

10 This section borrows extensively from the excellent analysis by Charles Harvie and Hyun-Hoon Lee, "Export-Led Industrialisation and Growth: Korea's Economic Miracle, 1962–1989," *Australian Economic History Review* 43 (November 2003): 256–86.

11 Ibid., pp. 260–61.

12 "Korean Economy 1981–2006: A Growth Theory Perspective," *Journal of International and Area Studies* 16, no. 1 (2009): 13.

13 Karl Marx, who borrowed copiously from the classical economists, called this phenomenon the "tendentially falling profit rate," in vol. 3 of *Das Kapital*.

14 Per capita income are taken from historical tabulation by Angus Maddison, http://www.ggdc.net/maddison/Historical_Statistics/horizontal-file _02-2010.xls. GDP figures are from U.S. Department of Agriculture, Economic Research Service, "Real Historical GDP and Growth Rates for Baseline Countries/Regions, 1969–2010."

15 Lawrence Lau, "Taiwan as Model for Economic Development," presentation at Stanford University, 4 October 2002, http://www.stanford .edu/~ljlau/Presentations/Presentations/021004.PDF.

16 *An Inquiry into the Nature and Causes of the Wealth of Nations*, 2nd ed., vol. 2 (London: Strahan and Cadell, 1778), p. 218.

17 For Taiwanese growth rates, see U.S. Department of Agriculture, Economic Research Service, "Historical Real GDP," http://www.ers.usda.gov /data/macroeconomics/data/historicalrealgdpvalues.xls. For capital accumulation, see "Gross Fixed Capital Formation-Annual at 2006 Prices," *Economic and Financial Data for the Republic of China*, http://win.dgbas .gov.tw/dgbas03/bs7/sdds/english/data.htm#top.

18 As quoted by Flora Lewis, "Japan's Looking Glass," *New York Times*, 8 November 1989.

19 Recall the title of the mother of all Japan hype, Ezra Vogel's *Japan as Num-*

ber One: Lessons for America (Cambridge: Harvard University Press, 1979),
which would spawn endless variations of Japan worship in the 1980s.

20 Sakura Shiga, as quoted in Richard Katz, *Japan: The System That Soured*
(Armonk, N.Y.: M. E. Sharpe, 1998), p. 20.

21 By George Friedman and Meredith LeBard, published by St. Martin's
Press.

22 As quoted in Maureen Dowd, "The 1992 Campaign: Campaign Memo,"
New York Times, 17 February 1992.

23 For a mildly laudatory account of this system by a British historian, see
W. G. Beasley, *The Rise of Modern Japan* (New York: St. Martin's Press,
1990), chap. 15.

24 William H. Overholt, "Japan's Economy, at War with Itself," *Foreign
Affairs*, January–February 2002, p. 135.

25 Fumiyo Hayashi (University of Tokyo) and Edward C. Pescott (Federal
Reserve Bank of Minneapolis), "The 1990s in Japan: A Lost Decade"
(unpublished paper, 2003), pp. 5, 6, 19.

26 This is the argument of the "authoritarian revival," for instance, by Azar
Gat, "The Return of Authoritarian Great Powers," *Foreign Affairs*, July–
August 2007, pp. 59–69. Accordingly, China and Russia embody the
"return of economically successful authoritarian capitalist powers" and
so "represent a viable alternative path to modernity."

27 It sounds more pithy in German: "Erst kommt das Fressen, dann die
Moral," from the ballad "What keeps man alive" in Brecht's *Three-Penny
Opera*.

28 *The Origins of Political Order: From Prehuman Times to the French Revolution* (New York: Farrar, Straus and Giroux, 2011), p. 353.

Chapter Five

1 *Dreaming with BRICs*, http://www.goldmansachs.com/our-thinking/archive
/archive-pdfs/brics-dream.pdf. BRIC stands for Brazil, Russia, India,
and China.

2 Per capita incomes was another story: by 2050, the United States still
would be almost three times richer than China.

3 "Broken BRICs: Why the Rest Stopped Rising," *Foreign Affairs*, November–
December 2012, p. 4.

4 *Dreaming with BRICs*, p. 14.

5   Thus a chapter heading in Martin Jacques, *When China Rules the World* (London: Allen Lane/Penguin, 2009), p. 17.

6   "$123,000,000,000,000: China's Estimated Economy by the Year 2040. Be warned." *Foreign Policy*, January–February 2010 (emphasis added), http://www.foreignpolicy.com/articles/2010/01/04/123000000000000.

7   For the numbers, see Angus Maddison, *The World Economy: Historical Statistics* (Paris: OECD, 2003), table 8-3, p. 249.

8   For one of the best short explanations, see David S. Landes, "Why Europe and the West? Why Not China?," *Journal of Economic Perspectives* 20 (Spring 2006): 3–22.

9   Jack Goldstone puts it thus: "The breakdown of hierarchies, and the onset of progress, were also once encapsulated into two great breakthroughs in Europe: the Industrial Revolution and the French (and other European) revolutions. The former gave rise to a massive urban working class, . . . altering the economic hierarchy; the latter eliminated the privileges of hereditary aristocracy and rulers, . . . destroying the old political hierarchy. After the eighteenth century, Europe could thus escape its feudal, agrarian heritage and move quickly to become fully modern, and enjoy the full benefits of modern economic growth." "Efflorescences and Economic Growth in World History: Rethinking the 'Rise of the West' and the Industrial Revolution," *Journal of World History* 13 (Fall 2002): 328.

10 *La bureaucratie céleste: Recherches sur l'économie et la société de la Chine traditionnelle* (Paris: Gallimard, 1968), p. 22, as quoted in Landes, "Why Europe," p. 7.

11 *What Went Wrong: The Clash between Islam and Modernity in the Middle East* (New York: HarperCollins Perennial Imprint, 2003), pp. 22–23.

12 The emissary was Lord Macartney in an episode related by John Darwin, *Unfinished Empire: The Global Expansion of Britain* (London: Allen Lane, 2012), pp. 122–23.

13 Landes, "Why Europe," p. 14.

14 Charles Horner, *Rising China and Its Postmodern Fate: Memories of Empire in a New Global Context* (Athens: University of Georgia Press, 2009), p. 72.

15 "China's Great Famine: 40 Years Later," *British Medical Journal*, 18 December 1999.

16 On the open culture between San Francisco and San Jose, see Annalee Saxenian, *Regional Advantage: Culture and Competition in Silicon Valley and Route 128* (Cambridge: Harvard University Press, 1994).

17 Aired in forty countries, the TV series *Parker Lewis Can't Lose* depicted the adventures of a high school student who went from triumph to triumph, no matter how daunting the odds.

18 *China's Economic Rise: Fact and Fiction*, Carnegie Endowment Policy Brief No. 61 (Washington, D.C.: CEIP, July 2008), pp. 8, 10, 12, 13, 4.

19 China ranks as No. 80, India as No. 94, out of 174 (the worst place) in the 2012 index of Tranparency International. At the beginning of the millennium, China ranked 57th. http://www.transparency.org/cpi2012 /results.

20 *Fault Lines: How Hidden Fractures Still Threaten the World Economy* (Princeton: Princeton University Press, 2010), p. 64.

21 Thus Xu Dixin, writing in 1981 and identified as vice-president of the Chinese Academy of Social Sciences. See "China's Special Economic Zones," *Beijing Review*, http://www.bjreview.com.cn/nation/txt/2009 -05/26/content_197576.htm. China watchers might note that this 1981 piece was republished online in 2009, reaffirming the same orthodoxy in the midst of rampant deviationism.

22 Numbers are taken from Yue-man Yeung et al., "China's Special Economic Zones at 30," tables 2 and 3, *Eurasian Geography and Economics* 50, no. 2 (2009): 222–40, http://www.espre.cn/111/manage/ziliao/China %26_039.pdf

23 OECD, "State-Owned Enterprises in China: Reviewing the Evidence," Occasional Paper, 26 January 2009, table 9, p. 17, http://www.oecd.org /dataoecd/14/30/42095493.pdf.

24 "The Visible Hand," Special Report on State Capitalism, 21 January 2012.

25 Richard McGregor, *The Party: The Secret World of China's Communist Rulers* (New York: HarperCollins, 2010), pp. 8–10.

26 Mark Kitto, "You'll Never Be Chinese," *Prospect* (London), August 2012, p. 29.

27 Mark Kitto, "5 Myths about the Chinese Communist Party," *Foreign Policy*, January–February 2011, http://www.foreignpolicy.com/articles /2011/01/02/5_myths_about_the_chinese_communist_party.

28 Andrew Szamosszegi and Cole Kyle, *An Analysis of State-Owned Enter-*

prises and State Capitalism in China (Washington, D.C.: U.S.-China Economic and Security Review Commission, 26 October 2011), p. 5. The study is the most exhaustive treatment of the SOEs known to this author.

29 Ibid., p. 3.

30 As reported by *Caijing Magazine*, 13 August 2010, http://english.caijing .com.cn/2010-08-13/110496984.html.

31 Thus Cheng Li, of Washington's Brookings Institution, "China's Secret Bosses," *Sunday Times*, 29 January 2012, p. B1.

32 Szamosszegi and Kyle, *An Analysis*, p. 7. The figures listed in the next paragraph are also from this study.

33 Ibid., p. 33.

34 The magazine adds, "This information is representative of only those central-level SOEs that can be published. There are actually 120 for-profit SOEs authorized by SASAC. Fifteen percent of them are legally prohibited from releasing this kind of information. If you include industries outside of those legal requirements, like the tobacco and finance industries, the scope of SOEs is even more alarming." "SOEs: Stifling the Nation's Vitality," *Caixin Online*, 1 December 2012, http://english .caixin.com/2012-01-12/100347961.html.

35 "The Visible Hand," January 2012.

36 Loren Brandt and Thomas G. Rawski, "China's Great Economic Transformation," in *China's Great Economic Transformation* (New York: Cambridge University Press, 2008), p. 18.

37 For the gist, see "The Wen Family Empire," *New York Times*, 25 October 2012, http://www.nytimes.com/interactive/2012/10/25/business /the-wen-family-empire.html. After the story broke, the government blocked search terms such as the Wen surname, "assets," "wealth," "family," and "prime minister." Also blocked were "2.7 billion," "Wen treasure," "Wen clan," and "Wen emperor."

38 "Corruption Up among Chinese Officials," *BBC News*, 8 January 2010, http://news.bbc.co.uk/2/hi/asia-pacific/8448059.stm.

39 "Chinese Officials Stole $120 billion, Fled Mainly to the U.S.," *BBC News*, 17 June 2011, http://www.bbc.co.uk/news/world-asia-pacific -13813688. The report has disappeared from the BBC website.

40 "Age Had Its Privileges at China's Eighteenth Party Congress," *Asia Blog*,

18 November 2012, http://asiasociety.org/blog/asia/susan-shirk-age-had
-its-privileges-chinas-eighteenth-party-congress.

41 As quoted in Edward Wong, "Family Ties and Hobnobbing Trump Merit at China Helm," *New York Times*, 17 November 2012.

42 Victor Shih et al., "Getting Ahead in the Communist Party: Explaining the Advancement of Central Committee Members in China," *American Political Science Review* 106 (February 2012): 180.

43 "China Questions and Answers," no date, http://www.china.org.cn/english /features/Q&A/161765.htm.

44 As reported by *Asia News*, 15 September 2010, http://www.asianews.it/ news-en/Crisis-in-China:-64-million-empty-apartments–19459.html.

45 Wayne M. Morrison, *China's Economic Conditions* (Washington, D.C.: Congressional Research Service, December 2009), p. 21.

46 John Lee, "China's Corporate Leninism," *American Interest*, May–June 2012, p. 43.

47 For the graphs, see Gao Xu, "State-Owned Enterprises in China: How Profitable Are They?," 2 March 2010, http://blogs.worldbank.org /eastasiapacific/state-owned-enterprises-in-china-how-profitable-are -they. After 2008, the state sector's ROI fell to around 3 percent, while the privates hardly suffered, earning close to 9 percent.

48 As reported by *Caixin Online* in "SOE Profits Tumble Again," 20 March 2012, http://english.caixin.com/2012-03-20/100370663.html.

49 Morrison, *China's Economic Conditions*, p. 21.

50 I am indebted to Minxin Pei of Claremont-McKenna College for pointing me to the source of these data: Ji Fongxiang, "An Empirical Analysis and Study of the System of Evaluating the Macroeconomic Efficiency of Investment," *Tongji Yanjiu* (Statistical Research) 24, no. 9 (September 2007): 64.

51 Edward Chancellor, "Corruption Threatens China's Future," *Financial Times*, 21 March 2012. Chancellor is the author of *Devil Take the Hindmost: A History of Financial Speculation*.

52 As quoted in "China's Economy: Apocalypse Soon?," *New York Times*, 9 July 2012, http://rendezvous.blogs.nytimes.com/2012/07/09 /watching-the-china-stress-index-its-rising/.

53 "Offshoring: Welcome Home," *Economist*, 19 January 2013, p. 11. (The article doesn't give a definition of "costs.")

54 Harold L. Sirkin et al., *U.S. Manufacturing Nears the Tipping Point* (BCG Perspectives, 22 March 2012), https://www.bcgperspectives. com/content/articles/manufacturing_supply_chain_management_us _manufacturing_nears_the_tipping_point/.

55 Ibid., p. 4. The authors add that their estimates for the future are "conservative," noting that some U.S. companies have experienced not, as posited, 18 percent wage increases, but up to 40 and 100 percent in a single year (p. 5).

56 "Thus the social order overthrown by a revolution is almost always better than the one immediately preceding it, and experience teaches us that . . . the most perilous moment for a bad government is one when it seeks to mend its ways. . . . Patiently endured for so long as it seemed beyond redress, a grievance comes to appear intolerable once the possibility of removing it crosses men's minds." *The Old Regime and the French Revolution*, trans. Stuart Gilbert (Garden City, N.Y.: Doubleday, 1955), pp. 176–77.

57 Explanatory note: A Gini of 0 is perfect equality; a Gini of 1 denotes perfect inequality, i.e., one person has all the income. The international data are patchy, but in the West, after transfers and taxes, the Gini is around .3; in the United States (the worst on the list), .38.

58 "A Distinctly American Internationalism," 19 November 1999, in John W. Dietrich, ed., *The George W. Bush Foreign Policy Reader: Presidential Speeches* (Armonk, N.Y.: M. E. Sharpe, 2005), p. 29.

59 Address to the Australian Parliament, 17 November 2011, as quoted in U.S. Department of State, *IIP Digital*, same day, http://iipdigital.usembassy .gov/st/english/article/2011/11/20111117144109nehpets0.8185999 .html#axzz1yzOHSMeS.

Chapter Six

1 Why the United States is tied for first place with Iceland in the West is a matter of lively debate. It cannot be state-provided child care, which is miserly in the United States compared with European nations with very low fertility rates. Factors might be high religiosity, which favors traditional family structures and thus childbearing; a flexible labor market economy that allows women to have both jobs and families; ample land that makes for low-priced housing; a culture that values flexible life

designs; a Hispanic immigrant population whose high birthrates endure for a generation or two.

2   Nicholas Eberstadt, "Growing Old the Hard Way: China, Russia, India," Policy Review No. 106 (2006), http://www.hoover.org/publications/policy-review/article/6783.

3   Richard Jackson and Neal Howe, *The Graying of the Middle Kingdom* (Washington, D.C.: Center for Strategic and International Studies, 2004), p. 32. This is the best short analysis of the data in the UN's *World Population Prospects: The 2002 Revision*, 2003.

4   "Growing Old the Hard Way," emphasis added.

5   *The Graying of the Middle Kingdom*, p. 13.

6   *Investments and Pensions Asia*, 7 July 2011, http://www.ipe.com/asia/china-expands-statutory-pensions-and-aims-for-system-convergence_41294.php.

7   "Pension Fund Deficits Grew to 67.9 Bln Yuan in 2010," *Caixin Online*, 23 December 2011, http://english.caixin.com/2011-12-23/100342018.html.

8   Lan Fang, "The Future Starts to Age: China's Elderly," *Caixin Online*, 9 June 2010, http://english.caixin.com/2010-09-06/100177574.html.

9   Figure 2, "Household, Enterprise and Government Saving as Percentage of GDP, 1992–2007" (latest available figures). Dennis Tao Yang et al., "Why Are Savings Rates So High in China?," NBER Working Papers 16771 (Cambridge, Mass., February 2011).

10 Total outlays in fiscal year 2013 were $856 billion. Subtracting $140 billion for veterans and $57 billion for foreign military and economic aid leaves $660 billion for strictly military outlays. See "US Government Spending," http://www.usgovernmentspending.com/us_defense_spending_30.html.

11 As Mark L. Haas puts it in his magnificent analysis of the impact of aging on military power, "each year that goes by in which the United States' military lead remains roughly the same increases the odds of the continuation of U.S. hegemony." "A Geriatric Peace? The Future of U.S. Power in a World of Aging Populations," *International Security* 32, no. 1 (Summer 2007): 133.

12 The title of a recent book by Diane Ravitch, *The Death and Life of the Great American School System* (2010), underlines the enduring theme.

13 "School Work," *New Yorker*, 27 September 2010, http://www.newyorker .com/talk/comment/2010/09/27/100927taco_talk_lemann.

14 The National Academies, "Broad Federal Effort Urgently Needed to Create New, High-Quality Jobs for All Americans in the Twenty-First Century," press release, 12 October 2005.

15 *Fortune*, 25 July 2005.

16 The first to dig deeper was Carl Bialik in the *Wall Street Journal* with "Outsourcing Fears Help to Inflate Some Numbers" (26 August 2005) and "Sounding the Alarm with a Fuzzy Stat" (27 October 2005). He was followed by Gerald W. Bracey, "Heard the One about the 600,000 Chinese Engineers?," *Washington Post*, 21 May 2006. At Duke, it was Vivek Wadhwa and Gary Gereffi, "Framing the Engineering Outsourcing Debate: Comparing the Quantity and Quality of Engineering Graduates in the United States, India and China," conference paper, 27 June 2006, citation on p. 11, http://www.nae.edu/File.aspx?id=10287. On the international competitiveness issue, see McKinsey Global Institute, "The Emerging Global Labor Market: Part II—The Supply of Offshore Talent," June 2005.

17 Explanatory note: Expenditure data for China and India are notoriously patchy. The World Bank's *Edstats*, the richest data set, does not show GDP percentages for China and India.

India: GDP figures are taken from the *National Accounts Statistics*, published by CSO. Education spending figures are taken from *Budgeted Expenditure on Education*, published by India Department of Higher Education.

United States: *Revenues and Expenditures for Public Elementary and Secondary Education*, 1970–71 through 1986–87; Common Core of Data (CCD), "National Public Education Financial Survey," 1987–88 through 2008–09; *Higher Education General Information Survey (HEGIS), Financial Statistics of Institutions of Higher Education*, 1965–66 through 1985–86; *Integrated Postsecondary Education Data System (IPEDS)*, "Finance Survey" (IPEDS-F:FY87-99); and IPEDS Spring 2001 through Spring 2011, "Finance Component." U.S. Department of Commerce, Bureau of Economic Analysis, "National Income and Product Accounts

Tables," retrieved November 28, 2011, from http://www.bea.gov/iTable /index_nipa.cfm.

China: *China Statistical Yearbook* (1996, 2003). For 2008, *The 2008 Statistical Notice on National Education Expenditure* (Beijing: s.n., 2009).

18 Program for International Student Assessment, the core of which is reading, math, and science skills.

19 *PIRLS 2011* (Progress in International Reading Literacy Study) (Chestnut Hill: Boston College, 2012), p. 37, http://timssandpirls.bc.edu/pirls 2011/downloads/P11_IR_Chapter1.pdf.

20 Tino Sanandaji, "The Amazing Truth about PISA Scores: USA Beats Europe and Ties with Asia," http://www.newgeography.com/content /001955-the-amazing-truth-about-pisa-scores-usa-beats-western-europe -ties-with-asia.

21 As quoted in Sam Dillon, "Top Test Scores from Shanghai Stun Educators," *New York Times*, 7 December 2009, http://www.nytimes.com/2010 /12/07/education/07education.html?_r=1&pagewanted=all.

22 "Our Generation's Sputnik Moment is Now," address in Winston, N.C., 8 December 2010, http://www.whitehouse.gov/blog/2010/12/06/president -obama-north-carolina-our-generation-s-sputnik-moment-now.

23 For the 2012 and earlier data, see *Academic Ranking of World Universities 2012*, http://www.arwu.org/index.jsp.

24 http://www.usnews.com/education/worlds-best-universities-rankings/top -400-universities-in-the-world?page=4.

25 The University of Michigan receives only 7 percent from the state, which is about par for other renowned public universities as well (e.g., Virginia). Berkeley gets 11 percent. To this, should be added ample federal grants, which push up the public share into the 30 percent range.

26 "Mehr Wert auf Wissen legen," interview with Christine Brinck in the German weekly *Die Zeit*, 12 July 2012, p. 63.

27 The Ecole Normale d'Administration, France's super-selective public-administration school, which trains the country's upper-level officials. Critics perennially contend that ENA teaches superb administrative skills rather than independent thinking.

28 Mark Kitto, "You'll Never Be Chinese," *Prospect* (London), August 2012, p. 31.

29 National Science Foundation, *Info Brief*, September 2010, table 1, p. 1, http://www.nsf.gov/statistics/infbrief/nsf10329/nsf10329.pdf.

30 Later in his life, Shockley unleashed a storm of controversy over his views on race, intelligence, and eugenics. For the whole story see Joel N. Shurkin, *Broken Genius: The Rise and Fall of William Shockley, Creator of the Electronic Age* (New York: Palgrave Macmillan, 2006).

31 Gregory Gromov, "A Legal Bridge Spanning 100 Years: From the Gold Mines of El Dorado to the 'Golden' Startups of Silicon Valley," *Net Valley*, n.d., accessed 7 July 2012, http://www.netvalley.com/silicon_valley/Legal_Bridge_From_El_Dorado_to_Silicon_Valley.html.

32 John Hechinger and Rebecca Buckman, "The Golden Touch of Stanford's President," *Wall Street Journal*, 25 February 2007.

33 Gromov, "A Legal Bridge."

34 By the National Commission on Excellence in Education, April 1983, and published by the Department of Education, pp. 5, 33, http://www.eric.ed.gov:80/PDFS/ED226006.pdf.

35 "What Export-Oriented America Means," *American Interest*, May–June 2012, p. 6.

36 Told by Adam Davidson, "Making It in America," *Atlantic*, January–February 2012, p. 65.

37 *Science and Engineering Indicators 2012*, Table O-13.

38 Ibid., chap. 5, section "Trends in Highly Cited S&E Literature."

39 The tally United States vs. China reads: 35 percent to .4 percent in astronomy, 57 to .1 in biological sciences, 54 to 1 in medicine, and 70 to .5 in "other life sciences." China isn't quite as outclassed in physics (37 to 6 percent) and computer science (44 to 10). Ibid., table 5-44, http://www.nsf.gov/statistics/seind12/c5/c5s4.htm#s4.

40 Titus Galama and James Hosek, *U.S. Competitiveness in Science and Technology* (Santa Monica: RAND, 2008), p. 28. The author acknowledges his debt to this most sophisticated analysis of America's global standing in one slender volume, which affirms some conventional wisdom while debunking most of it with a wealth of data, graphs, and tables.

41 OECD, *Compendium of Patent Statistics 2008*, p. 6, http://www.oecd.org/dataoecd/5/19/37569377.pdf.

42 Some figures in this chapter, extended in time, were inspired by Beckley's "China's Century? Why America's Edge Will Endure," *International Security* 36, no. 3 (Winter 2011/12): 41–78.

43 Ibid., p. 68.

44 See ibid., figure V.

45 Thomas Friedman and Michael Mandelbaum, *That Used to Be Us: How America Fell Behind in the World It Invented and How We Can Come Back* (New York: Farrar, Straus and Giroux, 2011), p. 17. This thoughtful book is fifth-wave Declinism with the classic double-punch: America will lose the race, unless ... The emphasis is on the how and the what that will preserve America's position. For some less judicious output during Decline 5.0, see Peter D. Kiernan, *Becoming China's Bitch: And Nine More Catastrophes We Must Avoid Right Now* (Nashville, Tenn.: Turner, 2012), and Mark Steyn, *After America: Get Ready for Armageddon* (Washington, D.C.: Regnery, 2011).

46 Richard Silberglitt et al., *The Global Technology Revolution 2020* (Santa Monica: RAND, 2008).

47 Thus the gist of the Silberglitt study, according to RAND's *U.S. Competitiveness in Science and Technology*, p. 37.

48 Isaac Stone Fish, "The China Threat," *Newsweek*, 24 January 2011, p. 22 (internat. edition)

49 This is the thirty-year average, as calculated from U.S. Department of Homeland Security, "Estimate of the Unauthorized Immigrant Population in the United States: January 2011," http://www.dhs.gov/xlibrary/assets /statistics/publications/ois_ill_pe_2011.pdf.

50 Samuel P. Huntington, *Who Are We? The Challenges to America's National Identity* (New York: Simon and Schuster, 2005).

51 As quoted in David Edwin Harrell et al., *Unto a Good Land: A History of the American People* (Grand Rapids, Mich.: Eerdmans, 2005), p. 214.

52 *Democracy in America*, vol. 2 (New York: Vintage Books, 1945), p. 279.

53 *Common Sense*, 1776, appendix to 3rd ed. Ronald Reagan used this sentence in his acceptance speech at the Republican National Convention on 17 July 1980.

54 For an elaboration, see my "The God Gap: Why Europeans Lose Faith and Americans Keep Praying," *American Interest*, November–December 2009, pp. 119–27.

55 "You'll Never Be Chinese," p. 30.

56 This is the title of Michael Lewis's 1999 book about Jim Clark, the founder of Netscape and other Silicon Valley companies.

57 As quoted in "Immigration Chief Seeks to Reassure Silicon Valley,"

USA Today, 2 February 2012, http://www.usatoday.com/tech/news/story/2012-02–22/silicon-valley-tech-immigration/53211162/1.

58 As reported in Matt Richtel, "Tech Recruiting Clashes with Immigration Rules," *New York Times*, 14 April 2009, http://www.nytimes.com/2009/04/12/business/12immig.html?pagewanted=all.

59 Vivek Wadhwa et al., *America's New Immigrant Entrepreneurs* (Duke University and UC Berkeley, 2007), p. 4, http://www.kauffman.org/uploadedFiles/entrep_immigrants_1_61207.pdf.

60 "The Chilecon Valley Challenge," *Economist*, 13 October 2012, p. 15.

61 Review of *Rising above the Gathering Storm*, pt. 3, 2 March 2006, http://cstpr.colorado.edu/prometheus/archives/gathering_storm/.

62 http://www.softwaretop100.org/global-software-top-100-edition-2011.

63 National Science Foundation, *Science and Engineering Indicators 2012*, appendix tables 2-19, 2-18, 2-28 2-35. Note: The figures are "S&E Net," that is, minus the social sciences.

64 National Science Foundation, National Center for Science and Engineering Statistics, special tabulations (2010) of *Survey of Earned Doctorates*, table 2-11. Note: Foreign doctorate recipients include permanent and temporary residents.

65 U.S. Department of Energy, "Stay Rates of Foreign Doctorate Recipients from U.S. Universities, 2007," January 2010. This figure marks the two-year stay rate (figure 1, p. 2). It declines to 60 percent after ten years (p. 1), http://orise.orau.gov/files/sep/stay-rates-foreign-doctorate-recipients-2007.pdf. For a quick summary, see David Wessel, "Most Foreign Ph.D.s Remain in the U.S.," *Wall Street Journal*, 27 January 2010, p. 12 (European ed.).

66 This is just a minuscule part of an almost endless list. For instance, the global dominance of America's film and entertainment industry might never have come about without scores of European immigrants or their direct descendants. Here are a few: George Cukor, Michael Curtis, Joe Eszterhas, Adolf Zukor (founder of Paramount), Peter Lorre (Hungarian-German), Yul Brynner, Kirk Douglas, and Samuel Goldwyn and Louis B. Mayer (founders of MGM). Extending the list to the third generation yields a Hollywood that is practically a European-Jewish colony.

67 Their share in IT was 84 percent, in pulse or digital communications 83

percent, in pharmaceuticals 79 percent, and in optics 77 percent. *Patent Pending: How Immigrants Are Reinventing the American Economy*, June 2012, published by the Partnership for a New American Economy (an association of U.S. mayors and business leaders), summary in http://www .renewoureconomy.org/patent-pending.

68 The number usually bandied about in the media is 100,000 per annum. These range from peaceful demonstrations to setting police stations ablaze. They do not foreshadow an imminent insurgency, because many protests are about wages and local corruption. On the other hand, Chinese history is replete with sudden, massive eruptions.

69 On this theme, buttressed by a wealth of historical detail, see the splendid work by Daron Acemoglu and James A. Robinson, *Why Nations Fail: The Origins of Power, Prosperity and Poverty* (New York: Crown, 2012). "The openness of a society, its willingness to permit creative destruction, and the rule of law appear to be decisive for economic development," writes the Nobel laureate Kenneth Arrow in a testimonial for the book.

Chapter Seven

1 The term was coined by Charles Krauthammer in his "The Unipolar Moment," *Foreign Affairs*, special issue titled "America and the World 1990," 70, no. 1 (1990–91): 23–33.

2 This is an oft-repeated phrase attributed to Barack Obama, which he never uttered. The honors go to an anonymous adviser, as quoted by a reporter: "Obama may be moving toward something resembling a doctrine. One of his advisers described the President's actions in Libya as 'leading from behind.'" Ryan Lizza, "The Consequentialist," *New Yorker*, 2 May 2011, last paragraph, http://www.newyorker.com/reporting/2011 /05/02/110502fa_fact_lizza#ixzz2GSLI5oAv.

3 "The Greatest Superpower Ever," *New Perspectives Quarterly*, Spring 2002, http://www.digitalnpq.org/archive/2002_spring/kennedy.html, originally published as "The Eagle Has Landed," *Financial Times*, 2 February 2002.

4 The *Enterprise*, launched in 1960, was deactivated in December 2012. With a length of 1,123 feet (342 meters) and a displacement of 95,000 tons, it could carry up to ninety combat aircraft. It will be reincarnated under the same name in 2025. Its biggest guns can fire fifteen projectiles

per minute. Some of its aircraft are or can be configured for nuclear missions.

5   Turreau, ambassador to the United States from 1803 to 1811, as quoted in Robert W. Tucker and David C. Hendrickson, *Empire of Liberty: The Statecraft of Thomas Jefferson* (New York: Oxford University Press, 1990), p. 18.

6   Multiply by about thirty and fifteen, respectively, to arrive at current dollars.

7   Richard N. Haass, "The Age of Nonpolarity: What Will Follow U.S. Dominance," *Foreign Affairs*, May–June 2008, pp. 44–56, passim.

8   These are the chip denominations usually found in American casinos.

9   Samuel P. Huntington, "The Lonely Superpower," *Foreign Affairs*, March–April 1999, pp. 35–49, passim.

10 For this term, see my *Überpower: The Imperial Temptation of America* (New York: W. W. Norton, 2006).

11 Alexis de Tocqueville, *Democracy in America*, vol. 1 (New York: Vintage Books, 1945), p. 131.

12 Ibid., p. 178.

13 "The Garrison State" is the title of a famous article by Harold D. Lasswell in the *American Journal of Sociology*, January 1941, in the middle of World War II, where the author foresaw a "world of 'garrison states'—a world in which the specialists on violence are the most powerful group in society" (p. 455).

14 I have elaborated on this theme in "Democracy and Deterrence: What Have They Done to Each Other?" in Linda Miller, ed., *Ideas & Ideals: Essays on Politics in Honor of Stanley Hoffmann* (Boulder, Colo.: Westview, 1993).

15 Historical note: Through a series of dynastic successions, Charles V inherited practically all of Europe: Spain, Burgundy, the Low Countries, and the lands of the (Austrian) house of Habsburg, becoming ruler of the Holy Roman Empire in 1519. Like a vise, his and his son Philip II's possessions squeezed France from the west and the east. For the next two hundred years, the French kings fought endlessly to break the stranglehold. This permanent conflict ended only in 1713, when Spain and Austria were formally separated, ending the encirclement of France.

16 "Avant-propos und Anfang der *Histoire de mon temps*," in Georg Kuntzel

and Martin Hass, eds., *Die politischen Testamente der Hohenzollern*, vol. 2 (Leipzig and Berlin: B. G. Teubner, 1911), pp. 89–90," digital ed. (in French), *Œuvres de Frédéric le Grand*, University of Trier, http://friedrich.uni-trier.de/de/droysen/2/30/text.

17 *Empire: The Rise and Demise of the British World Order and the Lessons for Global Power* (New York: Basic Books, 2002), p. xxv.

18 Winston S. Churchill, *The River War* (n.p.: NuVision Publications, 2007, originally published in 1899), p. 15.

19 *The Works of Edmund Burke*, vol. 7 (Boston: Charles C. Little, 1839), p. 267. For an account of the trial, see Ferguson, *Empire*, pp. 53–55.

20 "Government of India: A Speech Delivered in the House of Commons on the Tenth of July 1833," http://www.columbia.edu/itc/mealac/pritchett/00generallinks/macaulay/txt_commons_indiagovt_1833.html.

21 John Darwin, *Unfinished Empire* (London: Allen Lane, 2012), pp. 388, 389 (emphasis added).

22 The Homestead Act of 1862 marked a historical watershed. Distributing vast tracts of land at very low prices, it drew vast numbers of European immigrants to the United States, which the tenancy and peonage systems of Latin America did not.

23 *God and Gold: Britain, America, and the Making of the Modern World* (New York: Alfred A. Knopf, 2007), p. 193.

24 A classic is Alexander Gerschenkron's *Bread and Democracy in Germany*, first published in 1943.

25 "A Letter from Italy" (1701) in *A Complete Edition of the Poets of Great Britain*, vol. 7 (London: Printed for John and Arthur Arch et al., 1795), p. 181.

26 William Camden, *The History of the Most Renowned and Victorious Princess Elizabeth*, 4th ed. (London: M. Flesher, 1688), p. 233.

27 In a famous speech to the Conservative members of the House of Commons Foreign Affairs Committee in 1936 that laid out the balance of power as first principle of "four hundred years" of England's foreign policy. As reproduced in Winston S. Churchill, *The Gathering Storm*, Vol. 1 of *The Second World War* (Boston: Houghton Mifflin, 1947), p. 207.

28 "Lord Bathurst to Lord Castlereagh," 20 October 1818, in Charles William Vane, ed., *Correspondence, Despatches, and Other Papers of Viscount Castlereagh*, vol. 12 (London: John Murray, 1853), pp. 55–56. Castlereagh was foreign secretary from 1812 to 1822.

29 Letter to Madame la Duchesse d'Auville [*sic*], 2 April 1790, in *The Works of Thomas Jefferson* (New York and London: G. P. Putnam's Sons, 1904–05), vol. 6, http://oll.libertyfund.org/index.php?option=com_staticxt&staticfile=show.php%3Ftitle=803&layout=html#chapter_86751.

30 The term is from Tucker and Hendrickson, *Empire of Liberty*, p. 19—one of the best treatises on early American foreign policy.

31 As quoted in Gordon S. Wood, *Empire of Liberty: A History of the Early Republic, 1789–1815* (Oxford: Oxford University Press, 2009), p. 627. Chap. 17 offers an excellent analysis of early U.S. foreign policy, to which I am indebted.

32 On 2 April 1806, as quoted in Dumas Malone, *Jefferson the President: Second Term, 1805–1809* (Boston: Little, Brown, 1974), p. 76.

33 Letter to Thomas Pinckney, 29 May 1797, in *The Works of Thomas Jefferson*, vol. 8, http://oll.libertyfund.org/title/805/87090/1994133.

34 Wood, *Empire of Liberty*, p. 659.

35 For China, it is "exports first," a classic of mercantilism, plus direct investment in natural-resource extraction around the world—exclusive control, rather than reliance on open markets.

36 For a revisionist view of the Open Door as a tool of American business interests and power politics, see the influential works of William Appleman Williams, especially *The Tragedy of American Diplomacy* (Cleveland: World, 1959), and of Walter LaFeber, especially *The New Empire: An Interpretation of American Expansion, 1860–1898* (Ithaca: Cornell University Press, 1963).

37 "American Power: Hegemony, Isolationism or Engagement," address to the Council on Foreign Relations, 21 October 1999, http://www.cfr.org/world/american-power-hegemony-isolationism-engagement/p3600.

38 General Agreement on Tariffs and Trade; International Monetary Fund.

39 "Remarks by Secretary of Defense William S. Cohen at the Microsoft Corporation," 18 February 1999, http://www.defense.gov/speeches/speech.aspx?speechid=347. I am indebted for this quotation to Christopher Layne, *The Peace of Illusions* (Ithaca: Cornell University Press, 2006), p. 137.

40 For an elaboration of this argument, see my "Europe's American Pacifier," *Foreign Policy*, Spring 1984, pp. 64–82.

41 The bill includes the funding of a number of previously established

agencies, such as the Customs Service, Immigration and Naturalization, the Secret Service, the U.S. Coast Guard, and FEMA, the Federal Emergency Management Agency.

42 This author first employed the term in "The Default Power: The False Prophecy of America's Decline," *Foreign Affairs*, September–October 2009, pp. 21–35, from which some of the examples used here are taken.

43 The United States did, however, threaten intervention in case the Assad regime would use, or even prepare to use, chemical weapons.

44 "Second Inaugural Address," 20 January 1997, *U.S. Historical Documents*, http://www.law.ou.edu/ushistory/clinton2.shtml. "Remarks by the President at Univision Town Hall, Miami," 20 September 2012, http://www.whitehouse.gov/the-press-office/2012/09/20/remarks-president-univision-town-hall-jorge-ramos-and-maria-elena-salina.

45 When the stakes are significantly smaller, individual nations might deploy some forces in cooperation with regional actors, as France did in support of the Mali government in 2013.

46 A key example is the Seven Years' War, the first world war, which actually lasted from 1754 to 1763, having started in North America two years before it did in Europe in 1756. Against the French, the British masterminded coalitions that ranged from Prussia to the Iroquois Nation. French ambitions in North America and India were thwarted while the French fleet was decimated. Britain annexed Canada, Bengal, and Florida; France ceded Louisiana to Spain. In Europe the territorial status quo ante was restored.

47 In a 1936 speech, reproduced in his *Gathering Storm*, p. 207.

48 These are actually the words of Karl Marx and Friedrich Engels, "Address of the Central Committee to the Communist League," March 1850, which were Trotsky's gospel; see http://www.marxists.org/archive/marx/works/1847/communist-league/1850-ad1.htm.

49 "Remarks by Secretary Panetta at the Shangri-La Dialogue in Singapore," 2 June 2012, http://www.defense.gov/transcripts/transcript.aspx?transcriptid=5049.

50 Peng Yuan, assistant president and director of the Institute of American Studies, China Institutes for Contemporary International Studies. The following is adapted from the notes of Stapleton Roy, former U.S. ambassador to China, who served as moderator of the session at the

Woodrow Wilson Center on 19 September 2011. This author's debt is gratefully acknowledged.

51 On this distinction between the polarization of parties and electorate, see Morris P. Fiorina, "America's Missing Moderates: Hiding in Plain Sight," *American Interest*, March–April 2013.

52 "Remarks by the President at a Campaign Event," Virginia Commonwealth University, Richmond, 5 May 2012, http://www.whitehouse.gov /the-press-office/2012/05/05/remarks-president-and-first-lady-campaign -event-0.

53 "How Will History See Me?," *Economist*, 19 January 2013, p. 9.

Index

Page numbers in *italics* refer to tables and figures.